Praise for Mon

'Dan McCrum's deep dive into W
investigation of the decade. *Money M*
Wirecard's headquarters with entertaining drama and verve, but it
also unspools the high-stakes reporting process McCrum and his
colleagues carried out at the *Financial Times* against the odds.'
Bradley Hope, co-author of *New York Times* bestseller
Billion Dollar Whale

'A milestone in the history of investigative journalism.'
Olaf Scholz, Chancellor of Germany

'*Money Men* should be required reading for investors and financial
regulators. It is a compelling case study of a seemingly eternal truth:
when a business is built on lies, there are always clues.'
Economist

'*Money Men* is a rip-roaring ride into the underworld of the
global economy. Dan McCrum is a proper reporter: there is no
threat, con trick or hangover that will stand in his way. In today's
pandemic of lies, courageous journalism like this is the medicine.'
Tom Burgis, *Sunday Times* bestselling author of *Kleptopia*

'The culmination of years of careful investigative
work . . . A gripping tale.'
Evening Standard

MONEY MEN

A Hot Start-up, A Billion-dollar Fraud, A Fight for the Truth

Dan McCrum

PENGUIN BOOKS

TRANSWORLD PUBLISHERS
Penguin Random House, One Embassy Gardens,
8 Viaduct Gardens, London SW11 7BW
www.penguin.co.uk

Transworld is part of the Penguin Random House group of companies
whose addresses can be found at global.penguinrandomhouse.com

Penguin
Random House
UK

First published in Great Britain in 2022 by Bantam Press
an imprint of Transworld Publishers
Penguin paperback edition published 2023

A CIP catalogue record for this book
is available from the British Library.

ISBN
9780552178464

Typeset in 9.46/12.52pt Times NR MT by Jouve (UK), Milton Keynes.
Printed and bound in Great Britain by Clays Ltd, Elcograf S.p.A.

The authorized representative in the EEA is Penguin Random House Ireland,
Morrison Chambers, 32 Nassau Street, Dublin D02 YH68.

Penguin Random House is committed to a sustainable
future for our business, our readers and our planet. This book
is made from Forest Stewardship Council® certified paper.

For Charlotte

Contents

Cast of Characters

WIRECARD

Markus Braun Chief executive and, from 2007 onwards, largest shareholder. Partial to a black turtleneck.

Jan Marsalek Teenage prodigy who became chief operating officer. A fan of jiu-jitsu and military tactics who carried a solid-gold credit card.

Burkhard Ley Chief financial officer from 2006 to 2017. An unashamed dancer.

Hamid 'Ray' Akhavan Californian porn baron, friend of Jan Marsalek, Wirecard business partner. Maintained a personal armoury in Calabasas.

Paul Bauer-Schlichtegroll Entrepreneur, pornographer, founder of Electronic Billing Systems, owner of Wirecard from 2002 to 2005, supervisory board member until 2009. Known to some as 'Disco Paul'.

Christopher Bauer Manila tour bus operator and long-standing Wirecard business partner involved with Ashazi Services in Bahrain and PayEasy Solutions in the Philippines. Member of the Iron Cross Sons biker gang.

Oliver Bellenhaus — Early Wirecard employee. Teetotal racing driver who became head of Wirecard's largest unit, CardSystems Middle East, in Dubai.

'Colin' — Friend of Jan Marsalek, whom he met drinking champagne on the terrace of Pacha with Markus Braun. Ran Goomo, a travel business.

Simon Dowson — Paperwork guy, operated Brinken Merchant Incorporations in Consett, County Durham.

Andrea Görres — Lawyer, general counsel. Wirecard employee number thirteen.

Pav Gill — Lawyer, Wirecard's Asian legal counsel in Singapore. A product of his single mother's determination.

Dietmar Knöchelmann — Businessman, he sold G2Pay to Wirecard in 2007 then ran it for another year.

Alexander von Knoop — Bookkeeper, Wirecard chief financial officer from 2018 to 2020.

Edo Kurniawan — Bookkeeper, the workaholic head of Wirecard's Asian finance team based in Singapore. Prided himself on cleaning up the mess of others.

Henry O'Sullivan — Businessman, publicity-shy dealmaker, rambunctious entertainer, shooting enthusiast and friend of Jan Marsalek.

Ramu and Palani Ramasamy — Brothers. Original owners of the Indian business Hermes i-Tickets, purchased by Wirecard in 2015. Known as 'The Boys'.

'Mr Samt' — Spin Doctor, Jan Marsalek's personal PR guru. Lego enthusiast.

Simon Smaul — Irish head of sales for G2Pay in Dublin. Left Wirecard in 2010 to run an independent partner. Petrolhead.

| **Rüdiger Trautmann** | Salesman, Wirecard chief operating officer from 2005 to 2009, when he left to become president of a rival, Inatec Payment. Chatterbox. |

SPIES

Andrey Chuprygin	Russian. Former colonel, an academic at Moscow's Higher School of Economics with a speciality in Libya.
Hayley Elvins	British. Private detective. Ex-MI5.
Rami El Obeidi	Libyan. Former head of foreign intelligence for the transitional government in Libya. A loyal guest of the Dorchester Hotel.
Grey Raynor	British. His firm APG Protection was involved in multiple surveillance operations. Mancunian.

SHORT SELLERS AND ANALYSTS

Carson Block	Activist short seller based in San Francisco. Took down Sino Forest and the FTSE 100-listed NMC Health. Once ran a Shanghai self-storage business.
Matthew Earl	Blogger and short seller behind the 2016 Zatarra Report. A crusader persecuted by hackers.
John Hempton	Australian raconteur. Ran the hedge fund Bronte Capital.
Eduardo Marques	Brazilian short seller at Valiant Capital, San Francisco. Central casting's idea of a hedge fund manager.
Heike Pauls	Analyst, Commerzbank, Wirecard superfan.

Fraser Perring	Co-founder of Zatarra Research & Investigations. A struck-off social worker turned trader.
Leo Perry	Investor for Ennismore Fund Management, London. An early short seller of Wirecard stock. Softly spoken aficionado of accounting fraud.

'BANDITS'

The affectionate nickname for Paul Murphy's pool of sources

Nick Gold	Bandit, stationer, co-owner of Soho cabaret club The Box.
Gary Kilbey	Bandit, owner of Fabric nightclub in London, secret source of Paul Murphy.
Tom Kilbey	Bandit, son of Gary, former professional footballer and reality TV star.

FINANCIAL TIMES

Lionel Barber	Editor. 'Lionel the Movie'.
Nigel Hanson	In-house lawyer. A careful, rigorous badass.
Sam Jones	Investigations team. Schooled in spookery and Russian literature.
Cynthia O'Murchu	Investigations team. Expert tracker of paper trails.
Paul Murphy	Founder, *FT* Alphaville. Knows the value of lunch.
Stefania Palma	Singapore correspondent. 'Donna Stefania'.

Market cap history of Wirecard from 2003 to 2021

MONEY MEN

Prologue

B Y JANUARY 2019 I had spent two months cloistered in a bunker to one side of the *Financial Times* newsroom. I'd worked 'off the grid', beyond the reach of online hackers, and each night my air-gapped computer and notebooks had gone into a safe with steel walls six inches thick. The paranoia I took home with me, eyeing fellow commuters with suspicion, alert for signs of the surveillance I knew my sources were under. They were nervous and impatient, then one of them fell ill. She'd thought it was stress, but her doctor had bad news: it looked like brain cancer. Would she live to see justice done?

Head bowed, I waited for the verdict of the editor, Lionel Barber. We were in his office on the first floor of the *FT* building in London, perched above the Thames by Southwark Bridge, where he delivered pep talks and dispensed bollockings. Seated with my back to the river, I looked at a picture of him playing cricket with the Pakistani professional turned politician Imran Khan as I tried to control my drumming foot. A popular and respected editor, Barber was a renowned dropper of names, known as 'Lionel the Movie' for his habit of placing himself at the centre of dramatic events. Clubbable and enthusiastic when things were going well, he was forensic and ferocious when they were not.

It was dark outside, the end of the day, when the international edition was almost put to bed and he had time to see us. I watched Barber in his suit, tie and running shoes, the merest hint of grey at his temples, reading glasses on the end of his nose, marking up the story with a fountain pen as he called out errors and additions in a stern tone. He reached the end and paused for a moment, weighing it in his hands.

'This whistleblower, I don't want to know his name, but who is he? He's asking me to put the reputation of the *Financial Times* on the line.' A pointed finger jabbed the text. 'Tell me why I should trust him'.

Even in that inner sanctum, I was nervous about mentioning details. The target of our investigation was a renowned tech company, and some of the group's critics had found their private messages and emails plastered over the internet by hackers. There were no mobile phones in the room, a precaution against electronic eavesdropping. Was it possible the room could be bugged?

I took a deep breath. 'He's a lawyer, and he's put his career and safety at risk by talking to us. He wants to do the right thing, and I believe him, but the point is we don't have to believe him. We have the documents.' I had chapter and verse on every aspect of this particular story so I took refuge in the facts, reeling off details as Barber listened closely.

To my left was Paul Murphy, a senior *FT* editor who'd been with me every step of the way on this one. What we suspected, but didn't know for sure, was that Barber had his own ticking clock. Rumours were circulating that he was finally on the way out; what we did next could cap his legacy or, if we were wrong, wreck it entirely. Seeing Barber roll his eyes as I got bogged down in detail again, Murphy jumped in and cut to the chase. 'Look, even the company's own lawyers think they're crooks, yeah. It's there in black and white.'

Instinctively, he didn't mention the company's name, as if the invocation would summon it Voldemort-like into the room. It was an unspoken superstition Murphy and I had fallen into, lest we prompt any eavesdroppers to sit up and take notice. It was always 'The Company' or, for this investigation, *Ahab*; I'd been chasing it for so long it was a news desk joke, a great white whale I couldn't let go, like the captain in *Moby Dick*. Here's what I knew: The Company was called Wirecard. It had raised billions of euros as Europe's answer to Pay-Pal, a payment processing company poised to take a cut of the trillions of dollars of online payments flying through the air every year, but the truth was far stranger: taken to its stock listing by a porn magnate, The Company now had dozens of global subsidiaries, some of which didn't seem to be real businesses; its critics had been hacked, stalked and physically threatened. There were red flags all over the place, except that stock analysts were insisting that the emperor was very finely dressed – in fact, it had just overtaken Deutsche Bank in the stock market. Its billionaire CEO (chief executive officer) was feted as a technological visionary, champion of a future where notes and coins ceased to exist and all money was digital.

Initially I'd had trouble describing Wirecard to the *FT* lawyer, but over the course of five years of investigation I'd realized that was the point. Nobody, not its investors or regulators, really understood what was happening inside. I had become convinced The Company was run by Austrian gangsters who were, for reasons we couldn't fathom, protected by the German authorities. It was knee-deep in the worst kinds of porn, gambling and online scams. Its top brass appeared to be in bed with warlords, spies and mercenaries. Now, finally, I had proof that something inside The Company was rotten, a document which made me gasp the first time I laid eyes on it. At the top of every page was a tantalizing warning: 'Legally Privileged & Strictly Confidential. Please keep in safe and secure custody. Do not make copies or circulate.' It was a reporter's dream – I knew only the really good stuff got that sort of treatment. Squinting at my phone, I'd skimmed down a contents page written in block caps. There was a parade of strange company names, but then words started to jump out; FALSIFICATION OF ACCOUNTS; FORGERY; CORRUPTION; MONEY LAUNDERING. It was miraculous. I'd felt giddy, and I'd worked for months to have the confidence to put those words into print.

I followed Murphy's lead. 'Their whole business is moving money around the world. They've got their own bank, and it's wormed its way into the financial system. They're supposed to be whiter than white.'

Barber nodded. He looked to the fourth person at the table, Nigel Hanson, a sardonic lawyer in shirtsleeves who was taking detailed notes of proceedings on top of a thick file of papers. He'd already been through the story with a fine-toothed comb, and with every pass he found something new to consider, a loose word that might give one of London's most feared legal rottweilers, the law firm Schillings, something to sink their teeth into. He could often appear harassed, as the lone defender of the *FT*, and would generally take the opportunity to sand down a sharp edge if he could. Barber trusted him. 'What's the legal risk?'

Hanson put his pen down. For once he seemed relaxed. 'From a libel standpoint I think we've got strong grounds here: solid evidence, clear public interest, a reasonable belief that what we have is true. I think we do have to face the possibility that the story is so damaging they will sue anyway. They have unlimited resources.'

It was the final push. Barber bristled: 'I'm not going to be bullied. The story is good. If we get sued, so be it.'

It was our signal to leave. I felt a mix of elation and nausea at the prospect of testing the story in public after months of work. It would give the sources what they desperately wanted, but would also bring with it the risk of exposure. As we rose, Hanson threw in a final request. 'If it's OK, I'd like to get a second opinion, just to be sure.'

The next day, Friday morning, Hanson wobbled. On his cycle into work he dropped a hard copy of the draft at the law firm the *FT* used, rather than trust email. As soon as he got to his desk in the newsroom, barely visible under towers of case files, he took a call from the outside lawyer. It wasn't libel we had to worry about, it was an injunction. If we weren't careful The Company could make sure that the story would never see the light of day. A third opinion was needed, that of a barrister who would be called on to plead the case in front of a judge, if it got that far. A conference was hastily arranged.

At 6.30 that evening Murphy, Hanson and I waited outside Barber's office in the 'U-bend', the corridor of power at the end of the newsroom floor where the higher-ups had their offices. We were about to take part in the most expensive conversation I'd ever experienced: a phone call with a Silk, a Queen's Counsel ranked at the very top of the legal profession. Murphy issued quick instructions on how to handle this rare beast. 'They think they are gods. Colossal egos.

Whatever happens, don't get into an argument. A QC is used to being the most important person in the room. If you disagree with them they just harden their position.'

This one got straight to the point. 'I've skimmed the lawyers' report and the draft story. If I was advising the other side, I'd tell them to go for an injunction.'

Hanson prodded her into laying out just what that meant. Schillings would rush to the High Court in London, asking it to halt publication of the story, claiming breach of confidence in accessing internal company documents. We'd have to show up with what we wanted to run and try to convince a judge why it was in the public interest. We might get an immediate decision, but more than likely it would be stayed for six weeks to give both sides time to prepare their arguments, during which time we couldn't publish. It would be a disaster. The Company would get weeks to clear up and invent cover stories, and there was a danger we might be gagged altogether. We risked exposing our sources for nothing. Then there was the potential cost: the loser pays the bill for both sides, easily a six-figure sum.

The editor spoke deliberately. 'This is Lionel Barber here. You're telling me we can't publish. I can't believe this, we're exposing fraud at a large listed company and you're telling me it's confidential.'

'My advice is that you face significant risk that an injunction would be sought and granted.'

Barber had his arms out, appealing the umpire's decision. 'What about the public interest?'

Failing to hide my exasperation, I chimed in. 'This is clear evidence of criminality. Surely we've got a public interest in exposing it?'

She stood her ground. 'Is it clear? It says this is only an interim report. What were the final conclusions of the investigation?'

I wanted to scream. 'It was squashed. That's why the whistleblower approached us, there was a cover-up.'

'And would this person testify to that fact?'

The faces around the table were grim; we all knew the answer. I'd been a journalist long enough to realize the London courts were a disaster best avoided, a cudgel oligarchs and despots used to cow opponents and settle scores, but this was a new low. When the call finished we'd spent thousands of pounds of the *FT*'s money to shred my story. Murphy cursed the idiocy of the system. I was in shock; this was the best chance I'd ever had. What would I tell the whistleblowers?

Barber sent us off out into the darkness. 'We're not going to solve this one tonight, and I have to catch a flight to Tokyo. I want us to find a way of getting this into print.'

Five days after the QC torpedoed the story, my alarm went off at 5.30 a.m. It was Wednesday, 30 January. I'd slept fitfully that night, and as soon as I opened my eyes the adrenaline surged. This was the moment of truth. We had stripped the story down to its bare minimum and rested it on a presentation from my cache of documents which made no mention of confidentiality or legal privilege. A mid-level finance executive in the group's Asian headquarters had been investigated for cooking the books. Yet, instead of being suspended or fired, he was promoted.

All I had to do that morning was find out if it was actually true. In the months of work, one final detail had proved elusive: was this character still in the job? If he'd left, we had no story. We couldn't show our hand by making contact until the last moment. We had to give him and The Company a reasonable amount of time to respond, but no more. The risk of an injunction was still real.

It was too early to make coffee; the grinder would have woken the children. I settled for tea, sat at the desk in my threadbare dressing gown and prepared to make the call to his office line. The plan was to send questions at 6 a.m., early afternoon in Singapore and the start of the day in Munich, which was an hour ahead of London. I waited until 5.53, then dialled.

'Hello, is that Edo?'

'Yes, hi.'

'Edo Kurniawan?'

'Yes, can I help you?'

'And you're still head of International Finance?' There was an affirmative noise. 'Brilliant. My name's Dan McCrum, I'm calling from the *Financial Times*, I'm a newspaper.' No I wasn't, I should have made coffee after all. For a second I was thrown. 'Oh, sorry, the *Financial Times* newspaper. I just, um, I just wanted to talk to you about a story, er, which we've been reporting on. And what I'll do after this call is I'll send you some questions, which if you could take a look at would be very much appreciated. There's a relatively short deadline on it. If you want to get back to me that would need to be by 9 p.m. Singapore time today. By today, yes.' My heart was pounding. Here goes. 'OK, so the main thing is I understand you have been investigated for your involvement in suspicious transactions at Wirecard, backdating and forging documents.'

Kurniawan cut in. 'I am not aware on that. I'm in the middle of a meeting at the moment. I'm closing off the group audit, actually,' he said, politely trying to get off the phone as quickly as possible. 'Thank you. Bye bye.' Click.

I punched the air. We were on, the story was good. It was a tiny fraction of what I knew about The Company, the facts, theories and whispers I'd heard over the years: that it processed payments for extreme pornography; it was in bed with the mafia; it had regulators and politicians in its pocket; its supposedly thriving businesses were nothing but empty shells; it would stop at nothing to avoid being exposed. It was, however, a start, a signal to the rest of the world that something wasn't right. Would it work? Would we even get the story out? The questions were ready and I hit send. In seven hours we would have our answer.

1

Smoke in the Office

2003 – Hallbergmoos, Bavaria

Denis Wagner's Wirecard job interview in December 2003 exposed quite how little he knew about payments processing. He'd made the trek from Munich out to Hallbergmoos, where Wirecard occupied an expansive modern three-storey building on an office estate next to the airport runway, and found himself politely explaining to the interviewer that no, he didn't know anything about acquiring, or payment gateways, or any of the other bits of technical jargon a serious candidate might be expected to have thoughts on.

In his early thirties, Wagner was trying to escape a dull job at a Munich commercial bank. After university he'd spent the dotcom boom years at a start-up trying to revolutionize initial public offerings, by making it as easy for the person on the street to buy shares as to put money in their bank account. As it happened, Germany's finance industry had risen to the challenge of shovelling overhyped garbage on to credulous investors with the same gusto as Wall Street and the City of London. After the stock market collapsed, Wagner found work at a bank. If pressed, he might have been able to give the basic definition of a payments processor: it's the company that helps send money between businesses and their customers. But it was clear to both men in the room that Wagner was not equipped to manage relationships with Wirecard's banks.

Wirecard's finance director was serious but friendly, and he put a kind gloss on the disaster. 'Denis, you're really an honest man, I like your courage.' Wagner assumed it had been a wasted trip, so he was surprised to be called back to Hallbergmoos to meet the company's owner, and even more surprised when he met him.

Paul Bauer-Schlichtegroll did not look like the head of a financial business. He wore trendy trainers and designer jeans, and at about forty was slim, with a ruddy perma-tan, sun-flecked brown hair and a gravelly voice that gave him the air of an ageing rock star. Bauer apologized for the state of the office, where a giant ashtray was overflowing with cigarette stubbs. He seemed uninterested in Wagner's experience, instead asking about who he was and, more importantly, what he wanted. Wagner marvelled at a man who seemed totally at home with money – amassing it, displaying it and dangling it – as the inquisition quickly focused on the basic human desire for buckets of cash.

'OK, this would be your expected salary, of course, and what else do you want?' said Bauer, mentioning a number that prompted Wagner to blink. Bauer, not appearing to notice, continued to negotiate himself higher. 'You'll want a car, of course, I'll write that down. And that salary – fixed, or with something on top?' he asked.

'Yeah, it might be a good idea to get something on top, that would be nice,' mumbled Wagner, feeling that something very strange was happening. He was sure he'd come back to the same building. Was he in the right meeting, had Bauer confused him with someone else?

'OK I'll write down 30 per cent on top,' said Bauer. 'Now, where do you live? Do you need some money for changing apartments?'

Wagner declined; he already lived in Munich. Then, his head spinning and without actually being offered a job, he was ushered out. The whole exchange lasted less than twenty minutes.

The next thing he heard was bad news. The banking relationship job had gone to an internal candidate called Oliver Bellenhaus. The good news was another interview for the sales team. At his third attempt, Wagner was in.

He arrived at Wirecard for his first day on 15 January 2004. Waiting in reception while HR was summoned, a sharp click-clacking made him turn. Used to the conservative air of a bank, he was transfixed by a woman tottering towards him in six-inch heels, wearing make-up and a dress more suited to a certain kind of stage performance.

A pointed cough interrupted Wagner's gawping. 'You must be Denis. I wasn't expecting you till February.' The head of HR had arrived from the other direction. The sales manager who offered him the job no longer worked there, she said. She handed him some glossy brochures on the merits of Wirecard's payment processing expertise to digest while the disorganization was resolved. Finally shown to a small room, the door opened into a pall of smoke where three people were gabbing away on phones. To one side a man was puffing on a cigarette as he spoke while another, also lit and apparently forgotten, smouldered in an ashtray on his desk. The lone woman smiled and waved, while the guy closest to the door, middle-aged and balding, stood and shook Wagner's hand with a nod and a friendly wink before returning his full attention to the handset: 'So hardcore you say, how hardcore? Right, four men and full penetration . . .'

Wagner could only laugh. What had he walked into?

The hand of serendipity was a 1997 flight from Munich to Berlin when the conversation turned, as was natural, to the subject of pornography. At the time Paul Bauer was making a bundle from skate wear as the exclusive distributor for Vans trainers in central Europe, along with a handful of other clothing brands. The chatty passenger next to him was a photographer for the American skin merchant Larry Flynt, whose iconic *Hustler* magazine was the foundation of an adult entertainment empire. Bauer learned there was video, television and a stable of periodicals that included *Rage*, a Gen-X lifestyle magazine mixing alternative politics with pictures of women falling out of their edgy urban clothes. Here was something he could sell, Bauer thought. Yet it turned out Flynt lacked a German publisher, which is how Bauer found himself invited to the Beverly Hills headquarters of Flynt Publications.

Flynt's office was gargantuan and gloomy. Underfoot was a bright-green carpet, squares of stylized foliage, covered with a small palace-worth of gilded French rococo furniture, Tiffany lamps and marble statues. The effect was Louis XIV transported from Versailles to California as an ageing hoarder. Bauer found Flynt alone, in a gold wheelchair behind an immense mahogany desk. He negotiated in a murmur and the terms were straightforward: Bauer would pay a licence fee on whatever he sold. They shook hands and, just like that, Bauer became a pornographer.

Back in Munich, it took Bauer just three issues of *Hustler* to realize that print publications were doomed. Online was the future, and he had Flynt's vast inventory of material behind him. The question was how to charge for it. He started a new company, called Electronic Billing Systems (EBS), and hired a twenty-one-year-old local programmer who knocked up some rudimentary software to take direct debits and run what were called 'diallers'; it was the age of dial-up modems, so to access the adult material customers could switch their internet connection to a premium-rate number and pay via their phone bill. (If they forgot to switch back and continued browsing online at vast expense, bad luck for them.) Within a short space of time Bauer had diallers operating in more than twenty countries, which he monitored from a screen on the wall in his Munich office. The dashboard was mesmerizing, a torrent of money flowing into his pocket, but Bauer didn't stand still. He bought another payments processor to improve the technology. The system wasn't much better, EBS could barely reconcile transactions and the admin was a disaster, but the internet gold rush was on and the money pouring in for everyone was so great it didn't matter.

What transformed the business was the 2001 collapse of a rival on the other side of town. A payments processor called Wirecard went bust thanks to a combination of buggy software and a failure to win big clients. For just €500,000 and a commitment to keep on the staff, Bauer swooped in for the office furniture, the technology and the name. Wirecard quickly became the most valuable part of EBS due to its ability to process debit and credit card transactions. The message to his new employees was simple: chasing reputable blue-chip customers was out. One of the old Wirecard hands went from pitching Sony in Brussels to sitting at a formica table in someone's kitchen dealing with the proprietor of websites dedicated to 'assholes and armpits'. (He didn't stick around.) Others who made the transition recalled how calls to Wirecard customer service reflected the shift. 'I've been online for thirty minutes and I still haven't had sex,' a frustrated voice might rant, uninterested to learn that the helpline was for payment problems only. Some callers would be perplexed and angry, finding the number on their credit card statement next to a mysterious item.

'What's 2000Charge? I've never heard of them.'

'Well sir, have you by any chance recently used your credit card to subscribe to certain websites online, perhaps of an intimate nature . . .' the Wirecard rep would suggest. At this point the caller on the other end of line typically fell silent. A murmured 'ah' as the conversation barrelled into areas they'd prefer not to examine. Sometimes the muffled interrogation of a teenage son percolated through.

'Many of our customers prefer that a discreet reference appears on their bill,' the Wirecard rep would continue, if the line wasn't already dead.

When Denis Wagner joined the sales team in 2004, there was a chaos to Wirecard. Snap firings kept staff on their toes (the chain-smoker would soon be gone), but the company was growing fast and Bauer had loyal defenders among the staff who considered him a friend. The other man in Wagner's room was a former car salesman who looked after a weird array of small customers. He said it was his ex-wife who'd prompted Wagner's blushes on the first day; struggling for alimony, Bauer had helped him out by hiring her. Wagner had his doubts about staying on at such a weird company, but when he followed up with another business he'd applied to he mentioned that he'd started at Wirecard. The response was abrupt: goodbye, and good luck. Out of options, Wagner knuckled down and joined a team which was working on a new Wirecard product, an online wallet called Click2Pay, which brought him into the orbit of Jan Marsalek.

Marsalek ran the tech team of almost twenty people on the floor above Wagner. A Viennese whizz-kid of twenty-four who'd been one of Wirecard's first employees, he said he hadn't finished high school or learned to drive because he had better things to do. He was an athletic five foot eleven, a fan of jiu-jitsu with a buzz cut and brown eyes that flashed with charm. There was something special about Marsalek, thought Wagner, but with a decade more experience he saw hints of recklessness. In the evenings they often caught the S-Bahn back into the city together. Munich's light rail network operated on an honour system without gates, just machines to validate tickets and occasional checks by inspectors. So Marsalek didn't pay. When he was caught he didn't argue, he just produced €40 from his back pocket, said thank you very much to the guard and the next day started the game again.

After a few months their commute changed, when Bauer's collection of businesses moved to a low-slung octagonal building in Neukeferloh, an industrial estate in Grasbrunn, out on the eastern fringes of Munich. A bold stripe of on-brand company blue ringed the lobby walls. Electronic glass doors sprang open at the touch of a pass card. Management and high-risk processing moved into the first floor, where Paul Bauer took a large corner office with space for several people to meet, adorned by a striking coffee table book, a special edition of work by Helmut Newton, typically opened to a page of the arresting nudes for which the photographer was famous. Marsalek and his tech team were relegated to the basement, although he didn't confine his activities to software development. In August 2004, one of Wagner's most important London clients, responsible for a selection of online casinos, flew into town. As soon as he heard about the visit, Marsalek took charge. He knew the man – let's call him Jack – to be a stickler for detail and how to deal with him, he explained. On the last trip over he'd put him into a taxi at 4 a.m., a model in tow. At their meeting the next morning Jack was so exhausted and hung-over he'd barely been able to focus on the numbers he was there to review and had jumped on an early flight back to London.

This time, Wagner and another colleague tagged along. Dinner for the foursome was an avant-garde place offering experimental food to those with substantial expense accounts. A savoury mousse squeezed from a tube like toothpaste, vegetables in a liquorice broth, revelatory steaks. As the wine flowed Marsalek became caught up in the topic of his own success. He was proud not to have wasted time at a university, he said, getting ahead directly on the job while his peers sat in tedious lectures. Resolved to go far, Marsalek's hero in business was Dietrich Mateschitz, the Austrian marketing genius who had launched Red Bull in Europe in 1987. What really caught Marsalek's imagination was the intangible nature of it all. The business was worth billions, he said, but from the very first minute everything was outsourced, the production, the distribution. 'Behind the brand is nothing but air. Isn't it brilliant?' he enthused.

Wagner, a salesman finding himself out-talked and outshone, was fed up and attempted to leave once the meal was finished but was subjected to a charm offensive. 'Denis, please don't go home, Jack is here to see you. We're going to a club called Pacha. Come with us, we'll have a good time,' Marsalek promised, practically dragging him into a cab to Munich's party district.

Pacha was in high demand, a taste of Ibiza club life transplanted to Bavaria. The crowd lined up outside was young and casually fashionable, bouncing on that edge between excitement and anxiety in the balmy night air. The bouncers guarding the entrance were notoriously picky. Men in designer T-shirts and women in summer dresses palmed pills to each other in the queue, trying to gauge the level of scrutiny up ahead as the beautiful and the wealthy passed the test. Marsalek led the men straight through the side entrance, a high set of gates that opened into a grand courtyard. He was greeted like an old friend by the man guarding the VIP terrace. 'Jan, good to see you! Where's Markus? Come this way, your table is waiting.'

Raised a few steps, the terrace was just high enough for the group to take in the whole crowd, and for the crowd to admire them right back. With exaggerated humility, Marsalek made a suggestion: 'Gentlemen, would it be OK if I ordered a bottle of Louis Roederer Cristal?' As empty champagne bottles accumulated, Wagner realized that Marsalek's promise had been fulfilled; they were having a very good time indeed. Only the next day, once he'd peeled himself out of bed, did the thought occur that he might be on the hook for some of the bill, but in the office Jan reassured him. 'Don't worry, I'll take care of it.'

The client, meanwhile, was delighted with his night of fun. And when it was Wagner's turn to visit him in London, he found that Jack was delighted with the service from Click2Pay as well. Jack's business took care of legal matters, marketing and payment processing. 'Everything is going through, we're getting such a small number of blocked transactions, I really thought we'd get a lot more rejections,' Jack said.

Online gambling was legal in the UK, but there were plenty of jurisdictions around the world where it was prohibited or where the status of online casinos and bookmakers remained a grey area. In Germany, for instance, it was unregulated because no laws had been passed to address the new industry. Some banks around the world refused to allow payments for gambling via the debit and credit cards they issued. Do not pass go, do not collect the gambler's £200. To identify and block these transactions they used two key pieces of information which were attached to every payment on the Visa and Mastercard networks. One was the unique Merchant ID (MID), which identified the business taking the payment. The other was the Merchant Category Code, which described the type of commerce involved. Online gambling was coded 7995, and those four numbers represented a serious challenge, both to processing payments and to Wirecard's business model. Under Paul Bauer's guidance the company had become the pre-eminent payment processor for online gaming, which soon dwarfed porn in terms of the payments involved. However, Wirecard had started to lose business to Neteller, a rival with a solution to the problem of blocked 7995 transactions that was elegant in its simplicity. Instead of paying money directly to a casino, the would-be player transferred money into a Neteller online wallet – an innocent e-commerce transaction. The wallet was then used to load funds at digital slot machines and blackjack tables, without involving the card networks. In the unlikely event that anyone took an interest, the payment processor could adopt the pose of *Casablanca*'s Captain Renault: shocked, shocked, to find gambling going on in here.

Click2Pay was Wirecard's version of an online wallet, and judging by the reaction of Jack it was working as intended. Denis Wagner was uneasy on the flight home to Munich, however, as he considered the transaction volumes pouring through Click2Pay for online gambling. Millions of dollars of payments were flying through every month coded as innocuous business. It was great for Wirecard, which earned a fat commission, and as a salesman he had a happy client who would sing his praises to others, but was everything above board?

Paul Bauer didn't share Wagner's ethical misgivings about Click2Pay, but he was starting to think about the exit nonetheless. He'd run the company for almost a decade, made a fortune, and it now had far too many staff and pointless meetings for his liking. Selling to a rival was out. He'd taken over a series of those, and the serious competition left were American companies who wouldn't be interested in Wirecard's gambling-focused business; he certainly hadn't had any offers. Selling some of his shares to the public by listing on the stock market looked like the best route to maximize their value, and another deal he'd done at a bargain price had paved the way to do it. Shortly after he rescued Wirecard, Bauer had scooped up the bones of a second company on its way to the glue factory. InfoGenie was an almost defunct operator of call centres from Berlin that was beset by accounting problems. It was a near-worthless penny stock, but it had gone through the expense and so-called scrutiny of an initial public offering on Frankfurt's Neuer Markt in October 2000, a final piece of trash foisted on to the public in the dying days of the dotcom boom. InfoGenie's shares had little value and barely traded, as Bauer owned most of them, but they were listed. He decided to take Wirecard public by obliterating InfoGenie in a process known as a reverse takeover.

In December 2004, a couple of lawyers from the firm CMS oversaw the operation. Like a parasite devouring its host from the inside, Wirecard was injected into the corporate shell, emerging to walk the stock market in its place. Bauer could now cash in his chips at his leisure, selling his shares to stock market investors whenever the price was right. And he'd also used the process to boost his business, by attracting gambling operators to Click2Pay with a revenues-for-shares scheme: for every €10m of transactions sent through Click2Pay, they had got a handful of stock.

In the Wirecard office, Jan Marsalek handed Wagner a white plastic card, entirely blank on one side, a black magnetic strip on the other. It was an unbranded prepaid card. The idea, Marsalek said, was to link them to e-wallets maintained by Click2Pay. Gamblers would get the white card in the post, then they could take it to any ATM and withdraw their winnings in cold, hard cash without leaving a paper trail back to their bank account. Wagner mentioned his misgivings, but Marsalek was dismissive. 'No one is paying any attention, don't worry about it.' He had a point. A technical violation of rules laid down by Mastercard and Visa didn't even seem to be something the card networks were exercised about. Wirecard could also only operate with the help of a financial institution, which would have to bless the scheme. These banks were central to Wirecard's business, which is why the payments novice Wagner hadn't got the job of helping nurture such relationships. And the man who did, Oliver Bellenhaus, was the catalyst to bring Wagner's concerns to a head.

Bellenhaus had been one of the first people hired to work at EBS by Paul Bauer. A bloodless character, practically albino, he could look swamped in a suit and had a baby face with a fuzz of fast-receding hair. A specialist in banking technology, Bellenhaus was the card whisperer. He collected prepaid credit cards like other people accumulated business cards, asking for one at every meeting, taking prepaid cards when the banks were unwilling to give this polite but slightly odd, pale visitor a line of credit. He knew banking systems inside out, and that knowledge and position made him both a key figure inside the company and one of the most infrequently seen as he flew around cultivating banks, sometimes with Paul Bauer in tow. It was an elusive quality which caused aggravation, Wagner noticed. One day a senior member of the sales team marched into the Click-2Pay room, fuming. 'Can anyone in this company tell me where to find Oliver Bellenhaus?' he ranted, to shrugs. When Bellenhaus was spotted in Grasbrunn, it was in an office strewn with the boxes and packaging of whatever gadget had recently arrived. He'd either be on the phone or blowing off steam by playing *Call of Duty* on a big television attached to the wall.

The screen came in useful later when the porn site Live Jasmin was signed up as a client. The salesman involved mentioned it to Bellenhaus, slightly concerned. 'We just boarded this cam site, and morally it's not totally sound. You have South American people stripping all day on camera, and people paying to watch them, and this company brings them together over the internet.' Bellenhaus loved the idea of it but refused to believe it could all be live. 'It's probably fake,' he said. Resolving to find out, they grabbed one of his cards from the big book where he kept them and got the site up on the plasma screen. Logging in, they paid for a private session and the screen filled with a half-naked blonde woman. Suddenly aware that it was 10.30 a.m. in a busy office, the salesman asked her to touch her nose. At that moment another young guy walked in to find them sniggering like frat boys. 'Working hard in here, I see.' As they stood there, the woman on the screen did her best to sensuously meet the demands of this strange fetish, and 'touch your nose' soon became a running joke.

In the spring of 2005, Wagner was stewing. He had an inkling that his time at Wirecard was coming to an end as he'd practically been asked to train his replacement. There were four other men on the Click2Pay sales team, and one afternoon the head of it walked in with a despairing look on his face. 'Bellenhaus! That man has no scruples.' Without waiting to find out what particular affront prompted the outburst, Wagner was on his feet. 'You're not the one to say that about Oliver Bellenhaus.' He erupted, his contempt finally boiling over. 'Nobody working here can talk about ethics. We all know the adult business is not right. The gambling business is not right. The 7995 codes are not correct. Who are we to talk about scruples?' The manager's eyes bulged. He looked like he was about to respond but thought better of it, turned on his heel and left. It was Marsalek who eventually told Wagner he was out, trying to play it cool while his cheeks flushed nonetheless, for all his poise and responsibility still a young man.

Wagner's exit was just as disorganized as his arrival, meaning one good thing came from his introduction to the world of payments processing. He spent the next two years fighting and ultimately winning an unfair dismissal case which allowed him to enjoy the early years of his daughter's life at Wirecard's expense.

2

The Ponzi Guy

2008 – New York

STANDING IN MIDTOWN MANHATTAN, I could glimpse horse-drawn carriages serving Central Park tourists to the north. South, the Avenue of the Americas stretched into the distance, a canyon of skyscrapers. West, beyond an imposing but bland Hilton, was the direction of the sparse serviced apartment the *FT* had laid on, its sofa an impervious white plastic and its kitchen next to non-existent. Beyond that was Broadway and the lights of Times Square. East was the money, although I was to learn it was everywhere: a fifteen-minute stroll in any direction provided access to bankers, corporate raiders, lawyers, investors and assorted vultures in tailored suits with billions at their disposal. Craning my neck, I could see the illuminated *FT* sign atop the building, one of a handful allowed in a city where only newcomers ever stopped to look up. I couldn't believe my luck. I'd been a practising journalist for a shade over eighteen months and it felt like a dream.

Inside, fourteen floors up, was the newsroom of about twenty reporters overseen by Gary Silverman, a veteran editor with newsprint in the blood and an endless well of stories about the characters of Wall Street and the Mob, which were not always two separate categories. Here the pink newspaper was a plucky upstart, taking on its great rival the *Wall Street Journal* on its own turf. The *FT* had launched a North American edition in 1997 when its then owner,

Pearson, was thought of as a bold media conglomerate. In 2000 it paid *Ghostbusters* actor Dan Aykroyd to front TV advertising, and for one stunt had him drive a salmon-pink scooter down 6th Avenue to promote the launch of FT.com. The residual vestige of that confidence was the extremely expensive skyline advert above. Thanks to the *FT*'s global publishing schedule, the deadlines were intense. The newsroom gathered at 10 a.m., standing together around an island while Silverman asked 'What've you got?' in a Long Island drawl. Copy was filed a couple of hours later to make it into the Asian edition hitting the streets at dawn in Tokyo, giving the room a frantic energy.

When I showed up in July 2008 I was still largely mystified by what exactly it was the reporters did and where all the stories came from. My career up to that point had consisted of slowly evolving what I used to do at the leviathan investment bank Citi. I'd spent most days there writing short summaries of other people's research for the sales team: buy shares in this company, sell that one. Being a reporter seemed vaguely similar, except the report had to be printable. Learning the difference mostly involved discovering the things which caused editors to shout, such as spelling mistakes, starting sentences with the word 'That' and casually libelling large corporations. That, and keeping people waiting for copy on deadline. For six months I wrote for the *Investors Chronicle*, a share-tipping rag with a dedicated readership and an expert Marxist economist. Then I landed a terrifying job on the Lex column, where a team produced several 300-word-ish pieces of commentary on events in business and finance for the back page of the *FT*, the thing I'd been instructed to read religiously as a graduate trainee at the bank. On my first day in London I was dispatched to the gilded head office of a FTSE 100 CEO for lunch. Lobster thermidor rolled in on one trolley, a selection of drinks on another as I realized with a sinking feeling I was expected to have more than a passing knowledge of who this VIP was. What saved me was the lack of bylines, since the column was printed without attribution. The resident mega-brain, Patrick Foulis, was a Scottish former top-ranked telecoms analyst with a love of obscene puns who would casually throw together a rough valuation model in a morning if the piece required it, rescuing his bewildered colleagues. We'd get to sit there listening as he forensically skewered some poor banker, responding to lies with 'That's really a very cynical approach to take, don't you think.'

My ticket to the US was the work of the *Wall Street Journal*, which had poached two members of the New York Lex team. I was asked to step into the breach. Adding to the sense of being caught in a whirlwind was the swift (and secret) marriage which preceded crossing the Atlantic. I'd met Charlotte speed-dating in a bar by Oxford Street just before I left Citi. It was about the thirtieth two-minute conversation of the night and the moment I sat down I was captivated by the turquoise eyes and freckles of the woman in front of me, framed by her dark hair. We danced the night away and I called her the next day, keen for another date and entirely unsure how to proceed by texting. Our romance was a minor fraud – she was sold a banker and got a journalist – but then she was eager for a change and new horizons as well. Charlotte was a banking lawyer who wanted out, was drawn to public relations. We'd find out together how both sides of the media game were played. When the offer of New York came up we couldn't pack our bags fast enough, pausing only to rush to the registry office, encouraged on by the *FT*'s immigration lawyer. 'This really would be a lot easier if you were married . . .' (A year later we had a 'wedding' with friends and family where the vicar was in on it and quietly omitted a couple of key phrases.)

We spent the summer at museums, enjoying long brunches, walking by the river and picking restaurants at random. At work I'd bash out a Lex note in the morning then spend the rest of the time meeting people and trying to understand how the country worked. In London we could practically demand a senior executive be put on the phone, but in the US few outside banking had heard of the column. 'Lex who?' was typical, and a chastening 'What's the *Financial Times*, is that a magazine?' was not unheard of in some of the less-travelled parts of the country.

At a rooftop party in August 2008, I chatted to a former member of the CEO's staff for Lehman Brothers, one of the big investment banks. He had just left and was looking for a new job. 'I'm glad to be out of there, it's not going well at all. The next quarter is going to be a disaster,' he said. 'Yeah,' I nodded, 'it's getting tough isn't it.' I sipped on my beer, vaguely wondering to whom I should mention this titbit. Then Charlotte and I jumped into a yellow cab with some friends to go to another bar, cruising down an avenue marvelling at the lights and life of the city, and the thought evaporated.

When Lehman filed for bankruptcy a few weeks later, the global financial system teetered on the brink of collapse. The US housing market was in freefall, and financial products linked to mortgages had become time bombs exploding inside previously solid institutions. For a couple of months it seemed like anything was possible as household names teetered, previously renowned banks were shown to be empty vessels and the government in Washington bounced between letting the cards fall and diving in to save everything.

I was just along for the ride, trying to hold on and produce 300 words of vaguely coherent commentary each day on whatever was thrown in my direction. Everything was moving so fast that I could barely remember what I'd written the day before, although some of the older colleagues around me showed a greater awareness of events, conscious that sometimes the crowd rushes too far in the wrong direction. Spencer Jakab was a first-generation son of Hungarian immigrants who'd already had a successful career in banking, becoming the youngest managing director at Credit Suisse by advising companies in the former communist countries of Europe how to sell their shares to the public. A family man, he had a ribald humour suited to Lex and a well-developed sense of thrift, eating spicy chicken and rice for lunch most days from a food cart at the foot of the building. Not liking the look of financial markets, he'd put his entire pension and kids' college fund into cash in the summer of 2007. As the stock market approached a nadir, he decided the panic was out of hand. The person at Vanguard was alarmed by his proposal to now go all-in. 'Sir, this is your 529 plan not a brokerage fund. You're really not supposed to be trading your children's education back and forth like this.' Promising that this was the last time, he was allowed to make the trade.

The moment of maximum chaos came in December. News broke that investment funds run by Bernie Madoff, supposedly containing

$65bn, weren't able to meet requests for withdrawals. A former chairman of the Nasdaq exchange, Madoff was Wall Street royalty who had quietly amassed a reputation as a sensational money manager, producing incredibly reliable profits year after year. In the newsroom few people had even heard of Madoff or knew what was going on. At that moment in marched Henny Sender, a legendary reporter in her fifties, as usual in a skirt suit with trainers and a backpack over both shoulders. Personally recruited from the *Journal* by Lionel Barber, the *FT* editor, she was practically a clearing house for information, on first-name terms with every titan of finance. The news editor saw her and yelled, 'Hey Henny, you ever hear of Bernie Madoff?' 'The Ponzi guy?' she fired back. 'Sure, why, what's happened?' Sender operated at only one volume, and that morning her calls drifted across the room. 'I *told you* not to put money with Madoff . . .'

It turned out that Madoff had never done any investing, he simply spent the money on living the high life, a luxury yacht named *Bull* among the many trinkets. It felt like we were through the looking glass. If a fraud of that magnitude was hiding in plain sight, then anything could be fake.

3

Bloody Knuckles

2006 – Munich
Wirecard share price €4, market capitalization €300m

LUNCH, LIKE MUCH OF life in the Munich headquarters of the rebranded Wirecard, was a semi-improvised affair. The canteen was in the basement, illuminated by windows close to the ceiling, and the food was knocked up as a sideline by the women who cleaned the offices. They put out solid fare with limited crockery, meaning a water-glass full of carrot sticks next to the schnitzel. It was down there, in September 2006, that around 100 staff gathered to mark a milestone: Wirecard's admission to the TecDAX, an index of thirty listed technology companies maintained by Deutsche Börse, the Frankfurt stock exchange. A somewhat niche achievement, it was still a big deal for a company worth just €300m. It would bring them to the attention of investors, maybe even banks and analysts who might pitch Wirecard's prospects to their clients.

The chattering of the crowd was shushed and a tall Austrian in a suit and tie began to make a stilted speech. 'You know we are not going one mile, we are going two miles, we are going the extra mile.' The man speaking didn't really mix with the staff, and for a long time Wirecard's head of sales had openly mocked the Austrian's intellectual pretensions when they passed in the corridor. 'Oh hey *doc*. Hi, how are you doing?'

However, Dr Markus Braun had been the right man in the right place when Paul Bauer decided to take Wirecard public. Bauer wasn't interested in status, and he had no desire to be the CEO of a listed company. So he turned to Braun, whom he'd kept around since buying Wirecard out of insolvency. It was Braun's cropped blond hair, large forehead and blue eyes behind rimless spectacles that was pictured in the annual report sent to shareholders, above cod-inspirational quotes such as: 'Modern payment – both today and in the past – means one thing: communication'. It was also Braun's signature, as CEO, on the accounts.

Braun came from Vienna's middle class; his father ran a community college and his mother was a teacher. He'd trained as a computer scientist and was, by the standards of the technology industry, a slow starter. While his peers were founding companies and experimenting in the 1990s boom, Braun completed his doctorate working as a KPMG management consultant, an advisor rather than a practitioner. The struggling Wirecard had hired the firm in the autumn of 2000, and the thirty-year-old Braun walked in with the air of a surgeon resolving which parts of a dying body to amputate. Wirecard's software engineers had found Braun cold, not trusting a smile that failed to involve his eyes, but he soon took over and helped push the business into the arms of Paul Bauer. What Braun did in the three years between that moment and Wirecard's listing on the stock market is hard to identify. Nominally Marsalek's boss and in charge of the group's tech, Braun kept his small office on the executive floor almost entirely free of paper. He rarely sent emails, preferring to call people into his office to chat. In meetings he would take a few notes, only to screw them up and throw them in the bin at the end, appearing to trust his memory to retain important facts.

What can be said for sure was that Braun was ambitious (possibly stung by his sister's rapid ascent in the law) and ruthless. Five days before the reverse merger obliterated InfoGenie, he had walked into Bauer's corner office and demanded 10 per cent of Wirecard. He walked out with an 8 per cent stake.

Suitably incentivized, Braun was then the driving force behind a deal which would transform Wirecard, persisting for a year in a pursuit which Bauer would otherwise have abandoned. They raised €28m from stock market investors and spent €18m to buy XCOM, a tiny bank. The purchase meant Wirecard had a competitive advantage over other payment processors. As a bank, it could issue credit or debit cards stamped with the logo of Visa or Mastercard. Some raised eyebrows at the price, estimating it was possible to build a bank from scratch for as little as €5m, but inside the company the view was that they had to make membership of the Visa and Mastercard networks a *fait accompli*; if Wirecard didn't buy its way in, the door was unlikely to be opened when it asked for a banking licence in the normal way.

Perhaps most important was that owning its own bank gave Wirecard a level of control over its business that it had lacked before, when it relied on relationships with other institutions to get payments processed. One was an Israeli payment processor, ICC-Cal, and another was Germany's most important lender, Deutsche Bank, which was both competitor and partner. Deutsche Bank owned a rival to Wirecard, called Pago, but in Wirecard's early years another Deutsche Bank unit had supported its processing, until one day somebody inside that organization decided to freeze all of Wirecard's accounts. At 9 a.m. on a Friday morning Wirecard's legal team walked into the bank with a court order demanding a thaw. A lawyer came out to receive it, said he would be right back, then disappeared into the bowels. Bauer heard nothing till 11 p.m. on the Sunday evening, when he got an apologetic call: 'We're very sorry for the inconvenience, Mr Bauer. Everything will be switched back on first thing tomorrow morning.'

With Braun as the big-picture figurehead, Bauer moved to the supervisory board (the German equivalent of a non-executive director), and it was to Deutsche Bank that Bauer turned when he needed someone to take over the day-to-day running of Wirecard at the end of 2005. For chief operating officer, he poached Rüdiger Trautmann, the head of Pago, along with much of its business. Trautmann was the quintessential German salesman, a T-shirt under his shirt, suit off the rack, a pocket full of anecdotes. He'd learned his trade selling to banks at IBM and honed it with a spell at Deutsche Telekom. With the middle-aged swell of someone used to client wining and dining, he was a talker who roamed the office, prompting some to wonder how he ever got any work done. Others found him refreshingly effective, if a little in the abrasive mould of Paul Bauer. A couple of young salesmen made the mistake of meeting Trautmann at Heathrow on the way to a gaming conference in London. Unexpectedly, he showed up with Bauer. Rather than catch the Tube into the city, they piled into a black cab. One salesman was squashed between his superiors, with the other guy perched on a small fold-down seat, their knees clashing. Clearly, this made the juniors the only form of entertainment on a prolonged crawl through London traffic. 'So, do you like girls?' Bauer ventured by way of an opener. The younger men squirmed as he and Trautmann ran through the workforce, trash-talking the lazier and incompetent members of the organization and trying to force the young men into opinions on their peers. When they finally arrived at the conference, however, it was clear that between them Bauer and Trautmann knew everyone who mattered in the gaming world.

Bauer had also needed a credible numbers man. He found Burkhard Ley, a lanky and charismatic former banker with thick black hair and expressive eyebrows. At parties he would boogie unselfconsciously on the dancefloor with the finance team while Markus Braun sipped drinks at the side, tie removed to demonstrate levity, always the haughty figurehead. Ley's prime responsibility was external, charming investors, and he had a great story to tell. Wirecard sales rose from €40m in 2004 to €49m in 2005, and were heading much higher in 2006. Profits were fat, and growing even faster by the time Braun made his September speech to the group assembled in the basement canteen. He told them Wirecard Bank was the future, and with it the company would go far. 'The TecDAX is just the first step for us. One day Wirecard will join the DAX 30.'

Some in the crowd stifled laughter. The company was doing well for a chaotic start-up, but the DAX 30 was another universe, a collection of German household names employing tens, if not hundreds of thousands of people all over the world. The friends and family of most Wirecard employees barely knew what the company did, let alone the general public. Still, it was a celebration, and there was no harm in thinking big.

What none of them knew was that in a matter of weeks the United States Senate would change the rules of the game.

*

In September 2006 Washington DC was winding down and emptying out ahead of the Congressional midterm elections. On the last day of business in the Capitol, a Bill designed to protect container ports from terrorists prompted the opportunity for a deft piece of legislative extortion; an entirely unrelated amendment was tagged on. Rather than wreck a popular measure just before facing voters concerned about the war on terror, the amended Bill was waved through and, without notice or warning, the Unlawful Internet Gambling Enforcement Act sprang into being: it was illegal to take bets online. While the various US authorities were given a few years to work out the details, there were soon signs that a crackdown was coming. In January 2007 two founders of the 'virtual wallet' provider Neteller were arrested, one while on holiday in the US Virgin Islands. Six months later they pleaded guilty to conspiring to conduct illegal online gaming.

After the US authorities revealed their view of gaming the share prices of gaming stocks crashed. Wirecard made no mention of gambling, or any hit from the new law, in its annual report for the year.

Yet there was also opportunity, because poker was left in a legal grey area. The card game was one of the big winners from the early years of the internet, transformed by winner-takes-all tournaments. Anyone could pay a few bucks to enter from the obscurity of their own bedroom, then work their way from table to table accumulating chips until they walked away a millionaire. As games of skill were specifically excluded from the US legislation, some in the poker industry argued that play could continue. Continuing to take payments from American players would be risky, with the notoriously heavy-handed Department of Justice on the prowl, but with the retreat of operators concerned for their legitimacy it could also be highly profitable. The choice, for the senior men at Wirecard, was obvious. They were all in.

In 2007 Rüdiger Trautmann and Paul Bauer went to meet a German rival called Dietmar Knöchelmann, who ran the payment processor G2Pay from a back street in Dublin popular with junkies. Knöchelmann was an experienced, efficient and careful businessman with a background in the car industry. G2Pay was well run, with about eighty staff, most of whom looked after its technology in Toronto. The roots of the company were in managing payments for pay-per-view video options offered to hotel guests, but it had since become a specialist in online payments in general (a Miami cruise line was one large customer) and poker in particular, profitably managing payments for three companies: Absolute Poker, Full Tilt and Poker Stars. Before the change in the law G2Pay's options had included going public, but that was out of the window.

Knöchelmann had long viewed Wirecard with curiosity and wariness. Online payments processing had evolved in fits and starts as the credit card networks slowly introduced rules to curb the industry's worst practices. A few years earlier Visa had started to demand that payment processors hold merchants' passport details, to ensure they knew who exactly was using the network. Knöchelmann was surprised to hear back from some of his customers that Wirecard salespeople described it differently. 'Oh no, that's not a requirement for everyone, that's just something Visa has specified for G2Pay.'

The price was right, however. Wirecard announced in October that it would buy several European payment processors, including G2Pay, for €48m. Knöchelmann was contracted to stick around for a year to help manage the integration, and he and his fellow shareholders celebrated by buying new Audi R8 supercars.

As soon as the sale was concluded Wirecard fired G2Pay's auditor, the respected international firm Grant Thornton. Knöchelmann was told this was a question of cost; it didn't need an expensive brand-name firm if an IPO (initial public offering) was no longer on the cards. Wirecard itself still used a little-known Munich firm, RP Richter.

G2Pay mainly used the Israeli institution ICC-Cal to handle client money. Once Wirecard took control it could simply tell G2Pay to run some of that through Wirecard Bank, but it did something odd. G2Pay was asked to make a big upfront cash payment to Wirecard, in return for a discount on the commission it paid for processing by Wirecard Bank in the future. Wirecard was effectively moving money from its left pocket to its right. Knöchelmann was no accountant, but it seemed like a game to pull profits from the future in order to count them in the present.* He made a resolution: while he waited for the rest of his money, he wouldn't sign another Wirecard document without first running it past his own lawyer, just to be on the safe side.

Paul Bauer took precautions as well. He crossed the US off his list of holiday destinations and, while he remained on the supervisory board, as the chairman was a close friend, he no longer had money at stake. When the law changed he still owned a tenth of the company. By the end of 2007 he had sold up entirely.

Markus Braun might have expected a warm reception when he returned to Munich's Bayerische Wirtschaft for the tedious obligation of the annual general meeting in the summer of 2008. With the purchase of G2Pay, 2007 was a financial triumph. Wirecard revenues for the year rose 63 per cent, to €131m. Operating profits almost doubled for the second year in a row, to €33m. As 2008 unfolded the share price soared close to €11, giving it a market capitalization of more than €1bn, and it had started to attract more of a crowd to the conference centre, where any investor could show up and force management to listen to their concerns, suggestions and queries. Most sensible people had better things to do on a Tuesday, preferring to leave the task to the various investor associations dedicated to upholding the rights of individual shareholders. The day was proceeding with predictable lethargy when the head of one of those groups, the SdK (Schutzgemeinschaft der Kleinaktionäre), stood up. If most of Wirecard's operations were in Germany, why were almost all of its profits coming from the territory of Gibraltar? What was its obscure unit in the British Virgin Islands for anyway? Was Wirecard's balance sheet really fit for purpose? Markus Braun and Burkhard Ley waffled into their microphones, and it was a minor disturbance. It took two days for the concerns to trickle out to the stock market, at which point Wirecard's share price crashed 42 per cent, to €6.20.

Braun's response to this collapse in his personal fortune was to go on the attack by blaming an unloved minority: short sellers. Most

---

* Burkhard Ley said the agreement's purpose was simply to define the co-operation of G2Pay with other Wirecard subsidiaries.

investing is about slow accumulation, turning a dollar into a dollar and ten cents by buying a business on the way up, or assets like property, art and precious metals that get more valuable over time. The investor takes the long view, and hopes to surf the rising tide of financial markets a little faster than everyone else.

A short seller, by comparison, fights the tide. They bet on disaster, that everyone is wrong and that prices will fall. To do that they borrow the stock from a 'long' investor, then sell it, leaving themselves 'short'. If the price falls as predicted, they buy it back cheaply to close the trade and pocket the difference. They aim to profit from bad news, and the whiff of chicanery about the obscure financial process made short sellers ready villains.

'Wirecard AG is the target of an orchestrated short-sale attack of several hedge funds,' said Braun in a Wirecard press release. The company announced it was the victim of market manipulation 'obviously orchestrated out of London and Frankfurt', adding a small flavour of Anglo-Saxon conspiracy to its version of events. The German market regulator BaFin, Germany's equivalent of the Securities and Exchange Commission, was equally quick to announce an investigation into the market movements, but Wirecard had no intention of leaving the authorities to their work. 'Steps have been initiated against those who have intentionally spread false statements in order to trigger the decline of the share price,' it warned.

It didn't take long for Wirecard to land on two prime suspects for the attack close to home. The first was Tobias Bosler, an excitable writer of a stock market newsletter with an office in Munich's city centre who had previously been an officer of the SdK. He'd briefly recommended investors buy Wirecard stock when it first went public, then paid it little attention. What piqued his interest was something odd about its results for the first quarter of 2008. Wirecard reported sales and profits growing like billy-o as usual, but somehow on revenues of €41m money was flooding *out* of the business: its cash flow in those three months was minus €22m. Bosler investigated, but didn't publish. Instead he went short on Wirecard stock, betting the share price would fall, and passed his research to a friend called Markus Straub, the SdK's deputy chairman, who shared the analysis with his colleagues without mentioning his own substantial bets against the company.

A Wirecard legal advisor led the response. A practised lawyer who'd been involved with Wirecard since Paul Bauer took it over, he was soon armed with details of Bosler and Straub's trades from the loose-lipped broking community. So when the SdK returned to the fight with a press release detailing its concerns and warning investors to steer clear of Wirecard stock on 8 July, the lawyer called Bosler. He knew all about his trades, the lawyer said, and invited the newsletter writer to come to his office on the 10th to discuss the situation. Half an hour before the appointed time the lawyer was surprised when two Turkish boxers arrived at his door. One he recognized as Ahmet Öner, a fight promoter backed by Paul Bauer. 'We were asked to come here,' Öner said.

The lawyer showed the men into his office and said he would join them in a moment. As soon as they were safely inside he hissed at his secretary, 'Get hold of Bosler and cancel the meeting. He mustn't come. Once you've done that, come in and tell everyone that *he* called to cancel.' While she did that he called Wirecard's CEO for an explanation. 'Markus, what the fuck is going on?'

'Don't worry, we know them, we thought you could do with some moral support,' was the reply. The lawyer went back in to the heavies lounging in his office. When his secretary joined them to pass on the 'bad news', however, it made no difference. Öner shrugged and stood up. 'We checked this guy out before we got here. The office is only a couple of blocks down the street. Let's go and have a little conversation.'

Trailing along behind and alarmed at the direction of events, the lawyer texted Bosler a warning: get out of the office, you're going to have visitors.

Bosler worked in a ground-floor office with big windows which opened on to a large internal courtyard. A colleague saw the trio first, approaching fast. The lawyer was in a suit, flanked by the boxers. They were powerfully built, black shirts unbuttoned to display an abundance of hair, muscle and gold jewellery. Bosler stepped out into the courtyard to meet them. 'Why should I not be in the office?' he said with bravado, but quickly found himself backed up against a wall.

'We know everything,' said Öner. 'I'm an investor. I lost a lot of money because of your transactions. We know all about your positions,' he said, punching the wall next to Bosler's head to punctuate each point. Blood dripped from his knuckles.

The colleague had stepped outside and was frozen, unsure what to do. 'Call the police!' Bosler shouted, catching sight of him, and the man scurried back inside.

The lawyer belatedly tried to calm the situation. 'Look, we're going to talk about this later, we don't want this to escalate.'

To Bosler's ears it sounded like a threat, particularly as the other boxer stuck around after the lawyer and Öner left. He had one more thing to say to the terrified speculator: 'You should do what we want you to do. In Turkey, people die. It only costs €1,000.'

Bosler got the message. Two days later he closed all of his short positions.

Afterwards the lawyer was not happy. Paul Bauer apologized for putting him in that position, while Markus Braun was cold-blooded: 'Don't be such a pussy about it. It's part of the job, so what's your problem?'

The same tactics couldn't be used on the SdK's principled accountant Klaus Schneider, who refused to back down; on 18 July the association issued another press release announcing plans to sue to have Wirecard's annual accounts thrown out. The share price collapsed to its lowest point in two years, trading as low as €3.40. For the first time since it went public the company faced real scrutiny, and the controversy put pressure on the authorities to get involved. Except that, when they acted to thoroughly investigate this alleged abuse of free and fair markets, it was following a complaint lodged with Munich prosecutors by Wirecard's lawyer. Police raided the homes and offices of Klaus Schneider, Tobias Bosler and Markus Straub, who resigned his position at the SdK.

Straub and Bosler would be convicted more than three years later for trading in other stocks. What landed Bosler in prison was telling his newsletter readers that he *may* have had positions in the stocks mentioned, rather than clearly stating that he did. It was not the crime of the century, but the conviction was convenient for Wirecard. To anyone who asked, those old questions about its accounts were just the work of criminal short sellers.

4

Fake Trees

2010 – New York
Wirecard share price €8, market capitalization €800m

I KNEW I'D HAVE TO learn the grubby business of reporting with sleeves rolled up and hands dirty. In the autumn of 2010 there was a job going at the *FT* in New York covering the investment industry that seemed ideal. Thanks to crisis-era cost-cutting, the seat had been empty for a year, meaning any coverage at all was a plus. The beat was also absurdly broad, so newsworthy events were all but guaranteed. Stuart Kirk, the direct Australian who ran the US Lex team, helped me with a push. 'Given you've spent most of the summer researching an elaborate plan to spit-roast a pig, maybe it's time to try something new.'

My luck was in: as soon as I started, a crackdown began on insider trading. Preet Bharara, chief prosecutor for the Southern District of New York, set about earning a reputation as the new sheriff of Wall Street by prosecuting a few hedge funds, rather than the executives at banks who helped blow up the global economy. A series of billionaires were pursued for crimes such as finding out the results of drug trials by bribing doctors, then trading on the information before it became public. (There were some notable successes, including the prosecution of the former head of McKinsey, but a number of other convictions were later overturned on appeal.)

It was also my job to try to gauge the opinion of serious investors,

35

like hedge fund billionaires, and I was helped in this effort by Gillian Tett, the star *FT* journalist who had warned about the brewing crisis and developed quite a following. She ran the New York office, and she often invited me along to meetings with big-name investors keen to solicit her opinion on events and share theirs. Typically, there would be some chatty fellow underlings at these meetings who proved to be smart and useful. What we really cared about, though, were the big swinging dicks, the hedge fund maestros. Which is why one Wednesday morning in June 2011 Gary Silverman, the news editor, shouted in my direction, 'Hey Dan, there's something on the wires about Paulson and a Canadian company, take a look.'

John Paulson had just made billions from the financial crisis 'Big Short' by betting that the housing market would explode. He worked nearby and I'd occasionally spot him strolling down 6th Avenue in one of the billowy suits of American middle management. His hedge fund was the biggest investor in a Canadian company whose shares had dropped by a fifth that morning before trading was halted: Sino Forest.

The cause was a report by a short seller, barely older than I was, called Carson Block, a former lawyer with a mongrel accent, a hint of New Jersey roughness to go with his California tan. He'd tried to build a self-storage business in Shanghai, Love Box, but was so disgusted by the corruption which stymied it that he came home and started a new line of work exposing Chinese frauds.

Reading through Block's work was a revelation. In unsparing terms it laid out how Sino Forest was a long-running scam, backed up with photos of supposed business partners; one in a derelict building surrounded by overgrown bushes, another in a shoddy apartment block, the balconies caged in for security. Sino Forest claimed to have sold hundreds of millions of dollars' worth of trees it couldn't possibly have felled. 'Transporting the harvested logs would have required over 50,000 trucks driving on two-lane roads winding through the mountains from this remote region, which is far beyond belief (and likely road capacity),' Block wrote. I was jealous and amazed. Up to that point I'd just been trying to keep my head above water in the flood of stories flowing from the beat. *Wasn't this the sort of journalism I'd wanted to do?* a nagging voice murmured in the back of my head.

Except Block wrote with an absolute confidence that was unlike anything in a newspaper. Block said Sino Forest had always been a fraud since it listed on the Toronto stock exchange by reverse takeover in 1995, and when faced with problems it 'just lied'. Although its assets and business were in China, it was audited by Ernst & Young Canada. 'Sino Forest's board of directors appears to be the retirement plan for former Ernst & Young partners,' Block charged. With the help of banks, who hadn't checked that the trees or business partners existed, the company had raised $3bn by issuing bonds and shares to investors which were now worthless, he said.

Block wasn't writing to inform readers out of public spirit (or to sell newspapers, which sometimes coincides with that aim). He had laid large bets that he was right and was now inviting everyone else to do the same, helping him to profit. Humiliating one of the world's most famous investors at the same time was just a fringe benefit. The report had been timed for maximum attention, just as Sino Forest was due to discuss its first-quarter results. The conference call was a car crash, executives couldn't answer basic questions about their business, and within months the business had collapsed.

On a trip to San Francisco I sank a few beers with Carson Block. 'If you surprise the management, then it doesn't give them any time to come up with a good lie,' he said. It was my first introduction to a world view born of Block's experience in China. He wrote the book on the subject – *Doing Business in China for Dummies* – but that was before he tried the practice. 'One of my first mistakes was to actually pay invoices, which was immediately seen as a sign of weakness. Paying bills is a last resort. No one paid for gas, because they knew it wouldn't be cut off, people have to eat. But the electricity you paid for because that would be cut.'

The *FT* had a healthy culture of scepticism towards business. It's impossible to spend time with large companies and not see through the empty rhetoric of market forces and business dynamism when confronted most days with the mistakes, incompetence and happenstance of economic life. Many of the big industries were dominated by a few companies trying to protect their position, with management focused on maximizing their stock options. Yet short sellers like Block were something else. Executives weren't just greedy and self-interested; a significant minority were blatantly corrupt, manipulating rules, people and institutions to their own nefarious ends. Catching them was a game almost nobody played. There were far more leads and dead ends than real crimes, but the scuttlebutt was wild and tantalizing. Had I heard about the tech founder known to every maître d' in San Francisco for his wild spending on the company tab? What about the pharmaceutical giant where the CEO's jet kept showing up in locations more noted for their sex tourism than their medical-grade manufacturing? This sounded far more fun than diligently recording the opinions of very rich men on the future direction of interest rates. I was hooked.

5

Who is Jan Marsalek?

2009 – Dublin
Wirecard share price €4, market capitalization €325m

THE REAL TROUBLE BEGAN in 2009; before that Wirecard had just seemed a little strange to the Irishman who found himself running what was euphemistically called its 'Digital Goods' sales team. Simon Smaul's background was in mobile technology, so he thought he'd be working in mobile payments when he took a job at G2Pay. When it was purchased by Wirecard, he flew to Munich, and Oliver Bellenhaus offered him a lift to dinner with his new colleagues. Smaul, a blond, easy-going salesman with an affinity for numbers, was also a petrolhead and he recognized the power of the car, an Audi RS4 that to the untrained eye looked like an everyday executive saloon. Even so, Smaul clutched the handle of the door in terror, his foot reflexively searching for a brake, as Bellenhaus flung the car into a tram lane to overtake, weaving through traffic as if the laws of highways and physics didn't apply. Stumbling out and into the restaurant happy to be alive, Jan Marsalek and the Wirecard team laughed: didn't he know about Oliver?

There were various stories about Bellenhaus's driving (which he said were hearsay rumours). One was that as a party trick he'd collect clients arriving at the airport for Oktoberfest, the annual celebration of lederhosen and strong beer, in his racing suit. 'So you'd like to go fast?' he'd ask the eager passengers, who knew that

Germany's autobahn was a playground without speed limits and enthusiastically agreed. Then he'd reach into the footwell, pull out a racing driver's helmet and theatrically strap it on. 'OK, then we'll go fast,' he'd say, before roaring away, confidently powersliding the car around a roundabout on the way to the highway. However, the legend told and retold was about a visit to Wirecard's Gibraltar office, a one-man operation which held the contracts with gaming operators. Bellenhaus and a couple of colleagues flew into Spain and drove the rest of the way in a hired black Mercedes. Afterwards, running late for their trip home, they hit a huge queue of traffic at the Spanish border, where guards patrolled with machine guns. The other two men told him to relax, delays were notorious and there was nothing to be done, but Bellenhaus took matters into his own hands. He pulled the car out of line and floored it down an empty lane towards the frontier as his passengers screamed 'Oliver, stop! They are going to shoot us!' The tale no doubt grew in the telling (Bellenhaus said it was inaccurate, told by people who weren't there), but versions of it were a favourite of the clique Smaul encountered around the whizz-kid Jan Marsalek.

When Smaul first arrived, Marsalek was still in the basement with the tech team, where he was a popular boss. If morale was flagging in the evening he'd order pizza for the whole floor, or lead everyone to a nearby beer garden to blow off steam. He knew when he was asking too much. 'The problem with us Austrians,' he'd say with a smiling nod to Munich's most infamous resident, 'is we always want world domination.' All new joiners there were brought to meet him, and even in jeans and a T-shirt his authority was clear. Yet he also had an elusive quality. He used his own gadgets rather than the company's and preferred to float around instead of occupying an office. When approached about an issue, he had that rare ability to transfer his whole attention to the person at hand. He would slowly shut the lid of his laptop – the newest and lightest from Apple – then close his eyes, pausing for a second as if resetting. He'd turn to face the other person with a broad smile, only then opening his eyes with a spark of deep interest. For the next few minutes the other person would feel like the centre of Marsalek's world as he enthused about their work.

It would only be after they walked away that they'd realize they'd gone to him with three questions, and now they had four.

The truth was that Marsalek's coding had almost destroyed the company in 2000. Wirecard's first CEO had found him as a teenager working for a two-man Austrian start-up focused on the 'WAP' software mobile phones used to access the internet. Reasoning that mobile technology was the future, he'd hired Marsalek (experimenting with a goatee to hide his youth) as chief technology officer. The first warning sign was when the company's systems crashed and Wirecard's engineers traced the problem to Marsalek's desk. In an 'accident' he'd routed all of the company's internet traffic through his own PC, rather than the dedicated hardware in the server room – a set-up ideal for snooping. He couldn't be fired because his job was essentially rebuilding the software the company used to process payments from scratch, and the project was too important and too far along to start over with someone new. Instead the CEO kept a close eye on Marsalek, who was the picture of competence as he ticked off each milestone. With everything on track, Wirecard's salesforce began to pitch the new system to customers. A year in the making, it would be more secure, more transparent, easier to use. When the CEO asked for a demonstration, Marsalek demurred. 'I'm sure that's not necessary.' The man insisted and Marsalek offered more objections. It would be better to wait till the user interface was polished. There were still some bugs to work out, nothing serious. He kept talking, starting to protest as his boss practically backed him out of the room. Bit by bit, the CEO began to panic as Marsalek admitted that progress on each part of the system wasn't quite as far along as previously reported, that more work was needed. Halfway down the stairs between their floors, Marsalek finally came clean. He had nothing to demonstrate, only scattered pieces of code that didn't work. It was a disaster which almost killed the company: the problem which Markus Braun was hired to fix.

Under the two Austrians, Wirecard's systems were a series of improvisations as the salesforce upstairs sold features the company didn't yet have. A case in point was a project for a hotel chain, which wanted tiered access to details of customer payments based on employee rank. A mere clerk at reception would see relevant transactions for their hotel, the head of Europe would get everything, with various gradations in between. Technicians slaved away for a year, at which point the client was no longer interested. Not wanting to bin the system, it was repurposed as the Wirecard Enterprise Portal, an internal system for tracking customer business.

G2Pay's staff in Dublin and Toronto considered their systems and processes superior, and the business was far more stable. As head of sales Simon Smaul quickly deduced that at the profitable heart of G2Pay's business lay miscoded transactions. There were tens of millions of dollars' worth of payments going through every month, and while much of those were coded properly, with gaming recorded as 7995 transactions,* a significant part were not. If it was a moral quandary, it didn't seem like a very big one to Smaul, who had no influence over it and was only responsible for finding new business.

To much of the world poker was an uncontroversial vice, and everything was happening in plain sight. The customers knew what they were playing, and Smaul got the sense that Visa simply chose not to look too hard at the volumes. If it had, it would surely notice a lot of US transactions going through electronic wallets. Everything went through Visa, because early on in the decade G2Pay had been hit with big fines by Mastercard and so steered clear. The Israeli firm which handled most of the payments, ICC-Cal, was well aware and was paid a small premium, a commission of about 2.5 per cent versus 1.8 per cent.

Poker executives seemed professional, unlike some of the characters Smaul encountered at gaming conferences. In Barcelona he met the head of a Costa Rican company who was staying in the best suite at the Mandarin Oriental. Over thick Argentinian steaks the CEO talked about his colourful past as a bin man who worked his way up from the streets. It was clear that the true power at the company involved shadowy figures in New York, and this prospective client had no interest in the mechanics of payments, the software or the

---

* For instance, Smaul and others said that Poker Stars insisted on correctly coded transactions for its business.

questions of admin which characterized the concerns of legitimate operators. He wanted to settle for bets on US college football, which was flat out illegal, and to simply know how quickly the money would come through. G2Pay had nothing to offer him, Smaul was relieved to say. It had no need or desire to chase such business.

The digital goods business of Wirecard was less stable. To see it Smaul had to log on to a different database to that of the sales team managing everyday clients, which used a customer management system sitting on US servers (and so within reach of US law enforcement). Friend Finder, a dating site taking subscription fees from lonely hearts, was one of the more reliable large merchants. Wirecard also managed a lot of payments for gaming, airlines and porn, which was known in the industry as 'high-risk processing'. For a theatre or an airline, the risk was that they went bust having sold tickets for *Hamlet* or a flight to Budapest that now wouldn't happen; the transactions would all have to be refunded. In porn and gambling the danger was consumer complaints; *I didn't sign up for this; the game was rigged!* Credit card issuers want their customers to be happy and trusting, so in response to complaints they enforced refunds known as 'chargebacks'.

Some complaints resulted from disorganization. A career in adult entertainment didn't necessarily attract gifted administrators, and porn sites were often slapdash, failing to cancel subscriptions promptly when asked or actively making it hard to do so. High numbers of chargebacks then attracted fines from Visa and Mastercard, and a freeze on transactions through the offending Merchant IDs.

For Wirecard, Merchant IDs were a competitive advantage, and providing them was an important part of its growth. Visa and Mastercard split the world into regions, and Wirecard held a licence to process European payments. What made a company and its payments European, thus enabling Wirecard to process them, was a philosophical question answered with paperwork. It attracted gaming operators in particular by offering them a Merchant ID in the gambling-friendly jurisdiction in the UK, tied to a British registered shell company.

The unlikely location for many of these companies was a depressed former steel town of red-brick terraces on the edge of the Pennine hills, Consett, in County Durham. There a gruff, barrel-shaped twenty-six-year-old called Simon Dowson with a handful of GCSEs oversaw a paperwork factory cranking out the documents that Wirecard clients needed. A trading address at a business park run by the local council was available if needed. His firm, Brinken Merchant Incorporations, recruited hundreds of locals from the pubs of Consett to act as directors of the shell companies for as little as £50 a go. They passed on correspondence, signed the forms which had to be filed with the UK's Companies House, and didn't need to know what activity the shell companies served. Dowson was a familiar sight in Wirecard's Grasbrunn HQ, often seen playing *Call of Duty* with Oliver Bellenhaus, and the Wirecard sales team, which sent him clients, considered the service unremarkable and above board.

Still, having a paperwork factory on hand was no doubt useful if a business ran into trouble with its Merchant ID. The identity of Wirecard's clients was also protected from public sight by routing the paper trail of ownership from Consett back through one of the main secrecy providers, the British Virgin Islands, a tropical tax haven favoured by criminals, private equity groups and oligarchs. Payments to the various online casinos, pornographers and quack pill suppliers processed in this way went into accounts at Wirecard Bank in Germany in the name of the Consett companies, controlled by the unseen owners. It was a lot of effort to go to if you had nothing to hide.

Rüdiger Trautmann, Wirecard's chatty chief operating officer, was a regular visitor to the Dublin office. It had a small boardroom behind the reception, with a dour car park view. In early 2009, he seemed frustrated to Smaul. He'd always complained about Wirecard's lack of professionalism, about its direction under Braun. Now, as the 2008 group accounts were being finalized, Trautmann was concerned that as an executive board member his signature would be underneath them.

When the numbers appeared, they were excellent given the waves of financial crisis sweeping the rest of the world. Wirecard reported 2008 sales of almost €200m. Smaul estimated G2Pay was responsible for a good chunk of the €49m of operating profits declared. Yet by the time the figures were published in April 2009, Smaul and his colleagues in Dublin had noticed that G2Pay's biggest clients were making weird noises. They began talking about reviewing their infrastructure, or suddenly asking questions about long-standing aspects of the relationship. Then the volume of transactions started to drop. As the numbers declined each month, Smaul realized that G2Pay's golden geese had been wandering around discreetly collecting their possessions and remarking on how it was excellent weather for flying. Slowly but surely, some of Wirecard's best business was walking out of the door.

The poker companies couldn't leave overnight, because that risked Wirecard holding on to a pot of money called the rolling reserve. It was a sort of deposit for good behaviour held back in case of chargebacks or if the merchant went bust. By the summer, as transactions dwindled, it was clear Wirecard was losing the battle to hold on to its poker customers. Trautmann had asked Smaul a few times about plans for his future. Nothing direct, just casual conversations at work jollies, where a partner would hire a racetrack and fast cars for a bit of networking, but Smaul felt that he was being sounded out. Then came an invitation. Smaul had just got engaged and Trautmann suggested the couple take a weekend trip to Germany for an evening at a boxing match Paul Bauer was promoting. It would be a chance to get to know Bauer, and Knöchelmann would be there too. Given the history, Smaul thought it seemed like an invitation to side with Trautmann and leave.

Smaul didn't go, deciding to stick with what he thought was the safer bet of Wirecard given the economic outlook: the financial crisis had reached Ireland, exposing the rotten foundations of its building boom. Smaul wrote a new business plan for G2Pay with himself in charge. The days of highly profitable processing for online gambling were numbered, he reasoned. Germany had just got round to outlawing most online gambling, and other countries were set to follow suit or regularize and regulate. High-risk, high-profit grey would become outright dangerous black or low-margin white.

In August, Trautmann stopped showing up to work. Marsalek appeared in Dublin in a sharp blue suit and tie for the G2Pay board meeting instead. Smaul's pitch for a high-quality payment processor fell on deaf ears. Wirecard not only needed G2Pay to stop shrinking, it needed the 20 per cent annual growth expected by shareholders. The share price was what mattered, Marsalek said. 'We have to do it for Markus.'

Soon afterwards, Paul Bauer stormed out of a board meeting at the Kempinski Hotel by Munich airport. He had stayed on as a director after cashing in his stock, but the final straw was a set of growth projections Wirecard had prepared for its investors: a 45-degree line, an unstoppable upward expansion. 'All this cannot be possible, the guidance is not possible. That's it, I'm out of here.' Wirecard's chairman and Bauer's other remaining friends in the company departed with him.

It left in charge Markus Braun and the numbers guy Burkhard Ley, who had spent years working *on* the company, rather than in it. They presented its success, and helped investors understand it, but could they really claim to have created it? Wirecard had lost two men with deep connections to their best customers, and one of them was now an active competitor. Trautmann had gone into partnership with Dietmar Knöchelmann's future wife, setting up a rival payment processor in the Swiss canton of Zug called Inatec – which lured away G2Pay's juiciest clients.

For his new chief operating officer Braun turned to someone he could trust, the twenty-nine-year-old Jan Marsalek. Braun was, at ten years his senior, perhaps the older brother he never had. Marsalek's father was Czech, a worker in a linoleum factory. 'A small man with small ideas,' he said. He told people he hadn't seen his mother or much younger brother for many years, since the court hearing which confirmed his parents' divorce. Whenever Braun called, which was often, Marsalek would drop everything. The CEO was the one person who seemed to hold his attention, and he took care to fill his workmates in on what was 'important to Markus'.

Marsalek was clearly exceptionally intelligent, a product of Vienna's Lycée Français who spoke multiple languages, but he lacked formal qualifications and had never worked anywhere else. While he was cunning, knew technology and how to deal with people, he simply didn't have the rolodex or experience of the man whose shoes he had to fill. He also swaggered into the job just as the world changed. Along with the shift in attitudes towards gambling, ubiquitous free porn was upending the economics of skin. Meanwhile, the economic crash meant that in millions of households credit card bills were opened and scrutinized properly for the first time in years. Charges were queried, and complaints became a way to cut debt. 'I never subscribed!' became the clarion call, as consumers asked for refunds not just on one month's porn or pill subscription but a whole year's. Meanwhile Mastercard and Visa, like all large financial institutions which survived the crisis, faced pressure to know more about who they did business with because weapons of financial mass destruction had detonated inside Lehman Brothers and other banks for a simple reason: they got involved with people and products they didn't really understand.

Marsalek, summoned from the basement, was yet to learn that lesson. He needed a big new customer, and he needed it fast, which was the precise moment that the Acai Berry King walked into his life.

Martin Osterloh was the salesman Denis Wagner had trained as his replacement in 2005. He was in the room when Marsalek and a colleague faced a speakerphone emitting two Canadian voices. One played good cop, dangling the possibility of sending a big chunk of payments processing Wirecard's way for nutraceuticals, unregulated health supplements like acai berry powder and weight loss tea. The bad cop raised bogus complaints about Wirecard's limitations. The tactics were so blatant Osterloh couldn't help himself. 'Well that was a bunch of bullshit,' he said when they hung up.

'What do you mean?' responded Marsalek, offended.

'All of those reasons that guy presented for not using us were bogus, and they cannot be that stupid. None of that was realistic, it was basic psychological manipulation to get you to do a deal at the wrong price,' Osterloh said.

Marsalek looked at him like he was an idiot. 'No, this is a huge deal, we're going to make €120m a month in extra volume. We're going to do this.'

'Well I wouldn't touch it with a ten-foot pole,' said Osterloh, but it was useless against Marsalek's unbending optimism and it earned him a stern rebuke from the senior sales person once Marsalek had gone.

The money was so good it could get Wirecard back on track, offsetting the stolen poker clients. But there was also a personal element. If Marsalek had idolized Red Bull's Mateschitz, he was completely enamoured with the good cop on the line, Jesse Willms. A business prodigy and fellow high school dropout from the suburbs of Edmonton, Willms had already won and lost one fortune made from pirated software (surrendering his Lamborghinis in a settlement with Microsoft) and at the age of twenty-one was a private jet-flying, race car-driving, Las Vegas-partying, international snake oil phenomenon. Advertising for his company's interchangeable brands was the background noise of internet life – AcaiBurn, AcaiEdge Max, Ultra AcaiBurn, Detox Acaiburn, Extreme AcaiBurn, AcaiSlim and more. By the time he got to Wirecard he had extracted hundreds of millions of dollars from millions of customers (according to a Federal Trade Commission civil complaint for fraud that Willms would eventually settle by surrendering property and assets and promising future good behaviour, without admitting or denying the charges). Willms's game was to get hold of a credit or debit card number by offering 'risk-free' trials, then sting the customer with charges buried in small print that were nigh impossible to cancel. Chargebacks weren't a risk with his business, they were an inevitable part of the scam, and by the time he got to Wirecard Willms had already blown up ICC-Cal's processing business, landing the Israeli firm with multi-million-dollar fines from Visa.

Marsalek either didn't realize what Wirecard was taking on, or thought he could manage the chargebacks with tactics that had worked in the past. The credit card networks measured both the ratio of chargebacks and the absolute number, so Marsalek spread payments processing for the nutraceuticals over many different Merchant IDs, to keep the number of complaints below the threshold which drew attention. He also tried to keep the chargeback ratio low by using 'friendlies', bogus transactions from Wirecard-issued prepaid cards pumped through the Merchant ID to give the appearance of a lot of legitimate business.

The usual tactics didn't work. By October 2009 Visa was playing whack-a-mole more aggressively than in the past, quickly shutting down Merchant IDs with rising chargebacks. So Marsalek tried something new. He took to the skies by private jet, like Willms, telling the Wirecard accounts team to invoice this new star customer for the cost. He was on the hunt for partners who could take on some of the nutraceutical processing. In return, Wirecard would ask for a commission on the ongoing volumes, as a referral fee. What Marsalek reported back to Simon Smaul in Dublin were variations on the same conversation. However greedy the banker on the other side of the table, there would always come a point when the same question arose: 'This all sounds very interesting, but please tell me – why don't you simply process these payments through your own bank in Germany?' Unable to say, 'Chargebacks are through the roof and we can't keep the Merchant IDs open,' Marsalek struggled for traction.

In December, however, Wirecard celebrated Christmas as if everything was rosy. It threw a party for staff at the top of a Munich office complex, a row of ten towers linked by a gantry fifteen storeys up. The event space had bars and balconies for mingling and gossip. The hubbub ceased for a few minutes and Braun gave his standard short speech about Wirecard's bright future, this time in English with a couple of extra announcements. Marsalek was to formally join the executive board as chief operating officer. Braun had also arranged to buy a payments business in Singapore. Reflecting Wirecard's global ambitions, the whole company would now operate in English.

Smaul had flown in for the get-together and was gobsmacked by the relentless optimism in light of the brewing crises. He'd always found Braun superficial – he tended to change the subject if the Irishman talked about high-risk processing – but surely he had to know the true state of affairs? Marsalek was mobbed with congratulations, but later he and Smaul found time to discuss the problems in Dublin on the quiet corner of a balcony, the lights of Munich below wreathed in the evening mist. As well as losing clients, G2Pay was having issues with processing payments through ICC-Cal. The Israeli partner was suddenly asking for new information about Merchant IDs, cutting off totally normal, properly coded merchants until anti-money laundering checks were concluded. 'Something's going on. I need you to fly to Tel Aviv and find out what it is, get the lie of the land. I'll follow on in a few days. There's a problem with a trustee to discuss with them,' Marsalek said.

The issue was a few million dollars of stolen money. Early in the decade payment processors had handled client funds themselves. Then the rules changed and the responsibility went to the so-called acquiring banks. ICC-Cal's systems couldn't change overnight, so for a time money went into bank accounts controlled by trustees on behalf of each processor, including the pool of money held back for good behaviour, the rolling reserve. A temporary employee at the Israeli law firm acting as the Wirecard trustee had helped himself to a large chunk of cash, then disappeared.

Marsalek hoped to get ICC-Cal to cover some or all of the loss for the sake of its future business with Wirecard. When Smaul got to Israel, however, the situation was worse than they thought. The salesman he knew was practically packing his boxes. Visa's wrath was rumoured to be significant. 'We're in the shit,' was all he could say for sure.

Back at his hotel, Smaul was lying on his bed staring at the ceiling when a trill of the phone shattered the silence. 'Hello, this is air traffic control. Are you Mr Smaul? I need to speak to you about a Jan Marsalek.'

The astonished Smaul faced a curt inquiry. What was Wirecard? Who was this Marsalek and what business did he have in the country? Smaul's trip into Israel had been cleared with the notoriously paranoid Tel-Aviv authorities by ICC-Cal. Marsalek, however, was attempting to blithely fly a jet into one of the world's most tightly controlled airspaces. Not helping matters was the Austrian's fluid plans and loose sense of punctuality. While Smaul tried to make sure his boss was not shot out of the sky, he was at least consoled by Marsalek's promise of a lift back to Dublin in high-altitude luxury once their work was done. The Irishman also learned that Burkhard Ley was arriving on a scheduled flight; the missing millions were important enough to drag Wirecard's chief financial officer (CFO) away from Munich.

Two days after his first visit, Smaul sat outside the CEO's office at

ICC-Cal while Marsalek and Ley made their case inside. It was the evening, and the building was quiet. They came out with ashen faces. Not only was the business relationship dead, ICC-Cal was about to lose its licence to process international credit card payments. Visa was serious about cracking down on miscoding. Wirecard could whistle for the money: it was their trustee, their problem. Marsalek and Ley had to get straight back to Munich to tell Markus Braun.*

The trio got to Ben Gurion airport in the early hours of the morning. Smaul was exhausted, and jealously watched the two executives head to the private terminal. He was on the first commercial flight to Frankfurt, and then on to home. In the rush no one had thought to update border control and he wasn't in the system, meaning it was his turn to be viewed as a potential terrorist. At security, Smaul's laptop was taken away, to be encased in a special box in the hold. The Irishman stripped to his underwear in front of a couple of soldiers, then stood there shivering while his clothes and possessions were thoroughly and carefully searched. The young national servicemen escorted him to the gate and didn't let him out of their sight until he was safely on the plane. When he finally collapsed into his seat, Smaul thought to himself that it was the most eventful business trip he'd ever taken.

* In Burkhard Ley's recollection, Marsalek did not attend and the meeting was inconclusive.

6

The Entertainment Business

2014 – Honourable Artillery Company, London
Wirecard share price €33, market capitalization €3.7bn

IGLANCED AGAIN AT MY WATCH, extremely conscious that everyone crammed into the inflatable igloo was trying to sweat as discreetly as possible, and that escape was blocked. Bloggers, finance types and think tankers were stacked three rows deep at the entrance, straining to hear an earnest argument about governments giving their citizens cash every month, all taking place in a space roughly the size of a Volkswagen Beetle. It was the hottest day of 2014 and the igloo was one of three tucked at the end of a gigantic, sweltering tent.

The session came to a merciful close and the way cleared as people broke for relief next to an out-matched air conditioner, glancing at miniature programmes on orange lanyards to plot their routes through the chaos of the conference. I ducked outside and into the sunshine, hoping for a clearer path across the cricket pitch we'd hired for the day, a hidden oasis of green in the heart of London's financial district. Once an armoury, when the square mile of the City of London had walls and guards, it was now used mainly for events to build the camaraderie and connections of those who toiled in the skyscrapers surrounding it. As I passed an ice cream van and virtual reality game, where players could zip around the universe in a spaceship to trade commodities, I marvelled at what Paul Murphy had convinced the *FT* to spend its precious money on.

Pitched as a cross between a finance conference and a British summer music festival, the idea for Camp Alphaville was to present and discuss a melee of competing topics on grass and under canvas. It was the anarchic spirit of FT Alphaville, the *FT*'s finance blog, brought to life. Wonky, funny, unstructured, Alphaville was everything the conservative pink newspaper couldn't be and was generally treated as a misfit sibling by the rest of the organization. When I joined I could tell it was run by an old-school hack from the way he answered the constant calls to his mobile, an abrupt 'Murphy!', vestige of a craft learned in the days of landlines. Paul's primary weapon, for cultivating sources and motivating reporters, was the long lunch. A favoured spot was Sweeting's, just over the river from the *FT*, an archaic City destination that only served fish and only opened at lunchtime. You'd start by breaking bread, possibly with a black velvet, a mix of Guinness and champagne in a pewter tankard. After that the wine would flow without urgency. 'Another bottle?' Murphy would casually suggest and, without really noticing the hours pass, the last Tube home would have left while you sipped cocktails in CellarDoor, an underground former public lavatory on the edge of Covent Garden, taking in London's drag scene.

Murphy's forte was the mergers and acquisitions (M&A) scoop. In the late 1990s he'd been a finance hack at the *Guardian*, when he was recruited for the 1998 relaunch of the *Sunday Business* as a frontline deal reporter. The Barclay Brothers, a couple of billionaire businessmen, were throwing money at the paper with the aim of making it a weekly rival to the *FT*. Murphy spent a year catching limousines to fancy restaurants until, exhausted by the brutal deadlines of a Sunday title, he was delighted to be poached back to the *Guardian* as editor of the section he'd departed as a mere reporter. When he handed in his notice, a London stockbroker called Branston & Gothard had just gone bust, and one of the roly-poly brokers pinned its demise on a dispute within a City insider trading ring; he'd waddled up to Murphy with a carrier bag full of documents. The *Sunday Business* was run by a renowned editor called Jeff Randall, and he wasn't about to let Murphy out of the door with it.

'I know you've got this story. I want it,' he barked.

Murphy smirked. 'It can't be printed. The lawyers won't allow it, they'll have a heart attack.'

Randall wouldn't accept it. 'You're doing that fucking story. Get on a plane to Monaco.'

So Murphy did as he was told. He spent two weeks in Monaco at the Barclay Brothers' expense, meeting every fast trading scoundrel in town. He converted the story, furnished with details of financiers crossing borders with bags full of cash. As predicted, when he showed it to the lawyers they made small strangled noises. It couldn't be printed. Murphy tried briefing the London financial regulator on the whole thing, but nothing happened. In the end he reasoned that if he couldn't expose the bandits, he might as well turn them into sources.

One of Lionel Barber's first acts as *FT* editor was to hire Murphy, who launched Alphaville in 2007, the heyday of blogging before social media took over. Every morning he hosted a live online discussion with the 'Rabble', an unruly gathering of anonymous commenters among the readership, to pick over that day's corporate news and share gossip about takeover bids. He'd float titbits from his bandit sources, rated for their historical reliability on a scale of one (for gold dust) to ten (serious health warning), sometimes breaking major news. In 2008 Neil Hume, an ultra-competitive journalist then on the team, revealed that the Belgian brewer InBev was about to launch an audacious $52bn takeover bid for the iconic US beer maker Budweiser. Assembling the Rabble for a special chat session, Murphy told them to wait while he tested the story through official channels by phone. The 'felt-collared source', a senior PR advisor, was non-committal. 'I'm not going to comment on market speculation.' But as Murphy read through the confidential deal terms word for word, the PR man started laughing. 'Oh, very good,' he said. Taking that as confirmation, Murphy hung up and he and Neil briefed the delighted Rabble. They failed to endear themselves to the newsroom, however, by forgetting in all the excitement to let them know the story was coming. The editor in charge that day didn't fully trust Alphaville anyway, and a watered-down version of the blockbuster scoop was stuck inside the following day's London edition, as if the story was broken by a rival publication.

By the time I showed up in 2013, the blog had veered away from M&A. The near-death experience of the financial system prompted an explosion of interest from people trying to work out what on earth was upending their lives, which suited Alphaville's approach of throwing stuff against a wall to see what stuck. I read it avidly and wanted in. Charlotte and I had spent five years in New York and with a baby on the way it was time to head home. It was only after I got the job that anyone thought to mention it was the first time someone had moved to Alphaville from the newspaper.

At my first Murphy lunch he explained his philosophy. It's often said that journalists make bad managers, but actually the reverse is true: journalists are impossible to manage. So the job was a blank slate. 'Write about what you think is interesting. Look, we've got to keep the blog ticking over, but we're all professionals. If you think something's worth writing about, give it a go, the readers will soon let you know if they don't like it.'

He'd internalized the language and uniform of finance – dark, though moderately crumpled suit and white shirt – but never lost his punk spirit. At first glance I thought the silver on his finger was a signet ring favoured by those with old money, but it was actually a skull sculpted by a teenage daughter. Camp Alphaville had started with a typical Murphy flourish. He hired actors posing as an oligarch and his bodyguards to throw someone out of the main hall, a little theatre to set people on edge and give them something to talk about. 'We're in the entertainment business,' he always reminded the half-dozen reporters who wrote for the blog. I thought dubious companies were interesting, which was why on that summer's day I found myself dashing across the field in the heat. I ducked back into the main conference tent. Standing on a tiny stage which added only about a foot to his already considerable height, John Hempton was warming to his subject with the signature confidence of a successful Australian hedge fund manager: 'I've always said the best description for a mine is a hole in the ground with a liar on top.'

Hempton, whose curly grey hair indicated his experience, had his sleeves rolled up and microphone in hand. He'd spent months researching in excruciating detail the actions of a Canadian silver mine which didn't make sense, convinced the ore didn't exist. He took us through maps of remote train lines, obscure customs records, the process for crunching and grinding rock laced with precious metal. The only railhead nearby had none of the equipment for shifting tonnes of material. Even if you could get it aboard, why on earth would you send it in a loop hundreds of miles long to get it to Montana for processing? Every step indicated that this was a cast-iron fraud, except the last. Hempton spoke to a labourer from a Native American reservation who was part of a team that spent days at the railhead filling sacks of dirt and hefting them into a box car by hand. It didn't make business sense, but it had happened anyway. The mine was the greatest short that never was.

Not long afterwards, I was chatting to Hempton when he posed an irresistible question: 'Would you be interested in some German gangsters?' The company was Wirecard, a fintech worth about €4bn. He thought it was a fraud, but it was also rumoured to have a finger in every bit of dirty business online. 'If you are going to look into it, be careful,' he said.

It was the summer lull, and thoughts of danger seemed ridiculous in the genteel surroundings of a paper where reporters were more likely to doorstep a billionaire on a yacht than a thug. 'Sure, of course,' I blithely replied, jotting down the name with a question mark.

7

Friends Like These

2010 – Manila
Wirecard share price €10, market capitalization €1bn

AT THE TURN OF the decade Wirecard turned its attention to Asia. Martin Osterloh, the German salesman, got a chance to see the company's office in the Philippines shortly before the operation was moved to Singapore. Manila was a crowded, chaotic city, and inside the building was no different. A jumble of businesses were crammed in, a live casino among them. Wirecard had a small room with a mezzanine floor roughly inserted, where about 20 locals sat elbow to elbow, each with a beer crate's worth of space.

Osterloh was a specialist in gambling who'd thrived in the mad atmosphere of Wirecard. He was there for the Asian Internet Gaming conference, in search of new business. Ever cost-conscious, the Wirecard team had a stand set up, but had only purchased one $500 admission ticket. Security was light, so they'd pass the ticket to the next man over the low fence around the event under a piece of paper. It wasn't an unusual tactic, and they were soon busted by an organizer walking the floor.

'Gentlemen, what's going on here? You have three people and only one badge between you,' he said. The conference was hardly a sell-out success, so Osterloh bargained. He offered to pay for a second, and in the end the man handed it over for free as a gesture of goodwill.

The next day Wirecard had six people at the stand. The official appeared again, and as it was lunchtime he and Osterloh discussed the purchase of more badges as they strolled over towards the buffet. While the conference was ho-hum, the food the day before had been top-notch, an expansive selection of the region's cuisine. They arrived at the dining area to discover word had spread. At least a dozen people in Wirecard Asia polo shirts were tucking into large plates of food with gusto. Osterloh and the organizer did a double take in unison. 'Martin, this isn't on,' he said.

Once Osterloh sheepishly came to terms on extra badges, he introduced himself to the lone European among the Wirecard freeloaders, who stood out like a sore thumb. Middle-aged and flabby, the man wore a Wirecard polo but his business card was for a company called PayEasy Solutions. A German expat, he said he was partnering with the group on some sort of issuing project but was vague, almost shifty, about the details, like it was someone else's product. Osterloh was surprised he'd not heard about it, but it wasn't unusual for the company to use independent resellers. He pocketed the card and soon put the encounter out of his mind. It would be years before he ever heard the name Christopher Bauer again.

In Munich in early 2010, however, Osterloh was a salesman who couldn't sell. He'd slowly begun to realize that something was up, when for about a month and a half every new high-risk client he'd signed up had been blocked by the compliance team. He cornered his boss and asked her straight out what was going on.

'We have a small problem,' was all she would let on.

'It wasn't because of the pharmaceutical shit was it?' Osterloh guessed, correctly.

'Let's not talk about this,' she said, touchy.

But there was soon no way to hide it. Visa blocked all new high-risk clients for months (and sent a team from the international investigations firm Kroll to take a close look at Wirecard's processes). Osterloh asked if they should just sell Mastercard processing, but the answer came back that no, they shouldn't sell anything. Nobody in the stock market could know that Wirecard had been blocked by Visa.

*

In March 2010, Wirecard shares did crash, but not because of problems with Visa. Instead, news leaked about a Secret Service investigation into a German living in Florida, Michael Schütt, for conducting an unlicensed money transfer operation. Schütt had paid out more than $70m from Wirecard Bank accounts to US gamblers. Effectively his job was to spend all day signing and mailing out cheques.

When details of the indictment leaked, the Wirecard share price briefly slumped from €8 down to almost €5, until it put out a press release denying any connection to the case and threatening legal action. However, the moment of controversy did have one consequence: it caught the eye of a Brazilian hedge fund manager in San Francisco called Eduardo Marques. A laid-back surfer straight out of central casting, he'd been introduced to Wirecard's Paul Bauer-Schlichtegroll years earlier during an eye-opening day in Berlin dedicated to sex-related investment opportunities. Bauer had been open about Wirecard's business, that it processed some porn, but that the bulk of its profits came from gaming. Marques started to short Wirecard stock on the basis that it was lying, heavily involved in gaming, and the US authorities were likely to crack down.

In Dublin, G2Pay was running on fumes. In the early months of 2010 it was only thanks to the Irish taxman that Simon Smaul could pay the staff and keep the lights on. The company's profits had dropped so much in the latter half of 2009 as its big poker clients fled that a tax rebate arrived in the New Year. Just breaking even would be a challenge now, Smaul realized. Wirecard's Munich finance team had made it abundantly clear there were no funds to spare. When the going was good they had regularly called, looking for a dividend from Dublin. Now they demanded cost cuts and Smaul faced making a large portion of his workmates redundant.

Amid the gloom, Marsalek came to Smaul with a proposition: he should set up on his own, to deal with payments processing that Wirecard couldn't. Marsalek promised to send this new venture clients, and Smaul would send back a share of its commission on the transactions to Wirecard in return. It would be an independent partner, with no public connection to Wirecard, so Smaul could work with other banks.

The idea was sparked by Marsalek's struggle to offload the toxic nutraceutical volumes to other payment processors the previous year. With his background in technology, Marsalek also had a structure in mind. This new partner would pay Wirecard a licence fee for software, which made the accounting simple. The cost of developing the software was in the past, so any 'licence fees' would be pure profit.

Smaul had few alternatives; the Irish economy was a disaster. He persuaded himself that Marsalek's plan would be a chance to do high-risk processing properly. G2Pay was falling apart, so he would leave with a hand-picked team to start over. It would be a service provider, managing the merchants, the banking relationships, the settlements and risk management, not publicly linked to Wirecard.

Wary that the whole thing was another hairbrained notion of Marsalek's, Smaul and a colleague demanded a meeting with the top brass. Markus Braun was said to be unavailable, so they met Marsalek and the CFO, Burkhard Ley, in the basement of the Munich Hilton to talk through the plan. With Ley briefed, Smaul felt they had sign off to go ahead.* Back in Ireland, one of the last things he did before he walked out of the door at the end of June was to pass on a message from Marsalek, who wanted someone in the Dublin finance team to call him. The numbers for the quarter were going to be terrible, what with the cost of making about fifty of G2Pay's seventy staff redundant, but Jan said he had a piece of business in the Middle East for them to book which would help. Smaul didn't hang around to find out the details. He picked up his coat and left.

Smaul's new venture was called Sunsont, a random name assigned by the firm which incorporated it. It was founded on 6 July 2010, in rented office space in Sandyford, a well-to-do suburb favoured by tech companies to the south of Dublin. In the beginning, Marsalek

* Ley did not remember Marsalek attending the meeting, which he said covered Wirecard's willingness to work with this independent partner without discussing details of the arrangement.

visited every month. He went to Wirecard's Ulysses House office in the afternoon for the board meeting, then in the evening discussed Sunsont at a Chinese restaurant in Sandyford over a selection of traditional Sichuan dishes with an Irish twist, like stir-fried beef in a black pepper and merlot sauce. Smaul's focus was now technical operations and managing the relationships essential to the whole set-up, many introduced by Marsalek on the phone or via his personal email to keep Wirecard's name out of it. In November Smaul went on his first trip as the head of this new business, spending three days at the Peninsula Hotel in Manila for a course of frustrating meetings with one of his old Wirecard colleagues who had also become an independent consultant. The man was immaculately dressed, with a young girlfriend, and he liked to amble gently in the direction of business discussions over drinks. Smaul had found it frustrating when he was nominally the man's boss; now that Smaul was on his own he had no leverage whatsoever.

As Smaul tried to grow Sunsont, it didn't help that Marsalek was obsessed with the futile mission of winning back the poker business from Trautmann at Inatec. 'We have to burn their houses down! This is our money, our customers, we have to get them back,' he told Smaul repeatedly, obliging Sunsont to go through the motions of pursuit. Other introductions to potential new merchants from Marsalek were not encouraging. There were more acai berry sellers, pyramid schemes operating under the supposedly legitimate structure known as 'multi-level marketing', and online foreign exchange traders. With online gambling becoming harder, websites had popped up offering bets on the movements of financial markets with huge profits available for small stakes. The characters behind these trading venues weren't college dropouts launching a start-up. They were serious men with a range of business interests about which Smaul decided it would be imprudent to probe.

The question of which merchants to take on was largely moot, however, because banks weren't throwing themselves at an unknown Irish company. Smaul spent eighteen months in the air, back and forth to Panama, Eastern Europe, Asia. The meetings were almost never with a bank directly, always a partner. The most professional was the double act then behind PayEasy: Christopher Bauer* and James Bergman. They were at least not scary. Bergman was an extremely posh Englishman, making up in pleasantness what he lacked in sharpness. Most of what Simon Smaul talked about with Christopher Bauer involved possible projects in Bahrain and the Philippines, but no business for Sunsont ever transpired. At one point Smaul and a colleague jumped on a plane at short notice to meet Bergman at a Birmingham hotel. Marsalek had asked Smaul to go, and Bergman was there at Christopher's request, meaning that neither man was entirely sure what the point of the meeting was and the conversation went round in circles.

'Why are these people wasting our time?' Smaul ranted to his workmate on the way home. He was starting to feel like he was dealing with Derek and Rodney Trotter from *Only Fools and Horses*, constantly promised that 'this time next year we'll all be millionaires'. Were people taking meetings with him just to keep Marsalek happy?

Marsalek himself was in a manic, workaholic phase. Meetings with him became less frequent and calls were short, typically interrupted by a string of incoming calls or messages that grabbed his attention. Smaul noticed Jan would forget what he had said to whom as he projected relentless positivity. 'At least Mauritius is going well,' Marsalek said one day, when Smaul had briefed him the previous week that a project with a partner there really wasn't going well at all as essential paperwork was still missing. They were small slips, but some of Marsalek's brainwaves were truly heroic. On 15 April 2011, Federal prosecutors in the Southern District of New York unveiled a huge indictment against almost a dozen people involved in online poker. It was a death knell for the industry known as Black Friday, which made it plain that in the eyes of US law enforcement miscoded transactions for online poker amounted to money laundering. Marsalek's first instinct was to offer a job to one of those charged: Nelson Burtnick. The Canadian was a poker veteran in charge of payments processing at Full Tilt in Dublin. Until it was forcibly shut down by

* Christopher Bauer is not related to the pornographer and entrepreneur Paul Bauer-Schlichtegroll.

the US authorities, that is. Once the doors closed it became clear there wasn't nearly enough money left inside the company to repay the $360m its players thought they had on deposit.

'I can't hire him into Wirecard, you should take him on at Sunsont,' Marsalek said down the phone.

Smaul shook his head in disbelief. He was in Singapore and had breathed a huge sigh of relief when he saw the news.

'Are you crazy! He's all over the indictment. We can't give a job to one of America's most wanted.'

Marsalek refused to accept the premise of the argument, focusing only on the positives.

'Nelson knows everybody in the industry, he'll be sure to bring business. Plus, just think of his family, a job would be great for them, they could stay in Dublin. You wouldn't have to say what work he'd do for now, just get him in the door.'

'Have you got a screw loose?'

Smaul briefly wondered how it would look to write 'Ponzi scheme' in the box under former employment on the application form for an Irish work visa. Marsalek, as ever, didn't take it personally. Smaul wasn't sure if he treated these arguments like a game or really believed them, trying to talk the other person into submission. (Marsalek hadn't even sounded out Burtnick, who ultimately wound up working with Rüdiger Trautmann at Inatec, having first flown to New York to surrender and plead guilty to charges of conspiracy, bank fraud and money laundering in connection to illegal internet gambling operations, in a deal which saw Burtnick avoid prison.)

Marsalek and Smaul were involved in a delicate dance, with uncertain lines of obligation, control and commitment. Smaul put his foot down.

In Munich, Wirecard had outgrown the Grasbrunn location. The tech team held a ceremonial smashing-up party to say goodbye to their basement and everybody was handed hard hats and a souvenir mallet of yellow plastic and charcoal foam. Wirecard's new offices were in Einstein Ring, a nondescript development out in the quiet suburb of Aschheim. It took two of five buildings which formed a U, interconnected squat blocks of grey concrete and black glass. Inside, Markus Braun's wife Sylvia had a hand in the fit-out, designed to encourage a corporate identity. There were 'thinking cubes' covered in bright red to match the square dot of the 'i' in Wirecard's logo, scattered around the office as stools to foster impromptu collaboration. She wasn't the only female employee Braun had approached romantically over the years. As the value of the company rose, and Braun's fortune with it, another woman always joked at the rising cost of spurning his early offer of a date. Word of the union had spread only slowly, as Braun was intensely private and ever more removed. In Aschheim he had a secure area at the end of the underground parking garage, where a dedicated elevator whisked him to the top floor. Once there he sipped peppermint tea, formulated press releases and constantly checked the Wirecard share price on his phone. He travelled so little he was rumoured to be afraid of flying, which he left to his CFO Burkhard Ley and his protégé Marsalek.

Ley's responsibility was charming the analysts and investors, who were becoming enthusiasts for the stock once again. From a low of less than €4 in October 2008, the stock hit €13 in May 2011, valuing the group at €1.3bn. What wowed them was Wirecard's incredible financial performance. Wirecard's statements of results made no mention of the Visa freeze, or the more than $12m worth of fines it imposed for excessive chargebacks on nutraceutical business. At the time, Braun wrote to shareholders that Wirecard 'had a very successful start to the New Year'. For 2010 as a whole, sales surged by a fifth to €272m.

Braun spoke all the time to his right-hand man, but Marsalek was kept physically separate in Aschheim. Braun's corner office topped the building at the centre of the U. From there it was possible to see into Marsalek's quarters, which occupied a good chunk of the top floor of Wirecard's other building, to its left, close to the sales team. He had a large suite of three rooms accessed through a single door opening into the domain of his assistant in the middle. Marsalek had little in the way of a formal schedule as, unusually for a senior executive at a company with more than 500 staff, he had no real team. He was everywhere and nowhere, constantly travelling, usually alone.

Asked when he found time to sleep, he replied with a macho 'in the air'. He was a member of Lufthansa's top-tier Honours Circle, and claimed to fly more miles than the average cabin crew. He'd arrive in Aschheim with his carry-on straight from one flight, a copy of Sun Tzu's *The Art of War* or a book on the investing genius of Warren Buffett under his arm, then trundle back out again two hours later for the next departure. The two weeks of Oktoberfest were a grinding marathon of champagne consumption when he'd wear lederhosen to the office, ready for the next night of client schmoozing. Smaul's face-time with Jan was reduced to snatched meetings in airport hotels, when Marsalek would grab a club sandwich and fries, smothered in at least four miniature bottles of Heinz ketchup. By the summer of 2011, however, Smaul's replacement as head of 'digital sales' began taking over from Marsalek as the person sending referrals to him, and she too was projecting success, becoming noticeably more chic.

The partnership, however, proceeded in fits and starts, never really taking off. Sunsont managed to set up some relationships in Asia and Eastern Europe, but Smaul found there was a predictable pattern to the clients Wirecard sent. They weren't big enough, or were get-rich-quick schemes that wouldn't last due to chargebacks. Smaul knew they would mean a few good months of processing volume, followed swiftly by rising complaints that would eat up any profit; not a viable option.

Every so often a suitable prospect would arrive, but high-risk processing had got much harder. The sales team at a bank would say yes, sure, we'll give this site a go. Once the processing started, though, it became clear it was a 'yes, but . . .' Transaction volumes would be capped to begin with, or the holdback for the rolling reserve would be huge, handicaps which drove the potential client elsewhere.

Once again Smaul was struggling to keep the lights on, and as time passed the clients sent to him became weirder. The merchants reacted to setbacks with a level of personal aggression which Smaul found disconcerting; he certainly wouldn't want to owe them money.

Sunsont limped on to the summer of 2012. Marsalek was always pleasant, but Smaul suspected he didn't like to be reminded of his failures and had bigger fish to fry. Wirecard had just raised €139m from shareholders, who were delighted with its rapid expansion: €12m for the prepaid card unit of Newcastle Building Society; €47m for the Singapore business Systems@Work; €44m for Prima Vista Solusi, an Indonesian payments business. He'd hear from old workmates that Wirecard Dublin was struggling, but the overall group's financial performance was off the charts. It was heading for just under €400m of sales that year, and profits of €100m.

Smaul had just got back from a break to celebrate his wedding anniversary when he discovered Marsalek had sent through a significant offer. It involved processing for a big collection of Japanese websites, but the catch was that Sunsont would have to do it blind. They wouldn't have any connection to the customer, and even if they knew what the websites were they wouldn't be able to understand them. It could be for escorts, drugs, a Yakuza money-washing machine, anything.

'Come on, you guys need something to do, it's good business,' Marsalek said, upbeat as ever, trying to talk Smaul into crossing the Rubicon he'd set at the beginning. The whole point of Sunsont had been to retain control, and Smaul guessed that the only reason Marsalek came to them had to be problems with the processing. They went back and forth through July and August. Smaul had pretty much said no, and then the project died. The processing just wasn't there to do any more.

With it went Sunsont. Smaul had spent two years of his life chasing a Marsalek dream. He'd seen enough to know that there was no question of his going back to Wirecard. He would get out of payments processing and find something else to do. He sold the furniture, paid off the landlord and liquidated the business. Marsalek would have to find a new partner for his tricky merchants and crackpot schemes.

8

Ghosts in Manama

2014 – London
Wirecard share price €29, market capitalization €3.6bn

WHEN I WALKED INTO the Caffè Nero by Mansion House Tube station in September 2014, all I knew about the person I'd come to meet was that he'd seen my work on Alphaville and wanted to chat. Over coffee I discovered that Leo Perry was my age, in his mid-thirties, and was a softly spoken aficionado of accounting fraud. There were the tell-tell signifiers of an English hedge fund manager – beige cashmere jumper, a couple of days' stubble – with the thoughtful, almost academic quality of a career stock market investor. He chuckled quietly to himself as he explained how to fake profits, and the trail of breadcrumbs such financial crimes leave behind. From a neat black satchel he handed me a few pages of densely typed notes. What he had were more than suspicions. So far as he was concerned, everything about Wirecard was too good to be true: paperwork exposing the company's lies was littered halfway across Asia.

Once I'd found the documents for myself I could see what Perry meant. The question was what to do with it. Paul Murphy's response was straightforward. 'Pick one of these companies, go there and knock on the door.'

I soon had a destination in mind, Bahrain, a tiny emirate in the Middle East. 'This is it, Murph, I'm sure of it, this is the smoking gun.' The reason was a company called Ashazi Services. The name was flagged by a small audit firm at one of the businesses Wirecard purchased in Singapore. 'Somebody highlighted Ashazi on purpose, you don't go putting a customer's name in the accounts without a good reason,' Perry had said. From August 2010 onwards it was supposed to have paid Wirecard €4m a year as a software licence fee, but it looked like the money never arrived. Ashazi's limited online profile was stacked with lies – operations it didn't have, a business partner who'd never heard of it. This was the way in, I was sure.

A week later I landed in Bahrain, officially there as a consultant conducting due diligence. Since the Arab Spring spread across the Middle East, the paranoid local authorities weren't keen on foreign journalists visiting. I'd offered to help with some other reporting while I was there, but the decision was that trying to visit any of the political opposition would be a bit like arriving in Belfast during the Troubles and going straight to meet Gerry Adams: sure to attract attention. I'd chatted to a Scottish engineer on the plane, a regular visitor paid to maintain some of the equipment at the US naval base, and casually tried to attach myself to his party as we approached immigration, but I was told to wait while the immigration agent disappeared into a side room with my passport. I sat there, heart thumping, trying to look relaxed. One Google search was all it would take. For twenty agonizing minutes I watched everybody else pass. Suddenly the agent reappeared. 'Welcome to Bahrain, I hope you enjoy your stay.'

I set about tracing Ashazi, criss-crossing the capital city, Manama, trying to make sense of its bizarre organization in the blazing heat. There had barely been a country before oil was found, and building numbers and streets were haphazardly arranged. I was on a ghost hunt, shown to small empty rooms in apartment buildings, lonely places at the end of dusty roads. Yes, there had been a business here once, not for a long time though. Hoping for more records, I tried the official corporate registry in the gleaming business district. I strolled right in, and could have sat at one of the desks and started leafing through files. There was every indication of bureaucracy in action, just none of its people. It was the same story at my hotel. Paul Murphy had recommended the grand Bahrain Intercontinental, as its bar was where the journalists and diplomats hung out. The two other people there may have been at the heart of international intrigue, but they were focused on murdering Beyonce's legacy through karaoke.

Looking for Ashazi's lawyer the next day, I spent half an hour walking in circles. The building just didn't seem to exist. Pausing in the sliver of shade offered by a lamp post, I consulted the map for the twenty-seventh time. On the other side of the road was a car dealership; it had to be here. Between a car rental office and a Kentucky Fried Chicken was a narrow alley strewn with rubbish; looking down it, there was an opening, a set of stairs leading inside. A couple of flights up was a lawyer's office, cool and dim, the shades drawn against the sun. A man waved me in from behind a desk in one of the rooms beyond. He seemed to be alone, and I asked for the lawyer I was after, Kumail Al Alawi.

'Oh, sorry, he doesn't work here any more. He's set up on his own, I'm not sure where the office is but it isn't too far away I think. I'll call him for you if you like. Have a seat, would you like some tea?' he said, waving me in and already dialling the number. Someone answered and they chatted in Arabic for a minute, the man glancing in my direction as he spoke, then he handed over the handset. 'Here, he can explain to you the directions himself.'

It wasn't to an office. 'Yes, yes, I'm here now, I can see you, but I think it will be easier if I pick you up. There's a car park you should be able to find.' I scribbled down the way and his number, thanked the other lawyer and set off. I found myself walking beside a long highway past the backs of buildings into a desolate area, conscious that I didn't really know where I was, let alone anyone else. I shot Murphy a message with the scant details I had.

The car park was small, with only a handful of the spaces occupied. A dirty black saloon pulled in and beeped. I got in and said an awkward hello to Kumail. We drove a couple of hundred metres, turning into a construction site. 'They're still working on the building, nobody can ever find it,' he said. Inside we went to what appeared to be the only occupied office. It was obviously new, with white walls, minimal cheap furniture and a couple of large ferns, almost as if it had been thrown together as a set for a daytime soap opera. We sat at his desk and an assistant served us hot mint tea.

'Ashazi . . . Ashazi,' Kumail muttered to himself as he scanned the set of laminate shelves next to his desk. They were full of thick lever-arch files stuffed with paper, client names jotted on the spine in black sharpie. He pulled down a lone slim blue file, opened it on the desk between us and flicked half-heartedly through the contents. It was just a few registration papers, little more than I found online. He shrugged. Talk to the founder, he suggested, and jotted down her number on a scrap of paper.

Back at the Intercontinental I left messages for this Nasreen Sururi, a local actress, TV presenter and entrepreneur, and looked over the little I had. Another trip to the registrar's office had been fruitless. The receptionist at a Regus office provider in the business district remembered that Ashazi had taken some space there for a short period, but nothing else. There was evidence of a short-lived website online. Something had existed, but it hardly seemed to have had the scale to pay Wirecard €12m for software. There was no way to be sure. I'd got a phone number, learned that brogues were a terrible idea for shoe-leather reporting in desert heat, but not much else. Giving up, I thought I might as well go and have a look at a mega-mall out on the edge of the city I'd kept passing in cabs.

The cavernous halls were pleasantly chilly and quiet. I was brows-ing in Zara when the phone went – it was Nasreen Sururi. Crouching in an alcove by a fire exit, balancing a notepad on one knee, I asked about her business. Did she remember the contract with Wirecard in Singapore?

'No,' she said, pausing. 'No. I cannot recall anything. As you say, I cannot recall what I had for lunch. Literally I forget everything in my files.'

It was worth several million euros, I said. Surely she'd remember that.

Her business partner, Christopher Bauer, agreed to all the con-tracts, she said. 'I was running the company more on the management and marketing side.' Then she decided that if I had any more ques-tions I should email them. It wasn't much, but it was a start.

Back in London, I tracked down this Bauer. An old presentation for another payment company he'd run, PayEasy Solutions, was floating around online. It said PayEasy was a global provider of payment solutions with operations in the US, UK, Monaco, Hong Kong, Manila, Bahrain, Lebanon and Germany, and listed Bauer as CEO along with his personal email address. In a remarkable turn, Bauer had nothing to do with Ashazi's contracts either. 'I was more on the PR and marketing side,' he claimed when I finally reached him in the Philippines at the end of October. In his version of events Ashazi was a start-up trying to process payments in the Middle East. 'Most of the time it was her who did the work.' Somehow, a multi-million-euro licence fee deal with a Singapore branch of Wirecard had sprung into existence without any involvement of the people running the company. No wonder the money never arrived.

Bauer did know about Wirecard, however. 'I haven't worked for it, no, but I've been consulting on payments for a long time and they've got a great reputation here in Asia. Good technology. I've had a lot of experience in the industry, so let me know if you ever want to talk.'

'Sure, thanks, I will,' I said, hanging up. It was time to knock on the door at Wirecard itself.

9

That's All Bullshit

2014 – London
Wirecard share price €35, market capitalization €4.2bn

A T THE START OF the dance we both feigned polite interest. I called up the company's media relations team and expressed an interest in finding out more about this European PayPal. Wirecard's chief of communications was Iris Stoeckl, who had worked with the company since it was rescued from bankruptcy. She was pleased and polite, but of course I'd have to wait a month until the next financial results were published. Then I'd be welcome to visit Munich for a chat with a product manager about industry innovations. It was a fairly standard brush-off, if a bit strange from a small company that would normally welcome publicity from the *FT*. The tone changed when I sent her questions about Ashazi. Then Stoeckl wanted to know if I was corrupt or just naive.

'The only serious issue in this context is that obviously some short sellers (e.g. hedge funds) are trying to misuse you and the *FT* for their short-term speculative interest. We received various emails by our analysts and some investors in the last three months that they have been aggressively addressed by some hedge funds which were obviously short on the company. As this did not work because experts on the company saw at once that the questions raised had no ground whatsoever, it is our belief that you now have been targeted.' Confident that neither I nor the *FT* would want to be misused in such a 'dubious plot', she wanted to know what had triggered my interest and did I know anyone who was short?

Clearly I was on to something. Paul Murphy advised a terse reply. 'All I can say is that we examine a wide array of companies and situations as part of our regular journalistic operations,' I said, directing Iris to the *FT*'s code of conduct. Half an hour later, Nasreen Sururi popped back up. I hadn't heard from Ashazi's founder since I was in Bahrain. Something had jogged her memory because she wrote to say that the contract with Wirecard did exist after all. 'Please respect that because of non-disclosure agreements I cannot talk about details,' she said.

By then I had a well-developed theory. The Ashazi situation suggested Wirecard was faking some of its sales and profits, then using its purchase of Asian companies to hide the fraud, which is why the numbers got bigger every year. Leo Perry had explained the mechanics, fiddling with the lid of his coffee cup in the window of Caffè Nero.

'Faking profits, you end up with a problem of fake cash. At the end of the year the auditor will expect to see a healthy bank balance, it's the first thing they check. So what you have to do is *spend* that fake cash on fake assets,' he said. Imagine the auditor opens the treasure chest and finds it empty. We spent the gold on that building at the top of the hill, you say, handing them a telescope. So long as the accountant doesn't walk up there and discover the house is just a wooden façade (or, indeed, get on a flight to Bahrain), everything is fine.

Wirecard tended to announce its Asian takeovers right before the end of the year. Was that when it knew it had fake cash to make disappear? Instead of 'spending' the invented profits on an entirely fake business, it seemed to have found operations in poor shape which weren't worth very much. My working assumption was that the original owners of these businesses were either promised enough money to keep them happy, a few million euros, say, or Wirecard had someone else buy the operation first. Markus Braun could then effectively throw a press conference to present the sellers with a giant novelty cheque, an extra zero or two added to the price.

The challenge of such fraud is that each year the numbers get larger as the business grows; there is not much point in committing stock fraud to be boring and unnoticed. Each year Wirecard's deals got larger, and it had twice raised cash from shareholders to pay for them. If I was right, that money had been stolen. I was also mindful of John Hempton's silver mine; life was stranger than fiction and an explanation from someone senior could make all the difference. After weeks of persistence a date was set just before Christmas: 10 a.m. on 18 December.

'Good morning, Dan, how are you today? I'm sitting here with Markus, so may I introduce you to him virtually?' said Iris Stoeckl. I was in an out-of-the way meeting room in the *FT* office, a favoured spot for difficult conversations as the noise of arguments didn't carry too far. The voice of Markus Braun emanating from the speakerphone was positively cheery.

'Yeah, good to hear you. I appreciate the conversation. I heard some background of course, you were already in contact with our investor relations department, and I'm looking forward to being grilled.'

Chuckling, to indicate we're all friends here, I started gently. 'What is Wirecard, how should our readers understand what the company is, what you have been trying to do there, because you've been running the company for, it's what, is it twelve years now?'

'Yes, I came into the company at the beginning of 2002, the end of 2001, so I took over the company when everybody was coming out of the internet, because I'm a crazy person,' he said, launching into a fifteen-minute recitation of the factors behind Wirecard's success, so full of business-word salad that snatches of it might have come from *Succession*'s Kendall Roy: 'Our key claim today is of course internet technology to be used not only for online transactions but looking into the future there will also be a convergence . . . So we think that if you look into the future and the last five years we strongly believe in an omnichannel approach for the future merchant for all these transactions, for a strong internet platform, sales channels online, mobile and point of sale.'

I could tell why he was not a frequent subject of media interviews, although Braun claimed that was due to modesty. 'I'm not a big fan of companies where the CEO always puts himself in front of the media. I don't like so much this star-CEO approach.' Wirecard too operated largely behind the scenes, quietly facilitating payments for merchants, and what distinguished it from competitors was its technology, he said: 'We're an internet company with a bank as a daughter, and not the other way round.'

I was biding my time, dutifully scribbling down the empty phrases. 'Why do you buy small companies in Asia?' I asked.

'Being successful in payments is a little bit different to being successful in McDonald's, or a social network. You need a good combination of technology and local flavour, local understanding, local elements,' Braun said, adding a long list of countries where Wirecard operated.

Hoping to spur something quotable, I tried a left-field question about the architect Buckminster Fuller's geodesic dome. Wirecard's 2009 annual report had included a whole riff about how Fuller's design for a spherical building – the best-known of which is Disneyland's golf ball-like Epcot Center – somehow related to the practice of mergers and acquisitions. There was a baffled silence, then Iris interjected. 'I'll go and get a copy. Was it the 2008 annual report you said?'

Braun, clearly having no idea what I was banging on about, switched into management consultant mode: I caught 'learning curve', 'differentiating elements', 'philosophy', 'clear added value'.

What did it even mean? It was time to get to the meat. 'So just in terms of these Asian acquisitions that I've been taking a look at. Some of the ways that you buy them seem a little unusual.'

Trying to pin Braun down on details was useless, however. His answers were convoluted and contradictory. He would only talk in generalities, except when it came to the tenfold rise in Wirecard's share price. 'We are one of the most successful internet companies in Europe. Why are you so sceptical?'

I paused. There was nothing for it. 'What it looks like to me is that there are a few different possibilities about what is happening at Wirecard. One is that your accounts are sloppy. Another is that these acquisitions are being used to hide something.'

'What?' Braun interjected sharply as I pressed on. What I really wanted to know was if the dodgy takeovers were all fraud and fake profits, or if the money for them was real and he was looting the company as well.

'These deals are either being used to hide cash which doesn't exist, or are being used to send cash which does exist to third parties.'

'That's all bullshit, sorry to say it so openly. You must take one thing into account, [at] a successful company there are always people around who are jealous, who are full of emotion. I am absolutely sure you have talked to somebody like that. I can just give you some strong advice, we have seventeen analysts, we are audited by Ernst & Young. [On the] deals that we do the due diligence is done by an auditor and a high-profile legal company. With all due respect there is no ground whatsoever for this. I think the only real thing here is that there are some people that are full of emotions and full of jealousness and envy, they can be from the competition or something, I think that's the real issue here. Which is fair, I think around PayPal there are such people, around Google there are such people, it's part of success, I can take it.' He finished with a question – 'Why should I take this risk?' – and the strange thing was Braun's words were angry but his tone was not. He sounded almost weary, as if he was tired of having to explain yet again why he was not a fraudster. Then he said something casually, as if it was completely normal preparation for a newspaper interview. 'You're a smart guy, I think you're honest, we of course did some background checks.' I didn't really think about it at the time, wanting to get to the topic of Ashazi.

Wirecard's boss was again unaware of the details. I could hear him leafing through papers. 'I read here we had a relationship with this company between 2009 and 2012. Obviously in 2012 we had the activities in Bahrain associated with the Arab Spring.' He said Ashazi had paid its bills. 'What is your problem?'

'Ashazi never filed accounts in Bahrain. For a period when it was supposedly run out of its lawyer's office it was paying Wirecard €1m a month. I've been to that lawyer's office, it's tiny, it's above a car rental place on a small Bahrain back street. Other people involved describe it as in a start-up mode. None of the people could remember the contract until after I contacted Wirecard, and suddenly their story changed,' I said.

'You're a journalist, yeah,' he replied, invoking his status. 'I'm the CEO of a TecDAX company, what shall I say?'

'Hang on, I forgot the most important part. Ashazi claimed to be the official agent for a respectable Sri Lankan software company.

Ashazi put out press releases to that effect, its staff talked about this relationship in articles in Bahrain. That is a complete sham, that relationship did not exist, Ashazi was lying about it,' I said.

The problem was, for all the shoe leather expended, I'd caught Wirecard's customer lying, not Wirecard itself. Braun countered that he wasn't there to represent Ashazi, and Wirecard had got its money. 'I don't see any reason why for you as an *FT* journalist or for me running this company there is any significance to this thing,' Braun said.

Stoeckl moved to wrap things up. 'We are running out of time.'

If I was going to write something I'd have to put it all to him for comment. I offered him a summary. His was a company which showed the hallmarks of fraud: 'It listed by reverse takeover; you've had the same senior management in place for a very long time; the origins of the company seem opaque; the company has done a series of acquisitions which seem to have unusual aspects about them; and there are a series of accounting anomalies which if you start to look at Wirecard Gibraltar appear as early as 2005/2006. And that's why I'm looking at Wirecard.'

Braun laughed. 'Dan, with all due respect, couldn't this be the other way around? Couldn't it be a success factor that we have continuity in the management. We consistently have a strong net cash flow, we have a net cash position of over €500m. Couldn't it be exactly the other way around, that you had prejudice, that you tried to prove this prejudice, for whatever reason?' He carried on in that vein for a while, and listening to him I was conscious of a human trait: people prefer to lie indirectly if they can. Asking a question is a good way to avoid answering it. 'Markus, can I just point out that you didn't deny what was a very serious allegation that was just made.'

'I completely deny that,' he quickly responded, reaching once again for the professional opinion of others as bona fides. 'We are audited by Ernst & Young. The bank is additional-audited, so with all due respect it is simply not true. We are a very successful company.'

Our time was up and we all played at being friends again. I thanked him for his patience, and Braun urged me to stay in touch with a final encouragement: 'I would very much like to win you as a fan of Wirecard.'

10

On the Make in India

2015 – Chennai
Wirecard share price €35, market capitalization €4.3bn

MARSALEK WASN'T SUPPOSED TO be in India. Officially, on 7 July 2015, he was on company business in Thailand. Instead he landed in Chennai to meet one of his most important friends and business partners, Henry O'Sullivan, an extremely wide Englishman. For a long time O'Sullivan had lived in Monaco, pitching up in 2005 and spending money like it was water. He told friends he'd made a fortune working with David Vanrenen, a South African payments industry entrepreneur, and was busy making another one facilitating transactions for porn and gambling. The yacht from which he made important calls to the Wirecard sales team was *Sudelan*, what locals called a 'tart trap': a big, fast open motorboat with a few crew, ideal for the run down to St-Tropez. He told friends he'd backed a restaurant, Le Virage, in a prime spot on the Grand Prix circuit by the quay, and one year entertained Wirecard's CFO, Burkhard Ley, over a race weekend. For a long time O'Sullivan's business was clearly booming; a friend recalled him announcing his presence in a Mayfair hotel by barging in and slapping an inch of £50 notes on to the bar. 'Game's over, losers, I have all the money.'

On that sweltering monsoon day, O'Sullivan and Marsalek met in a hotel to put the finishing touches to a scheme that was months in the preparation. They had found an Indian business for Wirecard to buy, a chain of kiosks known as Smart Shops that were one step down from internet cafés; each had a computer, which the operator would primarily use to book bus, train and airplane tickets for customers. The name of the company reflected that focus, Hermes i-Tickets, and it was a business model suited to life at the fringes of modernity which was fast disappearing; the spread of cheap mobile phones was shrinking the population who needed a middleman to go online for them. If Wirecard truly had cutting-edge technology, Hermes' network of kiosks might have been a way to offer payments services to a billion potential customers. Instead, Hermes was a cutglass gem about to be sold as a diamond. At one level the plan was simple. Henry O'Sullivan had arranged to buy Hermes for €36m. He and Marsalek had given the company a quick polish, and were about to sell it on to Wirecard at a huge mark-up.

What complicated the plan was the need to establish a storyline that would pass scrutiny by journalists, short sellers, auditors and regulators. So in the hotel meeting room with O'Sullivan and Marsalek were a selection of Indian frontmen whose contribution was to hide O'Sullivan from sight. They'd set up a Mauritius investment vehicle with the nondescript name Emerging Markets Investment Fund 1A; it was this fund that would buy the chain of Smart Shops, then flip it on to Wirecard. To anyone who asked, 1A was a publicity-shy private equity fund.

Marsalek was the double agent. In the room with the Indian frontmen, his act suggested that the wool had to be pulled over the eyes of some or all of his colleagues who were already in the air, set to arrive on Lufthansa flight LH758 from Frankfurt that very night. Photographs of the 'VIP guests' had already been circulated, and Marsalek ticked off their responsibilities and expectations. Burkhard Ley, Wirecard's CFO, was leading the delegation to negotiate the purchase of the Smart Shop chain, accompanied by a collection of staff and external advisors. Marsalek warned who would be tricky and offered social tips about which of the German visitors preferred beer over wine, the better that both sides could rub along.

Two brothers in the room listening to this briefing were central to Marsalek's scheme, 'The Boys', as O'Sullivan called them. Ramu and

Palani Ramasamy were the faces of the Indian business Hermes; Ramu's with a broad, toothy smile, Palani's more reserved, wearing rimless glasses and a pencil moustache. Serial entrepreneurs, they had founded Hermes and the plan required them to stick around as managers once it was sold on to Wirecard. Leaving nothing to chance, Marsalek ran through the presentation Ramu was to give the next day, anticipating questions the Wirecard team would ask. All smiles, Marsalek was satisfied. Everything was in place for Wirecard's largest-ever takeover to begin.

Seeds for the deal had been planted three years earlier, when a contact of Henry O'Sullivan's took Marsalek on a scouting trip to see companies in Mumbai. He met one of the Ramasamy Boys for a chat at the Orchid, an extravagant airport hotel. It was friendly, high-level and brief. Hermes' chain of kiosks was interesting but too small for Marsalek's purposes, and he swiftly moved on.

When nothing else fitted the bill, O'Sullivan's contact, who had played tour guide, tried again, introducing Marsalek to a couple of banks in Hyderabad. The pitch was a bust, but afterwards Marsalek pulled a neat little bit of kit out of his bag to show off, a prototype credit card reader which could be attached to a mobile phone. A light bulb went off in the mind of the guide; here was the perfect device for a country with millions of small traders. It was Wirecard's version of Square, the company disrupting the US payments industry with a white plastic box that made it easy and cheap to take card payments. 'I'd love to launch this here,' he said.

Marsalek gave an easy shrug. Sure, he said, he'd discuss it with O'Sullivan. The guide persisted, and in early 2013 he found a bank and a taxi firm with 10,000 cars prepared to work together on a trial. The project was off the ground, and the company Bijlipay was born. Wirecard funded it through an €8m convertible loan, yet it was O'Sullivan who took control, somehow ending up with three-quarters of the shares – in the name of a Singapore company – while his new partner, the Indian guide, kept the rest.

O'Sullivan saw enough promise in the project to uproot his life, family and entourage from Monaco to Chennai, including an old friend and consigliere who joined Bijlipay as a director. By July 2014 the product was finally ready for launch, so Wirecard trumpeted the roll-out in a press release and conference call with investors. It was a promising entrée into a huge market and the long-term potential was significant, *if* they could make it work. (Square would soon raise investment at a $6bn valuation, making it substantially more valuable than Wirecard.) Yet Bijlipay's progress was slow and patience wasn't a Jan Marsalek virtue. He wanted Bijlipay to start buying up the competition.

Hermes' chain of internet kiosks was run from Chennai as well, so O'Sullivan and his Indian partner knocked on the Ramasamy brothers' door. A merger made sense; the tens of thousands of Smart Shops could use Bijlipay card readers, updating their technology and expanding the brand. Down the line the whole thing could be sold to Wirecard. O'Sullivan offered about €24m, plus a bonus dependent on profits, for Hermes (through Santego Capital, a Singapore shell company), but the brothers didn't bite.

A November attempt to reopen talks with Hermes was delayed by a nasty attack of dengue fever in the O'Sullivan household. Marsalek was then engaged in something more important: lavish celebrations for O'Sullivan's fortieth birthday on Benguerra Island, a tropical idyll off the coast of Mozambique. Guests flew in from around the world, encouraged to bring champagne, Bombay Sapphire gin and Sky vodka with them. Marsalek and his girlfriend went for the weekend, along with the head of Wirecard's digital sales team and her husband, who worked in the company's technology team.

A week later it was back to business. On 8 December O'Sullivan wrote to the brothers: 'It's a shame that our deal never culminated in anything, but that's business, no hard feelings.' Instead, a December meeting was set for one of the brothers with Marsalek at Vienna's imperious Hotel Sacher, home to Austria's most famous cake. As the conversations continued into the New Year, it would transpire that Marsalek and O'Sullivan had something ambitious in mind for Hermes.

Henry O'Sullivan was extremely careful. Like Jan Marsalek, he conducted important business over Telegram, the encrypted messaging app made famous by Isis terrorists. WhatsApp was for wives and girl-friends, O'Sullivan told business partners who tried to use it. There were companies which his friends and associates knew he controlled, even though the signature of Singaporean citizens appeared on official documents. Little trace of the man was to be found online. However, bank heists and international M&A are similar in that both require careful planning and a trustworthy team. For the latter there are lawyers, staff and a thousand small tasks of administration. Frontmen need careful instruction on how to proceed, and it was impossible to quietly whisper in their ear when there were thousands of miles between Singapore, Chennai and Port Louis in Mauritius. So, to manage the purchase of Hermes from the brothers and its sale to Wirecard, O'Sullivan used Fleep, a messaging and file-sharing service. What neither he nor Marsalek appears to have realized, however, was how to properly delete the archives of their activity. For instance, on Friday, 13 February O'Sullivan started the day in energetic mode, updating his team on progress and dispensing compliments: 'I am impressed at your grasp of Fleep already Amit, your protestations of techie illiteracy were clearly over-cooked!'

On the receiving end of the praise was Amit Shah, the man providing the fund, 1A, used for the deal. Shah was a hefty figure, physically and financially. Almost forty, he was a co-founder of IIFL Wealth, an Indian fund management group with offices all over the world. Under Shah's direction IIFL set up 1A and arranged Mauritian directors to administer the fund and deal with all correspondence. Lowly operations guys, they did what O'Sullivan told them to. On that unlucky Friday, however, O'Sullivan was personally involved. He went to see The Boys in Chennai with a USB stick full of the documents needed to purchase Hermes from them, keen to get things moving before Ramu Ramasamy left for a spiritual retreat in the Himalayas. A deed was signed on 25 March for The Boys' holding company to sell 94 per cent of Hermes to 1A. Something had changed their minds and persuaded them to sell.

April Fools' Day saw Jan Marsalek lend a hand in Munich. The Hermes website was outdated and focused on its travel agency arm. If the company was to be presented as a glittering and valuable fintech, a rebrand was needed. He sent a local web designer a detailed layout for a slick new Hermes website, brazenly using his Wirecard email account. At one point he shared some feedback from India: 'The Boys have requested the new logo to be incorporated in the banner images.' The web designers worked regularly with Wirecard and were surprised to deal directly with one of its top executives and by the urgent pace of the commission. They simply assumed Hermes was part of the company, particularly when the €25,000 bill was settled by Wirecard.

Next was for O'Sullivan and Amit Shah to meet 'The Buyer': Jan Marsalek. Amit Shah pushed for Goa, where he liked the Park Hyatt and the weather, but they settled on Dubai for 16 April.

Work began on the cover story that 1A was a private equity fund. 'We want to show investments going into fund for storyline,' O'Sullivan told the team.

In May, The Boys caused trouble. They had received an advance payment of 120 million rupees in March (worth €1.7m). Yet for the sale of Hermes to go through certain paperwork had to be rubber-stamped by a deadline, otherwise the payment would have to be recalled. One of the brothers was in Penang, and unable to find a witness willing or able to sign papers for a foreigner. The whole deal was on the cusp of unravelling and O'Sullivan was furious that the Reserve Bank of India, which tracked all money flowing in and, particularly, out of India, might notice. 'In the course of attempting to keep our heads under the parapet, we're about to pop ourselves up to [the Reserve Bank of India] and yell "here we are",' he wrote on Fleep. He suggested accepting a small transfer of shares in Hermes in return for the money, then sorting the rest of the paperwork out later, which prompted the fund's lawyer, Katherine Ardiss, to intervene.

'Red light,' interjected Ardiss, a petite M&A specialist from O'Sullivan's Monaco social scene. The fund was arranging to buy all of Hermes, and without the right papers to complete the whole transaction it risked being left with a minor shareholding it couldn't sell. 'My duty remains to [1A] and I will step down when red light is crossed,' she said.

'I would rather lose [€1.7m] and still have a deal right now than scupper the whole deal,' replied O'Sullivan. But the lawyer responded that letting the money go would also kill it, just more slowly.

'I have no answer for an impossible situation knowingly created by the sellers,' she wrote.

Amit Shah, ever the banker, invoked the stakes. The payoff from selling Hermes on to Wirecard was 'disproportionate' relative to the money the fund would risk, he said, while the paperwork problem was a 'technical issue which is not intentional'.

O'Sullivan seemed to have been persuaded of the need for caution with The Boys. 'The problem is if it is intentional, Amit. They have had twenty-four hours to arrange a witness. More.' He demanded an 'idiot's guide' for what had to be signed, and where, and the team scrambled to find a solution.

Shah was a problem solver. The brother came to Shah's Singapore office, where the pages were finally signed, witnessed and stamped. Shah then took Palani out to lunch to mark the occasion. There was no turning back now. Two days later, Jan Marsalek informed Burkhard Ley of the good news: he'd found an exciting new company in India for Wirecard to buy.

On the morning of Wednesday, 8 July, Amit Shah had breakfast with Wirecard's due diligence team at the Chennai Park Hyatt, then accompanied the group to see Hermes. The offices were dingy, on an industrial estate close to a major highway. Its staff were packed in, their monitors almost touching. Lacking a separate canteen, they ate at their stations, which gave the atmosphere a certain robust aroma. The meeting room was also crammed with almost twenty people to discuss what Wirecard called Project Peacock. The walls were thin and traffic noise filtered through. Disregarding the humble surroundings, Amit Shah ran the show. Acting like the owner, he kicked off proceedings by talking about 1A. He said the fund had an agreement to buy Hermes, but the deal hadn't closed. He didn't mention the price. Then he handed over to The Boys. Their presentation practically channelled Markus Braun. It was a high-level sprint through the wonders of Hermes and its network of 100,000 Smart Shops. There was barely any detail on the business itself, just a single page of financial figures with bold projections for the future, filled out with guff about financial inclusion and meaningless statistics. *Rural households account for 83 per cent of total domestic remittances in India but urban households are expected to exceed 30 per cent in the coming years*, ran one large-type bullet.* There was little interaction, just a few questions from Burkhard Ley. After a working lunch, there was a trip to see a few Smart Shops in action. To a cynical eye the pristine blue and white English-language banners at these locations, draped over the dirty Tamil signs of other stores, might have looked suspiciously new and out of place.

Day two removed proceedings to the calm surrounds of a business hotel. It was time to get into the figures and the Hermes CFO didn't use a laptop. Instead an assistant carried in and reassembled the various parts of his PC on the meeting room table. The CFO was an older gentleman with grey hair and thick spectacles. He squinted at the computer screen, where barely nine cells of a spreadsheet zoomed to giant size were visible. He delivered a rapid-fire monologue about the economics of Hermes in a thick accent that some of the Germans found hard to follow. After lunch the party broke into smaller groups to focus on the various technical, financial and legal aspects of the deal, at which point the value of KPMG became clear. Two partners from the accounting firm were advising 1A, and they had already conducted extensive due diligence for its purchase. Such work by one of the world's most reputable accounting firms left their counterparts at the accounting firm advising Wirecard, Baker Tilly, largely free to focus on expansive projections for the future. The story was that 1A intended to carve out the travel agency part of Hermes, which Wirecard did not want, leaving behind the payments operations, remittances arm and technology.

Satisfied with their progress and with plenty to be getting on with, the Wirecard team set off back to the airport. All they needed now

---

* The Ramasamys' lawyer said they were told by O'Sullivan the purpose of the meeting was to discuss Wirecard's investment into their technology business with the aim of establishing an Indian payments bank, and that shortly beforehand O'Sullivan said representatives of 1A would attend as he wanted them to meet Wirecard.

was for Jan Marsalek to negotiate the price. The sellers had asked for $500m, claiming private equity interest, which raised a few smiles on the Wirecard side. They were considering something much more reasonable as a starting point: just €250m.

Marsalek was in charge of those conversations, and he gently walked the price up to the maximum Wirecard was prepared to pay: €326m for Hermes, plus a €14m injection of capital into a related business, GI Technology. (A Bangalore chain of currency exchange shops valued at around €1m and some other entities of minimal value were also bundled into the deal.)

By October, Jan Marsalek and Henry O'Sullivan were starting to look ahead. Marsalek appeared back in Chennai with an old friend from Munich in tow – 'Colin' – who was part of their plans for 1A once Hermes was sold to Wirecard. Colin, whose default setting was enthusiasm, was a slight and amiable German who'd spent his career in the tourism industry. It had never taken him to India, and he was thrilled by its assault on the senses: the heat, the heady mix of dirt, spice, petrol and sweat which filled the air. People were everywhere, and parts of the city had an open, unfinished look to them, improvised pipework and electrics on full display. He marvelled at a man stretched out asleep on a flat piece of concrete by the roadside, a piece of cloth stretched over his face as if he were a corpse. The next moment they were ushered into the cool marble of a luxury hotel, where Marsalek thought nothing of dropping $1,000 on a bottle of Château Haut-Brion '94, or whatever exclusive wine label caught his eye that day. Marsalek would rattle off the wines, not for the flavours but for the prices and the power, appearing to enjoy the look of anxiety on a guest's face in that brief moment of uncertainty when a stupendous bill arrived. The less he liked someone, the longer he'd let them sweat before swooping in with a thick wad of notes. 'Please, if you'd allow me it would be my honour to take care of this.'

Colin was there to meet O'Sullivan, who introduced himself by his first name: James. (In some groups he'd be Henry, in others James, perhaps to help keep his complicated business arrangements compartmentalised.) In this small circle there was no attempt to hide the fact that Marsalek and O'Sullivan were arm in arm as they explained their plans for 1A. Left with the unwanted travel offcuts from Hermes, they intended to buy another travel business, Orbit, for a few million euros, then inject a big chunk of cash. Colin's job would be to run this new operation, called Goomo. He was game, but as they discussed Hermes a thought occurred. 'So, you want to buy this company for €300m. But have you checked out any of these Smart Shops?' he asked. Marsalek said no. Colin looked at Marsalek and O'Sullivan in turn. 'Wait, so you're buying, and you're selling, and you've never even seen one?'

'OK. I think that could be a problem,' Marsalek said. The three of them jumped into Henry's blue tuktuk, enjoying the breeze and the novelty as he puttered through the dust to a bustling flower market. Amid the riot of colour, three white men in white designer shirts stuck out like a sore thumb. They found a man sitting underneath a Smart Shop sign holding a giant, ancient laptop with a plug-in 3G connection. He could make money transfers, like Western Union, or print out bus tickets. A couple more stops brought similar results. Their fact-finding mission complete, they retreated back to the hotel to toast their efforts with vintage champagne.

The effort to get the deal over the line did come at a social cost, however. O'Sullivan and Marsalek missed a weekend's shooting in Ellingham, a village on the Northumberland coast, with a small group of O'Sullivan's friends.

Wirecard announced the €340m purchase of Indian businesses on 27 October. There was no mention of 1A in the press release, just that the cash would go to The Boys, Ramu & Palani, who intended to stay on as managers, and non-specified 'financial investors' in two parts: €230m initially, followed by €110m more related to profitability.

Within a week a €75m down payment appeared in 1A's account and O'Sullivan was impatient to see it disbursed to the two Singapore shell companies which had invested in the fund. 'For heaven's sakes I wanted that processed and released today. This is becoming increasingly frustrating can you PLEASE get that redemption processed tonight and released. This is too much,' he wrote on 4 November.

The next morning he let someone else ask. 'Thank you for beating me to the question, Amit, I was slowly pulling the arms off my chair,' he replied, and this time his patience was rewarded with the news that payments of $58.9m and $12.6m respectively were dispatched to the two companies. 'Thanks, will ask the investor to keep an eye open for it,' Henry said.

There was also the matter of paying 1A's advisors, which included one of the world's top law firms. Hugo Stolkin, a Linklaters partner in Singapore, slung in a bill for legal fees of $459,946. The biggest invoice was from a Dubai business of Ramu's father-in-law, Veerappan Narayanan, whose consultancy received an initial $5m 'finder's fee' on the purchase of Hermes by 1A, €2.8m more from the onward sale to Wirecard, plus a share of the future earnout payments. Did the money explain why the brothers were willing to sell all but one of their shares in Hermes to 1A, then take part in the sale of the business to Wirecard for eight times the price?* For all the brothers' co-operation, they continued to cause headaches for O'Sullivan. The role of 1A was supposed to be confidential, but the Indian law firm used by the brothers bragged to a legal trade rag about advising on the sale of Hermes to the fund, prompting a scramble to get the story taken down.

His work in India almost done, O'Sullivan was in the process of moving to Singapore, tying up a few loose ends to get the travel company Goomo in motion. Colin, the travel expert, returned to India in January 2016, this time meeting Marsalek and Henry O'Sullivan in Mumbai. He tried to talk them out of buying Orbit, a travel agency whose main operation largely involved sending groups of Indian businesspeople to trade fairs, including one in Hanover each year. It was too late. 'The deal is done,' Marsalek said, and the meeting was simply to bring the $3m purchase to a close. KPMG had been hired to advise on carving travel out of Hermes and merging it into Orbit.

Afterwards the whole party went to the Four Seasons Hotel for a slap-up celebration, where Colin met The Boys from Hermes. One of the guests claimed to be involved in distributing the Indian version of

---

* The Ramasamys' lawyer said Narayanan's services to 1A were independent commercial arrangements, and that they had to 'deal' with Wirecard because of their ongoing roles at Hermes and its investment in their other company.

Viagra and sat a large carton of 'Vigora' pills on the table as a talking point. The food was theatrical pan-Asian: tuna tartare atop cubes of ice a foot high; chicken teriyaki draped over giant spring onions. It was, of course, washed down with the best of the cellar. A Château Mouton Rothschild '95 and another Haut-Brion, this time the '99, which Colin thought was particularly delicious. Money was no object, in entertaining and hiring. Varun Gupta, the KPMG partner who'd overseen the due diligence on Hermes for 1A, was offered a $100,000 signing bonus and $360,000 annual package to join Goomo as finance director. Now all they needed was a suitable base for Goomo's European headquarters, and Marsalek already had an appropriately grandiose address in mind.

11

Rabble and Strife

May 2015 – Mansion House
Wirecard share price €41, market capitalization €5bn

IT WAS LEO PERRY'S turn to think he had the smoking gun. I arrived at Caffè Nero to find the hedge fund manager on our usual perch in the window overlooking the tangle of roads that converge at Mansion House. There were two coffees waiting, and he was smiling with a look that said he'd found something.

'This is it, this is how they're doing it,' he said, putting a sheet of paper in front of me covered in numbers, no words. I'd asked him about Wirecard's cash flow a week earlier and here was the answer. It meant nothing to me, and the situation wasn't much improved the first few times Perry explained. The general thrust was that Wirecard hid an accumulation of fake sales by a subtle bit of misdirection. Because it was a strange hybrid of technology company and bank it had weird financial statements. Some of the money flows recorded there related to the huge volume of payments coursing through its systems from credit card issuers to merchants, while the rest described Wirecard's actual business: the commission it kept from each transaction and all the various costs and investments and profits and other details of activity at a normal company. To simplify everything, Wirecard's CFO, Burkhard Ley, provided analysts with adjusted versions of the cash flow statement. It was like he took a knife and carefully cut Wirecard the machine away from the giant spinning wheel it powered. The engine generating the profits was what investors cared about. Leo Perry reverse-engineered that process to look at the wheel, and he found something. Sitting there, left behind unnoticed, was a pile of unpaid invoices. The amount was small in proportion to the wheel, but large compared to the engine: about €250m worth of sales where the money hadn't arrived. (Accountants call these trade receivables.) If he was right, pretty much all the profits Wirecard had declared as a public company were fake.*

Nobody had noticed because trying to visualize the wheel was head-spinning. Perry was unusually diligent at the hard parts of accounting. He'd had the good fortune to land early in his career at a hedge fund, Ennismore, run by two of the top investors in the 1990s. They threw books in his direction and told him to ask when he had questions. He'd discovered that London's junior market, AIM, had plenty of examples of dubious balance sheets, and he liked the certainty that came with finding them – as well as the tendency of such companies to collapse overnight once someone exposed them. (Hence why Perry was helping me to get to the truth.)

When I tried to explain the theory to the readers of *FT* Alphaville, however, the reaction was similar to the first set of blog posts in the House of Wirecard series we published. The company set Schillings on us, the aggressive London law firm specializing in reputation defence work. 'Mr McCrum now suggests that there may be "underlying problems" with our client's business or that it may need to "restate previous accounts". As with all his previous allegations of wrongdoing, these conclusions are, at best, based upon fundamental misunderstandings of our client's business.' I didn't have enough proof to use the f-word, fraud, in print and many readers were stumped. One commented, not unreasonably, 'This article could do with a paragraph that states, in plain English, what the author's point

---

* Ley denied any knowledge of or involvement in alleged fraudulent accounting while he was CFO. His lawyer said during that time Ley had no indication financial statements were prepared on the basis of false financial data. He said additional information was provided in the adjusted cash flow statement for the effect of reporting dates, which was precisely stated and justified in each instance.

is. There are a lot of facts presented, but their significance is lost on me (sorry). I feel a bit like I've just watched a French film – I've read all the subtitles, I've paid attention, but I have no idea what that ending was all about.'

Hedge funds and accounting nerds seemed interested, but most investors trusted the company to explain a complicated situation. I was also on a ticking clock, having taken a pay rise and a promotion to run a team of market reporters on the *FT*'s equivalent of the sports pages: the section at the back which tracked the gyrations of asset prices and the performance of the teams involved in trading them, garnished with expert opinion on what might happen next. The impact of a year's work was to see Wirecard's share price go from €41 in April 2015 to €37 at the start of September. I'd taken the horse to water; there were other stories out there. I'd have to wait for something more attention-grabbing to show up.

While I spent the summer fiddling with spreadsheets, a twenty-five-year-old American investigator in her first job out of university was knocking on the doors of Wirecard offices across Asia. Or at least Susannah Kroeber had tried to. In Laos she found nothing at all. In Cambodia only traces. At Wirecard's branch in Ho Chi Minh City, Vietnam, the reception area was like a school lunchroom; the only furniture was a picnic table for six. An open bicycle lock hung from one of the internal doors, a common security measure but one usually removed at a business expecting visitors. As she peered through the glass she saw that the inside was gloomy, with most lights off. A handful of people were visible and many of the desks were empty. Wirecard had paid €21m for the business three years before. It was a similar story in Kuala Lumpur: less than a dozen people inside a huge office in a glitzy location. Kroeber could tell something was up, but as she'd gone half mad looking for non-existent offices on dirt roads she'd also realized how the company could get away with it: who in their right mind would go to the lengths she was just to check out a stock investment?

Her photographs of desolate roads and empty rooms were published by J-Capital Research just after Wirecard announced its big

Indian takeover at the end of October. As soon as I saw Kroeber's snapshots I had flashbacks to the collapse of Sino Forest. I should have gone further afield than Bahrain, I cursed. Except changing minds is hard when money's at stake. When Carson Block took on Sino Forest he was pushing on an open door. The investing public already had an image in their mind of China, the cliché of inscrutability combined with the obvious corruption of a one-party state. Forestry was an industry with a long and distinguished record of hucksters, never mind the broader record of the Canadian investment industry; Vancouver once had a stock market that was a byword for scams. Sino Forest's trees literally weren't there.

Germany was different. It was the well-adjusted, highly educated manufacturing heart of Europe. Its coalition politics, tortuous to the outsider, suggested a robust institutional weight. Its record of consensus-building extended to business, with unions and executives engaged in grand projects for prosperity. Germans' sober culture of thrift was renowned, and thanks to the European debt crisis German government debt securities – known as Bunds – were about the safest financial asset going. If an international investor gave it any thought at all, they would probably have ranked German institutions among the best in the world. There were many Teutonic stereotypes available, but incompetent crook wasn't one of them. So, whether it was a subtle question of accounting or a photo of an empty office, the reaction of many investors and analysts was the same. They turned to Markus Braun and Burkhard Ley for reassurance. If Braun was too esoteric for their liking, Ley was the safe pair of hands with every number and detail at his fingertips. It didn't really matter what the answer was – Wirecard claimed it ran the Cambodian business from Singapore, for instance – so long as there was an answer. Kroeber found that when she presented her findings to potential clients of J-Cap they were often met with outright disbelief. 'These are reputable people, they have a good auditor, why would they be lying?'

'Because there's a lot of money at stake . . .', she would venture, realizing to her frustration that the other person was simply operating on a different wavelength, looking for explanations instead of suspicions. Some investors were less credulous, but didn't care because the dodgy deals in question were small, while Wirecard's valuation was in the billions and its growth was so rapid.

At a Wirecard meeting for investors held soon after J-Cap published, Leo Perry listened to a French fund manager tell the room of fellow professionals he was happy with his own due diligence. He'd just asked his secretary to call Wirecard's Singapore office, he said, and was pleased to announce that someone there had picked up the phone.

Wirecard anyway soon laid on a trip to Asia for a selection of investment bank analysts to see for themselves, bypassing most of the locations visited by J-Cap. In Jakarta the offices were thronged with staff and the analysts were treated to presentations from every layer of the Indonesian business, from call centres and IT all the way up to the top management: catnip for overworked analysts. There was plenty of time for taking photos, to pepper the glowing reports laying out what they learned for clients back home. They stopped in friendly Singapore, home to Wirecard's Asian headquarters, then it was on to Chennai to discover more about the go-getting operations of Hermes (now relocated to modern, well-ventilated quarters). Wirecard said J-Cap's report wasn't worth the paper it was written on. And, in a sense, there was nothing to check. The entire business was intangible, electronic money zipping through the air. So long as the profits were good, why should investors care how Wirecard did it?

A consequence of Wirecard's Indian deal was a meeting of minds in a Pizza Express behind Cheapside, the broad avenue running from St Paul's Cathedral to the Bank of England. First there was Matt Earl, an Essex lad done good with a nose for financial shenanigans. He'd studied Pure Maths at St Andrews, enjoying the logic of an elegant proof, and his introduction to banking was the solution to a problem: money, or, more precisely, his lack of it. A stock analyst by trade, he'd gained a small degree of fame in financial circles by daring to attack the accounting of an outsourcing company, Connaught. In 2010 it accused him of being in the pay of hedge funds, said his work was 'a masterful feat of incompetence', then collapsed into administration. He'd chafed at being told what and how to write inside an investment bank, so struck out on his own. For a few years he'd enjoyed leafy Surrey, played golf, invested his own money and shared thoughts about suspect companies on his blog, Lordship Trading.

In November 2015, Earl blogged about Wirecard's India purchase, declaring a short position in the stock. A scan of LinkedIn showed that only a handful of the claimed 900 employees had profiles. One was an HR manager interested in hiring those with travel industry skills. 'What ticketing operators, tour package experience and these other types of hires have to do with electronic payment processing I am uncertain,' Earl wrote, calling it 'an altogether strange acquisition'. It prompted the invitation for lunch, where he was joined by a hedge fund guy who went by the nickname Roddy, and a struck-off social worker called Fraser Perring.

Earl didn't know what to make of Perring. A balding, grinning, rough-shaven oddball, he hobbled around with a crutch, one ankle encased in a plastic brace. Never knowingly undersold, Perring claimed to have been on the right side of every notable trade going, helping to expose fraud by putting the occasional anonymous dossier in the post. His eyes bulged behind his glasses as he talked and his pronouncements verged on the conspiratorial, but his enthusiasm was infectious. As they tucked into small pizzas Earl found the presence of Roddy reassuring. He lived near Earl in Surrey and was a seasoned professional, rigorous, careful and prepared. He spoke quietly and deliberately, as if letting the other person in on an important secret. Roddy was one of those kids who'd caught the bug early. At age twelve he'd picked three stocks to buy – Tesco, Simon Engineering and WH Smith – and religiously tracked their progress in the financial pages of the *Daily Mail* until the investments were sold to pay school fees. He cajoled his family into participating in the stock offerings of Margaret Thatcher's privatization wave in the 1980s, but had no idea a career picking stocks existed. The son of immigrants, he was to be a doctor. In 1991, while on a particularly tedious course at medical school, he found himself killing time in a Holborn bookshop. On the counter were two investment classics: *Security Analysis* by Graham and Dodd, with a foreword by the billionaire Warren Buffett; and Schwager's *Market Wizards*, a series of interviews with industry greats. Picking them up to browse, he was hooked. The tales were an inspiration, but when he marched into the university careers office the only job ad was a small thing for an unnamed investment firm. It asked candidates to fax an essay on economics. Roddy was deflated; what did a doctor know about tax and spending? But a couple of weeks later he was tinkering with his computer and purchased a fax card. The only number he could find to test it was on the job ad. He dashed off an essay written as if he were the chancellor announcing that year's budget and hit send. Roddy heard back the next day; he'd got a job at one of the famous hedge funds he'd read about. A broker called him Roderick by mistake, which so delighted the fund's head trader the nickname stuck, but it didn't matter, he was on his way.

What Roddy didn't mention in Pizza Express was how he came to be lumbered with Perring in the first place.

Perring and Roddy were both vocal and long-standing members of Paul Murphy's Rabble, hooked on his daily market chats. They'd sparred online, graduated to phone calls, then finally met at the first Camp Alphaville in June 2014. Roddy warmed to him, trusting Perring to keep an eye on his teenage son who was dragged along for the day. The two men stayed in touch, chatting every so often, and when the following June rolled round they were both keen to catch up at the second Camp Alphaville together. At the time Roddy was a couple of weeks into a job at a new hedge fund, so he suggested meeting there first. Perring limped through the door and introduced himself to everyone with typical bravado. He said he had a natural gift for trading and investing he'd discovered late in life and spent most of his time managing money for a friend, an extremely rich commodity trader called Ian Hollins. Roddy eventually extracted Perring and made it to Camp Alphaville, where I met them for the first time after a panel I was chairing.

The next week Roddy was stunned to discover his boss was so impressed by Perring he'd offered him a job. Apparently, Perring was the source of Roddy's best investment ideas. Roddy felt differently and quietly seethed, reluctant to pick a fight with his new boss or to prompt legal headaches by backing out of a job offer. Perring had somehow negotiated himself a remarkable deal – a much higher basic salary than everyone else at the fund, who were paid primarily as a share of profits, plus a first-class season ticket for travel from his home in Lincoln, two hours north of London. So Roddy and his boss resolved a compromise. He and Perring would find a project to collaborate on as a trial run for working together. The stock they chose was Wirecard.

In Pizza Express, any questions about Perring disappeared from Earl's mind as they became caught up in the topic of Wirecard. As well as the whiff coming from India, Roddy was interested in the old Florida Secret Service case against Michael Schutt, who was convicted for unlicensed money transfers for online poker in 2010. Maybe there was something more there? The trio resolved to pool their resources from that point on. Earl was the master of internet sleuthing, and everywhere he looked there was more material; rabbit holes in which to disappear. They were soon spending their evenings online together, sitting with a Skype chat or call open as they pieced together a picture of Wirecard and its various associates, partners and former executives. Every new discovery was an endorphin hit, another brick in the wall of their growing confidence, and the investigation soon had the character of an obsession. Revisiting the Schutt case led them to a company called Bluetool, set up by Simon Dowson's paperwork factory in Consett. From there, an administrative short cut laid out a huge network of corporate shells: Dowson had used the same British Virgin Island entity, Bournewood, as the corporate secretary for 738 different companies. The paperwork also led them to Rüdiger Trautmann, Wirecard's chief operating officer, who had left to join Inatec in 2009, but whose departure was only announced in 2010. The overlap suggested that perhaps he never really left? They soon had the outlines of a theory, a network of companies and individuals in and around Wirecard all working together to facilitate suspect payments for online gambling in the US. If they were right, the company could face the same fate experienced by the poker companies on Black Friday: a dramatic and very public prosecution by the American authorities.

Sometimes the trio spent the weekend brainstorming at Earl's house in Surrey. 'Where's the Bentley?' he asked when Perring turned up in a Mazda. Hollins's motor, which he usually drove, was at the garage, replied Perring. Earl let it go, but other odd moments stuck in his mind. Perring had a flair for the dramatic. He would animatedly hang up his mobile, as if hearing incredible intel. 'Jesus. I know why Rüdiger Trautmann left. He was in a homosexual relationship with Markus Braun. That's the reason he doesn't wear a wedding ring!'

'Er, right. OK,' Matt replied, starting to wonder about Perring's sources.* One minute Wirecard was deep in bed with an Israeli billionaire, the next it was the Russian mafia. Perring could get aggressive if challenged, so Earl tended to let the contradictions pass given how much other material they had found. As 2015 came to a close, the full dossier ran to about 300 dense pages. Roddy had seen how J-Cap's report on the empty Asian offices fizzled. The lesson he took was that theirs had to be more comprehensive; a relentless onslaught of facts would force shareholders to come to their senses. He spent his time removing Perring's wilder speculations and insisted on detailed footnotes, so keen readers could check the source of the information themselves. Yet the three men had different ideas about what they should do with the fruit of their labours.

Perring began to talk about a new job of sorts. He told the other two he'd started advising the private investment office of a billionaire, a team of investors which he referred to as the 'Wise Men'. Supposedly his involvement had already boosted the profits of these Wise Men, and they were interested in funding the Wirecard report. Although, when Earl asked for a meeting with the Wise Men to discuss this idea, Perring kept putting it off.

Talk of selling their research set alarm bells ringing for Roddy. Publishing a short attack wasn't in his business plan. Running a hedge fund portfolio came with professional obligations, such as reporting suspicions of money laundering to regulators. He wanted to hand the

---

* In Perring's version of events he was joking around, based on intel from a German source who claimed to have seen (the introverted) Markus Braun spraying a bottle of champagne on a young man in a nightclub after a day at Oktoberfest.

dossier to the authorities first, and only then go public if nothing happened. He told his fund to stop trading Wirecard, to avoid any complications down the line. As Christmas approached Roddy reached out to an acquaintance, a senior man at the Financial Conduct Authority, for advice on how to proceed.

'You only get one chance at this. You have to lay it on a plate. Explain exactly what rules or regulations have been broken, and present the evidence,' the friend said. Roddy knew the draft was in no fit shape for that and promised to be in touch.

Earl saw the project as a chance to put the information he'd found out there, as he couldn't believe Wirecard had got so far without being exposed. As soon as the research pointed to money laundering, he abandoned any idea of writing about it in his own name. White-collar stock fraud was one thing, but who knew which gangsters might be upset if their laundromat ran into trouble. Meanwhile Perring, who didn't face the same professional obligations as Roddy, seemed to be focused on the business opportunity. 'The brand, we're creating a brand,' he would cackle, talking up the possibilities of using their work on Wirecard to build a short seller reputation to rival that of Carson Block. As they moved towards publication in the New Year, Earl suggested running the report past a lawyer. Perring assured him it was fine, that he would send it to a Harvard Law professor he knew.* Earl thought it was odd that, if anything, the language came back even stronger than before, but he was confident in the evidence he'd found. Perring was also taking care of the IT, cleaning up the report and preparing a website to host it. In February 2016 he called Alphaville's Paul Murphy, who was on holiday in Mozambique. For years Murphy had been involved in a quixotic effort to build a lodge on an unspoiled piece of coastline occasionally swept by hurricanes. He was strolling along the sand enjoying the warm breeze off the Indian Ocean when Perring called, even more excited than usual.

---

* Perring said he actually spoke to a German professor, whom he declined to name, and said that he ran the report past his local lawyer, whom he used for matters such as his divorce.

'This is the big one, Murphy, it's a €5bn fraud. I've got the whole thing. I've spent the last six months digging. You won't believe it, it's all public information for anyone to find. Somehow the market has missed the truth here.' When Perring finally spat out the name of the company, however, Murphy was nonplussed. 'Wirecard? Haven't you seen the stuff Dan's written about it? I thought it was all out there, you should go talk to him.'

Days later I walked down the steps into Kurumaya, a basement restaurant in one of the side streets near Cannon Street station. It offered a reliable bento box within reach of the *FT*'s expenses and was small enough to be discreet. Half the floor was given over to traditional low Japanese tables. Earl and Perring had somehow folded themselves (complete with ankle brace) underneath one of them, and they were beaming. As soon as we'd ordered and the waitress left, Earl conspiratorially passed a Tesco carrier bag underneath the table. It held a thick wodge of paper, unbound, and it was clear from his behaviour that I shouldn't pull it out in public. Keeping it in my lap, I looked at the top sheet and raised an eyebrow. 'What's Zatarra Research and Investigations?'

'That's us,' said Earl, eyes twinkling. 'I think you're going to find it very interesting.'

Roddy, preoccupied with other matters and unaware of the rush to publish, was still hoping to go down the official route, tapping up another contact over breakfast in an expensive restaurant near the Bank of England. The friend had long been involved with international policing. As Roddy talked the man pulled out a small notebook and started peppering him with questions. 'How do you know these things? How do you know Perring? How do you know Earl?' Eventually Roddy explained that he thought Wirecard was rotten from top to bottom, a front for money laundering, and he wanted to know whom to alert. The friend paused, thinking. He put down his pen. 'I've trained many of the investigators in fraud across various of the German states. This Wirecard is in Munich, you say; that would be the Bavarian prosecutor's office.' He sighed. 'It's not even worth me sending a notification to them. They'll just wipe their arses with the fax.'

12

The Façades Shake

December 2015 – Munich
Wirecard share price €45, market capitalization €5.6bn

On Tuesday, 1 December 2015, the Bavarian police showed up at the Wirecard office in Aschheim. If it was a raid, it was an unobtrusive one, failing to break into the regular gossip that circulated around the windswept Einstein business park, or a mention in the local press. The officers were armed with a court order, and the digital haul they took away included inbox archives for Jan Marsalek, Rüdiger Trautmann and other key employees stretching all the way back to 2007. It was enough to lay bare the inner workings of the company for anyone who cared to look. The days of processing poker payments finally threatened to catch up with the company.

The threat was not from Roddy, but from the other side of the Atlantic. A criminal money laundering probe was under way by Federal prosecutors in the Eastern District of New York. They had found more than 1,000 examples of so-called transaction laundering. According to the German court order, when a payment coded 7995 was declined by a US bank, Wirecard would resubmit a transaction for an almost identical sum under a different code, sometimes within seconds of the first attempt. When a bookmaker was turned away, it was as if he stepped out of sight for a moment then knocked on the bank's door again wearing a hat and false moustache. Wirecard was alleged to have run the scam on an industrial scale, processing $1.5bn worth of illegal

transactions between 2007 and 2010. US prosecutors had also identified a string of Wirecard clients about which they wanted information,
including the three poker companies that had been served by G2Pay
from Dublin, and WalPay, an Isle of Man payments company associated with Henry O'Sullivan. All they needed to make the case was
evidence from inside Wirecard, and that was now safely in the hands of
the Bavarian authorities. Once they began to dig, there was no knowing what an inquisitive detective might stumble upon.*

Wirecard's immediate response was to bog the investigation down
in German court proceedings. The data couldn't be allowed to cross
the Atlantic. In its stead CFO Burkhard Ley and Andrea Görres,
Wirecard's fearsome general counsel, flew to New York in January to
assist lawyers at the firm Blank Rome on a charm offensive. The tactics were those used by most financial institutions facing criminal
inquiries. A former prosecutor from the Department of Justice, Car-
los Ortiz, was hired to present Wirecard as a good corporate citizen,
ethical and capable of investigating itself. He was highly experienced,
also working on a FIFA-related matter for a foreign company. Wirecard would offer to short-cut the tangled legal proceedings in Munich
by reviewing the documents itself and handing over anything relevant.
The game here relies on the unimpeachable character of lawyers; at all
times their motives, honesty and conduct are not to be questioned.
The trick is to give them careful instruction, and this fell to Görres,
who had developed into a canny defender of the company's interests.
She was another long-term employee, number thirteen, hired by its

---

* For instance, at the time Wirecard processed payments for a Maltese casino
called CenturionBet. The Italian courts would later judge that CenturionBet was
controlled by Francesco Martiradonna, a member of the Puglian mafia convicted
for being a kingpin of mafia money laundering. The casino was found to have
washed millions of euros of criminal profits by an 'Ndrangheta group from Cal-
abria, one of Europe's most dangerous criminal gangs. Its activities included
taking control of one of Europe's largest refugee reception centres and siphoning
off European Union funds intended to provide care for migrants arriving from
North Africa. It is possible that Wirecard staff had no knowledge of Centurion-
Bet's role as a mafia laundromat. See https://www.crotonenews.com/cronaca/
ieri-linchiesta-jonny-a-presa-diretta-gli-affari-della-cosca-arena-nelle-scom
messe-e-nelle-slot-machine/

original CEO. She applied for a lowly assistant role, having previously worked for Lufthansa at the airport. Looking at her CV, Wirecard's first CEO saw that she had legal training. 'You're made for better things,' he said, deciding to hire her and push her forward. A decade and a half later, as head of the legal department, she would instruct Wirecard's US law firm to remove a selection of key words from the proposed search of the data – *avoid*, *circumvent*, *disguise*, *hide* – in favour of the presumably less incriminatory *cascading* and *recycling*.

As Wirecard threw resources at its legal counter-offensive, business proceeded as normal. It had aspirations to be a global company, but its corporate culture was firmly German. It didn't maintain a help desk for clients out of hours, and at the weekend the office was nearly silent. On Saturday, 6 February a technician was there in a corner of the IT department, methodically ticking off jobs on a list of routine maintenance. Just after 2.30 p.m. he made a small but significant typo as he decommissioned a Linux server. He unleashed a notoriously powerful *rm* command, not on the one machine but on all of them. The technician immediately realized what he'd done and frantically tried to intervene, but it was too late: he'd hit the self-destruct button. Payments processing systems, testing systems, quality assurance systems, issuing, risk assessment, email – none of them were spared. Without notice or explanation, Wirecard was suddenly out of business.

Various Wirecard salespeople were quietly enjoying the weekend. As they paused at the bottom of a ski run, opened their locker in the gym or got back to their car after a hike in the woods, they discovered phones exploding with calls from angry customers. The more advanced clients were fine; they tended to have multiple payments processing relationships in place and could adjust. It was the loyal merchants who relied entirely on Wirecard who were stuffed. 'What is going on?' they screamed down the phone, and Wirecard's staff had no answer. To begin with they had no idea, and some simply turned their phones off for a respite. Later, even if they did, they weren't allowed to say.

'Well, we only have some hiccups,' an exhausted underling was told by Markus Braun when he asked how to respond. As the emergency response got under way any employee with an ounce of technical know-how was dragooned into Aschheim and put to work setting up servers around the clock, crashing at the hotel across the road for a few hours' sleep. It took days for the most important services to restart. Monday was the Lunar New Year in Singapore, for instance, and staff there complained about the lack of updates from Munich while they faced the wrath of restaurateurs feeding holiday crowds without working credit card machines. Attempts to win new business went out the window, as the sales team urgently attempted to repair the relationships they already had. They placated customers with discounts, cuts to the commission paid on processing designed to compensate for the lost business. Even so, multiple staff remember that a small but significant portion of the customer base abandoned Wirecard.

Helpfully, while Wirecard was in crisis the local authorities appeared to have better things to do than investigate the company. On 12 February, Wirecard's Munich lawyer reported that an informal conversation with the Bavarian State Attorney went well. The goal, he said, had been 'to further reduce the StA's (already low) appetite for the evaluation of the files'. Clearing up headaches caused by the fight over the transfer of the data to the US would be convenient for the prosecutor, reported Wirecard's lawyer, who wrote: 'After all, no one is interested in the case.'

Still, disruption from the IT crisis threatened Wirecard's careful US legal approach. Burkhard Ley had promised documents to the US lawyers and, late in the evening on 16 February, he bollocked the head of digital sales for failing to deliver. 'Thank you for the interim reply, but we are not all living on Mars. I also know what has been going on for the last 1 1/2 weeks,' he wrote. Asking her to urgently turn to the topic, the normally calm CFO warned that 'the façades we built may shake' and that while there was 'an attempt to keep damage away from all involved . . . my former optimism dwindles massively'.*

For those at the top, the company must have felt under siege. And then, a week later, on 24 February, the Zatarra Report appeared.

---

* Ley disputed the translation of the word '*Kulisse*' as 'façades'. He said from his point of view Wirecard had nothing to hide, he was merely referring to the procedural strategy agreed with the US lawyers and his aim was to ensure documents were submitted in good time.

13

A Rush of Blood

February 2016 – London Bridge
Wirecard share price €43, market capitalization €5.3bn

THAT WEDNESDAY I WAS eating eggs and pancakes in a pastiche of an American diner on the edge of London's Borough Market. To be honest, I was still a bit fuzzy from the weekend. With a young daughter, and a son on the way, I didn't get out much any more, but there'd been a blowout farewell to an old friend emigrating to Australia. I wasn't used to partying all night. Slurping black coffee, I tried to focus on what the source on the other side of the booth was saying. Yousef Majali was a corporate investigator, a fast talker with a new business. A US hedge fund, Dialectic Capital, had hired him, and the results were spread out over the table, a deep dive into GI Retail and the businesses Wirecard had purchased in India. Majali was explaining why the whole thing stank like a Chennai sewer, but I was only half paying attention. I knew the Zatarra Report, packed full of bombshell allegations, was about to drop, and right on cue a message arrived: the report was out. 'I'm sorry, I've got to go,' I said, putting my phone away and hastily gathering up the pile of corporate paperwork. 'Something big's about to break. I think you'll be interested.'

Borough Market was quiet, the tourists drawn to its faux authenticity yet to arrive. I practically skipped back to the *FT* office. I took the stairs three at a time up to the first floor, threw down my bag and bashed out a short story. This was the moment I'd been waiting for.

Finally, I was sure, the truth would come out. It wasn't the accounting fraud I'd been focused on. There was some of that, but mainly Zatarra accused Wirecard and the people around it of involvement in a grand money laundering conspiracy. The assumptions were laid out near the top: 'If Wirecard employees have allegedly defrauded Visa Inc. and Mastercard Inc., helped orchestrate the violation of the US Wire Act, and disregarded standard levels of decency, it is doubtful much concern will have been directed to the interests of Wirecard's shareholders.' The shares were worthless, it claimed. In the few days I'd had to review the 100-page report the evidence seemed solid. I was convinced this would bring the authorities to Wirecard's door. Maybe even the formidable US Department of Justice.

I left a voicemail with Wirecard's press office, asking them to get back to me with any comment. Then I urged Murphy to read and publish what I'd written, conscious that Zatarra's work would already be circulating among traders. I'd considered writing up some of the research in the report, but had unwisely agreed not to contact anybody before it went live. I knew I couldn't write a story without giving them a chance to respond, so thought the sensible thing to do was to draw attention to what was obviously a short seller attack and leave readers to draw their own conclusions.

As soon as the blog was posted the Wirecard share price crashed, wiping more than €1bn off its stock market value.

A sinking feeling set in. Perhaps I had been a little hasty. The rule is a simple one – if you think *Should we run this by the lawyer?* then you already know the answer.

Every other word we'd published on Wirecard went through Nigel Hanson, the *FT*'s scrupulous in-house counsel, for legal approval. He sat only metres away and was expert in keeping hacks like me out of trouble. Approaching him after the fact, he raised his eyebrows as I handed him a copy of the short post, swiftly noting its shortcomings. I'd assumed it would be safe to simply direct readers to the report, who could then read it and make up their own minds. I hadn't paused to consider how bad Zatarra's anonymity would appear, or explained the smash-and-grab tactics of such short sellers – I thought Zatarra's aim to profit by crashing the Wirecard share price was transparent.

How long had I given the company to comment on this 100-page report, exactly, he enquired?

A furious response soon arrived from Wirecard's lawyers at Schillings. Apparently the €1bn worth of value which had gone up in smoke that morning was my fault. The *FT* had effectively published Zatarra's report, was caught up in the unlawful manipulation of Wirecard's share price, and so was on the hook for every loose word and wild allegation, argued Schillings.

Within days it became clear that we faced serious litigation risk that would get very expensive, very quickly. I'd put Lionel Barber's cherished track record in jeopardy. In a decade as editor, no one had actually filed suit against the *FT* on his watch. Readers were piling in. 'Accuracy is the journalist's job and one of your most cherished values. Shame on you, Dan McCrum.'

I wanted to go on the attack, as it seemed unlikely that many people had actually read Zatarra's dense report, particularly as its website kept mysteriously disappearing, taken offline by hackers. But I'd tied my own hands, as digging into the contents would have dared Wirecard to litigate. We'd given the document to the *FT*'s outside lawyers at Reynolds Porter Chamberlain (RPC) for a second look, prompting much sucking of teeth. Instead of careful questions, Zatarra favoured bold conspiracy. 'You really don't want to have to stand up and defend this in court,' the expert said, adding that Wirecard would have a whole year to file suit.

Thanks to my rush of blood, we went from chief critic to vacating the scene at the moment of maximum controversy, a silence which appeared to speak volumes. My 'Hey, look at this' blog post was replaced by a heavily balanced article explaining that twenty out of twenty-six investment bank analysts rated Wirecard stock a 'buy', and that the company had previously been the victim of a short seller attack in 2008 but came through unscathed. It further noted that the man responsible for that incident (Tobias Bosler, the Munich newsletter writer) was thrown in jail by the German authorities. The implication that such a fate could lie in store for Zatarra's authors was obvious. Markus Braun was emphatic: 'We have investigated all allegations. Every single point is wrong.' Wirecard was off the hook.

Just when our story hit a dead end, things behind the scenes started to get strange. Bryce Elder, a dishevelled veteran deal reporter, was given Jan Marsalek's phone number by a source and told to call it to confirm details of a merger which would blow the short sellers out of the water: Ingenico, a rather pedestrian French payments company which specialized in the credit card machines found on shop counter-tops, was going to bid for Wirecard. Elder reached Marsalek, who said he was in a Moscow hotel room and gave a full briefing on the transaction as if creating a European payments powerhouse was in the bag. The price would be in the region of €60 a share, almost double the level Wirecard stock had slumped to. As sources go, it was straight from the horse's mouth, but Elder was extremely wary. He knew that any story from us, Wirecard's chief public antagonist, would send the share price soaring. In the *FT*'s London office Elder sat with the Alphaville team, a clutter of burner phones and empty Diet Coke cans strewn across his desk, the office line propped slightly off its receiver to divert incoming calls straight to voicemail. He turned to Murphy. 'OK, something very strange just happened,' relaying the chat with Marsalek.

They decided to dig further and were dumbfounded when Ingenico's spokesperson gave the *FT* an emphatic on-the-record denial: 'There are absolutely no M&A discussions with Wirecard at all, whether initial, advanced or whatever.' Then reporters started to pick up new rumours circulating, that the *FT* was about to run a pro-Wirecard story and apologize. It was almost too brazen to believe. A senior executive at a large publicly listed European company had tried to spoof the *FT* into running a highly price-sensitive story. Speculation about a takeover would have sent the share price soaring, blowing up the short sellers with a blatant piece of market manipula-tion. We'd had suspicions before, but this confirmed it. Wirecard was not a normal enterprise.

As a hit job, the Zatarra Report was a resounding success. The price crashed profitably and for weeks it was all anyone could talk about. Yet Matt Earl hoped to get the attention of the German authorities, and the response was not quite what he'd expected. Prepared to hand

over the acres of material he'd gathered, instead an email arrived
from the German financial regulator, BaFin, with a bureaucratic
query. BaFin couldn't find Zatarra registered to provide investment
advice. Earl was baffled, he couldn't believe that was all they wanted
to know. At this stage he was relaxed about his own position, even
though BaFin quickly let it be known it was looking into the possibility of market manipulation. Everything in the Zatarra Report was
based on public information, so Earl was confident there was no
inside information. It was, to the best of his knowledge, true. Earl
was sure that regulators would realize when they actually read the
report properly, and he and Perring tried to interest London's Financial Conduct Authority in their work as well.

Yet in the court of public opinion the anonymity didn't help, nor
did the disappearance of Zatarra's website in distributed denial of
service (DDoS) attacks which forced Perring's IT guy to hire Cloud-
flare, a specialist in defending against such assaults.

Wirecard tried to squash discussion by threatening to sue and talking up its search for the culprits, yet even good-faith attempts to
engage with the Zatarra Report ran into problems because of its
weaknesses. A veteran Wirecard analyst, Jochen Reichert at War-
burg, was upfront about his process. The appropriate response might
be to suspend his buy rating, but that would 'play into the hands of
the authors', he wrote, after two weeks considering the document.
'Zatarra takes several different facts, throws them together and tries
to connect those facts in a way to make it look as if everything was
operated by Wirecard. This approach makes it quite complicated (for
us) to verify the evidence of Zatarra's allegations.'

Earl and Perring shot out a series of rebuttals which screamed,
look, we've caught Wirecard in a lie. It was an application of cockroach theory. *There is never just one cockroach in the kitchen.* But their
work was vulnerable to the same approach. All Wirecard had to do
was knock one brick out of their wall of information to raise doubt
about the strength of the whole thing. One of those bricks was Kirch
Media, a conglomerate which had collapsed into insolvency. Burkhard Ley worked there before he joined Wirecard. The Zatarra Report
implied, without evidence, that Ley had something to do with the

collapse of Kirch, so why should investors trust this anonymous attack? As Reichert wrote, 'Strangely enough, Zatarra is the alias for Edmond Dantès in the 2002 film *The Count of Monte Cristo*. Again, maybe it doesn't mean anything, but having read the report several times, one could potentially get the impression that to some extent it seems to be a personal vendetta against Wirecard.'

The media could have clarified the picture, but the *FT* was absent and much of the German press took the company line, which was to trumpet how well the business was doing. It was one of Germany's big success stories, after all. As Markus Braun told it, Wirecard's business had never been stronger. Sales in the first quarter of 2016 were a third higher than the same period the year before. Profits grew even faster, and Wirecard forecast it would deliver about €300m of Ebitda (earnings before interest, tax, depreciation and amortization) for 2016 as a whole, sparking a renewed share price recovery.

Risking their anonymity, Perring and Earl began to talk using what they dubbed the 'Bat Phone', a specialist secure handset to make calls and send messages. During these conversations Perring adopted a bizarre accent which veered somewhere between war film Gestapo officer and Stavro Blofeld. For some of them Earl put on a South African voice. (He would make a reasonably convincing apartheid-era Krugerrand smuggler.) The combination may not have offered the greatest reassurance. Perring also wasn't always the best advocate for his work. At one point Earl queried some research Perring had shared on transaction laundering. The text was fully formed, but his answers to questions about it were garbled, as if he didn't understand it himself.

'Look, Fraser, where has this come from? Who's given you this?' Earl had asked.

Perring was defensive. 'It's all come from me, it's all me. Why do you say that?'

'Well it has to come from someone else, because you're incapable of explaining it. Can I please speak to the person who's written it?'

Earl persisted and eventually Perring gave in. There was another contributor who'd shared his work with Perring. This fourth man had found signs online of historic miscoding for US poker transactions by Wirecard in violation of the American ban, such as instructions for call centre operators. It was one of the Wise Men. He hadn't employed Perring, the two of them had just been quietly comparing notes for months. Once Earl was introduced it took him about thirty seconds to grasp the point.*

In May 2016, Roddy went to a full-day Wirecard presentation for investors in London. The pressure of the moment had dragged Markus Braun away from seclusion in Munich. Held at FTI Consulting on Cheapside, the PR firm's room was packed with investors of all types, most of them supporters for whom the Austrian had prepared red meat. He confidently predicted Wirecard would triple in size by 2020, when it would process €160bn of payments and keep €2.1bn of that as revenues. With a profit margin of more than 30 per cent, the business would be more profitable than Apple. It was a particularly unusual prediction because payment companies typically could either grow fast or show good profit margins, but not both.

The explanation for how Wirecard was to perform this miracle of productivity was almost absurd. One of the three prongs of Braun's strategy was simply 'globalization'. Other bullet points were Zen in their ambiguity: *Payment will be the data carrier*. After every half-hour presentation there was a brief interlude for questions. Roddy tried to ask something pointed, but as soon as they started to have any bite at all the head of PR, Iris Stoeckl, jumped in to move things along. Ramu Ramasamy talked about Hermes and its chain of Smart Shop kiosks he now ran for Wirecard in India. He was mobbed at each break, but Braun was always at his elbow to jump in and revisit the attractions of such a rapidly changing country if Ramu fluffed his lines.

During lunch, while all attention was on the scrum around Braun trying to get out of the door, Roddy sidled up the podium. He pulled out a sheet of yellow Zatarra stickers and stuck one on to the table sign bearing Braun's name as a little joke to needle the CEO. That

* In Perring's account both he and Earl struggled to understand the explanation on the late-night Skype call with the Wise Men.

afternoon he kept an eye on Braun, who eventually moved the folded piece of card and spotted the logo. The Austrian appeared to blanch for a moment before quickly regaining his composure. Roddy chuckled quietly to himself, but his humour turned to anxiety as Braun surveyed the audience with suspicion. He had a vision of Braun interrupting proceedings. 'Zatarra is here among us. Lock the doors, nobody is to leave.' It was totally irrational, yet feelings among shareholders were still running high. Was he noticed? Roddy slipped to the toilet and locked himself in a cubicle. The incriminating sheet of stickers wouldn't flush, and there was no cistern, but there was a partition wall. He prised a panel ajar. Slipping the sheet into the gap, he breathed a sigh of relief. His pulse slowing, he returned to the meeting, just another hedge fund manager interested in the world of electronic payments. When the day finished, Roddy had a final scan of the crowd looking for Perring's rich patron, Ian Hollins. Perring had insisted he'd be there and Roddy wanted to put a face to the name he'd heard so much about. Perring hadn't made an introduction or passed on a number, just said to watch out for someone who looked part-Lebanese. Roddy shrugged; maybe Hollins had better things to do.

In June a fresh takeover rumour surfaced. Citing 'well-placed sources', a UK blog reported that 'A mystery Chinese company is in talks with German payment processor outfit Wirecard about a deal to buy a significant stake in the business or even purchase the group outright.' It pushed the share price up 6 per cent to €41, closing in on its €47 peak. The effect of Zatarra had proved transitory.

Still, Perring and Roddy were in good spirits. I saw them a couple of weeks later on another sweltering day on the cricket pitch at the final Camp Alphaville. At the third iteration the newspaper's conference division had asserted control, rebranding it the *FT* Festival of Finance. The cabaret dancers and sweaty igloos were long gone, but Carson Block was back. He was attempting to expose accounting problems at a French supermarket chain, Casino, but was finding the European market far less amenable to tactics that were commonplace in the US. The Parisian establishment had closed ranks behind the billionaire owner of the group, and the stock market regulator seemed more interested in the rectitude of Block's own fund than what he had to say about the French company.

On stage, Block and I chatted about financial fraud in a white marquee with a representative of J-Capital Research, dancing around the subject of Wirecard due to my extensive collection of threatening legal letters, in spite of a few loaded questions from Perring and Roddy in the audience. Dave, the IT guy, was there as well, and afterwards I caught up with them over a few beers in the sunshine (with a mild level of paranoia towards other conference attendees). As the bar crowd grew, we kept edging further into the field, suspicious of unfamiliar faces, shuffling our pile of bags with us to avoid being overheard. We were relaxed and happy, however. The day had gone well, and Perring told hair-raising stories about a lavish wedding in South Africa he'd recently attended thrown by a billionaire; cocaine on silver platters in the bathroom, that sort of thing. It wasn't his cup of tea, he assured us. Wirecard sailed on regardless, but we told each other it would only be a matter of time. The authorities were yet to have their say, and we could hope that they were working away behind the scenes. One day, surely, the truth would come out. We would just have to be patient.

14

Friend or Foe?

March 2016 – Munich
Wirecard share price €31, market capitalization €3.8bn

Jan Marsalek's first response to the Zatarra Report was to set a thief to catch a thief, or in this case a junkie insider trader to snare a short seller. He turned to James Harris, a heavily tattooed former tea boy who was the lynchpin in a network of bankers, lawyers, brokers, art dealers and oligarchs spread across two continents. It was the bandit world from which Murphy's secret sources came, and while he never let their names slip the bandits themselves weren't quite so discreet. Marsalek wanted a way into the *FT*, to bend an ear himself, and Harris knew whom to target: the owner of one of London's biggest nightclubs, Fabric. He found him next door to the club in Smiths, known for serving the pick of the Smithfield meat market opposite, and stuck a tiny Post-it note to the table. 'Look, ring this fella, there'll be a lot of money in it for you.'

Gary Kilbey looked at the scrawled digits. He usually steered clear of Harris, a loose cannon with a heroin habit that would eventually kill him. Kilbey was a greying Essex businessman, a careful and successful one, but he was also an incessant trader. He'd run an arm of British Telecom before it was privatized, and then a haulage business which he'd sold in the 1990s when he realized he could make more money on a single stock trade than working for a year. He became a turnaround expert, buying struggling businesses and selling them on for a profit. The mega-club next door was one which hadn't turned. His vice was spread betting, a stock trading activity the UK government considered gambling and so wasn't taxed. At the tap of a phone the bet would be on, and there were bandits all over the world, exchanging rumours, hunches, scuttlebutt and, sometimes, very well-informed information about stocks. They would team up, sharing accounts to trade together for a while, or exchanging tips for a share of profits. The question was always: 'Do you have any margin?', meaning capacity left to make another trade. Brokers were just as leaky, and if a spread betting account became hot, with a string of winners, it would soon have a crowd copying its every move. Intrigued by Harris, Kilbey rang the number on the note.

'I've been told that you're good friends with Paul Murphy,' Marsalek said. The *FT* was ruining Wirecard's reputation, he wanted to set the record straight and thought a warm introduction would help.

Kilbey was bemused, but he agreed to try. He didn't know anything about Wirecard, but he did know some people who had shorted the stock. He spoke to Murphy and reported back the blunt reaction: not while Wirecard was threatening to sue the *FT*.

Stymied, but armed with information, Marsalek moved on to countermeasures, which he orchestrated from his new personal base of operations. At Wirecard HQ Marsalek had three rooms accessed by a single door, guarded by his assistant Sabine. Most visitors were directed right into his personal conference room. Few were allowed left, where Marsalek's spotless glass-topped desk was set at an angle at the far end of a large room, larger even than Markus Braun's. To the left of the door, the other side of a pillar which obscured them from view, was a low set of cabinets bearing a collection of Russian *ushanka* hats picked up on his travels to Moscow (where Wirecard did not have a business). It was a sanctum, but insufficiently private for Marsalek's expanding personal interests. With the bounty from the Mauritius fund 1A, Marsalek installed himself at P61, an elegant villa of oak floors, white columns and four-metre-high ceilings on Prinzregentenstrasse, one of the grandest avenues in the centre of Munich, a fifteen-minute drive from the Wirecard campus. Practically a small palace, P61 matched the Russian Consulate opposite in grandeur, and was surrounded by high hedges which afforded privacy. The rent was €680,000 a year, paid by the travel business Goomo for use as its European headquarters. Colin worked there, as well as Marsalek's assistant for his private affairs, also called Sabine. If it was a coincidence it was a useful one. He could discuss personal business in front of Wirecard staff and they assumed he was on the phone to Sabine in HQ, although his professional and extra-curricular activities were frequently intertwined. For instance, he attended the Tripoli board meetings of a payment card provider that Wirecard supported in Libya, while also investing alongside some of the backers of that business in a set of cement plants in the war-torn country. Marsalek moved seamlessly among investors, oligarchs and spies, and to combat Zatarra he turned to his network of contacts inside and outside the Austrian state security apparatus.

In a document dated Tuesday, 8 March 2016, Marsalek was presented with a buffet of hacking options by a Vienna security firm. He had given them my name, as well that of a London playboy said to have shorted Wirecard stock days before Zatarra's attack, Brett Palos, stepson of the retail billionaire Philip Green and a friend of Matt Earl.

The private detectives suggested using a so-called 4G IMSI Catcher, which posed as a mobile phone mast to track the location of particular handsets. The investigators also urged the purchase of a backpack-sized hacking kit for sucking information from mobile phones, and a 'conspiratorial car' for use in the UK. It would take two weeks to fit out the vehicle, the firm warned, so a quick decision was recommended.

Marsalek also suspected a leak, because to those with insight into the history of Wirecard the Zatarra Report was a deeply strange document. There were surely too many connections, too many glimpses of dirty laundry in its pages for it to be based on public information, as the anonymous authors claimed. Yet at the same time its central premise was flawed. Yes, Wirecard had shovelled payments for US gambling through its systems, but Zatarra made a leap too far. It cast Rüdiger Trautmann's Inatec as a conspirator, not a competitor who had stolen Wirecard's best poker clients. Casting around for the mole,

Marsalek initially settled on someone just outside the inner circle, a contact of Henry O'Sullivan's who ran Wirecard's UK business in Newcastle. With upper-class connections and plenty of friends in London, it was assumed the manager had the opportunity to conspire with the speculators behind Zatarra. The man could be examined within days, said the private detectives, but they wanted more information. Who else at the company might have a motive? Had anyone just been through an expensive divorce, had he noticed colleagues living beyond their means?

That same day, Markus Braun threw the resources of Wirecard at the hunt as well. He hired the blue-chip corporate intelligence firm Kroll for an above-ground investigation of me, Zatarra and Brett Palos. Braun also wanted Kroll to look into a friend of Palos's who had also shorted Wirecard stock, Nick Gold, the flamboyant co-owner of a notorious Soho nightclub called The Box, famed for its star-studded clientele and outrageous cabaret entertainment.

At around the same time the dirty tricks began. A fake apology email was sent to analysts and investors pretending to be from a Zatarra employee undergoing an attack of conscience. The allegations about Wirecard were 'concocted and wrong', and Zatarra's friends in the media were crooks. The email was an unsophisticated spoof, yet whoever wrote it shared Braun and Marsalek's theory about the protagonists. It said that 'the inner circle' of Zatarra were Palos, Gold and several other individuals, who had 'repeatedly bribed and attempted to bribe journalists of several newspapers in the United Kingdom and the United States'. The beginnings of the counter-attack were coming into view.

Markus Braun, meanwhile, really did spend the weekend talking to the French about a merger. Codenamed Project Elysium, the idea was that Ingenico would swoop in to buy Wirecard. The early efforts involved grandiose codenames: Ingenico was a Parisian 'Zeus' to Wirecard's Bavarian 'Poseidon'. Yet given the speed with which Marsalek leaked the transaction on the Monday morning, it's unlikely Wirecard saw the talks as anything more than a ploy to revive the share price. At the time he briefed the *FT*'s Bryce Elder from Moscow as if everything was agreed, lawyers for Zeus and Poseidon were still sparring over the non-disclosure agreement needed to start the discussions.

Regardless, Marsalek had another idea. What if he could pay Carson Block, the famous American short seller, to come out in support of Wirecard?* For the pitch, Marsalek sent an old friend called Sina Taleb, a fixer and a dealmaker who split his time between Paris, the Middle East and LA. In San Francisco Carson Block said, 'We're not going to take any money. If the company is as clean as fuck and there's something to do, then we'll go long and write a report.' Taleb seemed uncomfortable that Block's colleagues joined the meeting and was vague about his ties to Wirecard. He left, and Block never heard from him again.

Another old ally offering Marsalek help was a porn baron, Hamid 'Ray' Akhavan, an Iranian-born US citizen who liked fast cars, guns and helicopters. He lived in Calabasas, a city on the edge of LA in the Santa Monica mountains, where he maintained a walk-in armoury stocked with automatic weapons. He'd made a fortune in high-risk payments and was a long-standing Wirecard customer – in 2013 he controlled almost 200 Wirecard Bank accounts held in the name of companies from Consett, Country Durham, for instance. He offered to put Marsalek in touch with a former CIA officer who might be able to advise on the company's US legal issues. A different friend of Akhavan's appeared to interest the Wirecard top brass: a senior figure in Mastercard's compliance team. Akhavan had cultivated the figure, taking business associates to meet him when out for drinks in New York. To those in the high-risk processing world, a friend at Mastercard who might influence how and when enforcement actions were taken would be the best possible friend. In May 2016, after he'd spoken to Wirecard's external lawyers, Wirecard CFO Burkhard Ley suggested that it might be helpful for Marsalek to 'activate contacts' at the top of Mastercard.

* The introduction to Block was made by a Turkish businessman and stock market trader with a traumatic past. In 2015 he was trying to resolve a Corsican property dispute when he was kidnapped by an Algerian gang dressed as police and held in a Paris basement for six days while they demanded he transfer millions to them through stock sales made at the wrong price. When police arrested an alleged conspirator he was dumped, bloodied and beaten but alive, at a train station.

To be fair, at the time it wasn't hard to find people willing to sing Wirecard's praises. Kroll named a few of Wirecard's greatest fans in a May update on its search for Zatarra, including Antoine Badel at Alken Asset Management, a large shareholder. 'Badel has been extremely helpful since our interview; our ongoing correspondence has reinforced our investigation and has provided us with potential leads,' Kroll said. As for the tricky assignment of identifying Zatarra's authors, Kroll's investigators preferred to discuss such tactics over the phone.

Wirecard's law firm, Schillings, raked in the fees as well. In an investigative report for the company it wrote: 'We have not been able to identify any evidence in McCrum's personal life to suggest he has become more affluent recently.' They were presumably looking for evidence that I'd been paid off by short sellers, and the basis for that assessment wasn't offered.* The document offered three options, of which the third was: 'Depending on the next steps taken by McCrum, and/or any additional research conducted, we may wish to seek other options for dissuading McCrum/Alphaville from publishing further articles in the same vein.'

Fraser Perring had at least thrown the gumshoes off the scent a little. Kroll's report to Wirecard on 15 July said: 'We have spoken to several people who spoke to Zatarra and have had the Zatarra person described on one occasion as having a London or British accent, and on other occasions as having a European or East European accent.' Yet Kroll was closing in. It suspected two people were involved, and from one of those conversations it had obtained a recording.

By the end of July Kroll's bill for the Wirecard project came to €379,618. From Braun's perspective it was perhaps money well spent. Their investigators shared three photographs: two long-lens shots on a street in Mayfair, and a close-up from inside Victoria Tube station. The men pictured were in sports jackets and jeans, clearly in conversation. One held a leather laptop case. The other had a weekend bag in his right hand, while his left rested on a crutch. Matt Earl and Fraser Perring. Kroll didn't know their names yet, but that was only a matter of time.

---

* Schillings told me it acted entirely properly throughout, in compliance with its legal and regulatory obligations.

15

Freaking Out

2016 – St Albans
Wirecard share price €45, market capitalization €5.5bn

ONE SUNDAY AFTERNOON IN November 2016, I was concerned about the remains of our house. An ugly 1970s bungalow of red brick at the end of a cul-de-sac, it was half demolished, the ground in front scarred by muddy trenches in preparation for the foundations of the family home we intended to build. We'd picked St Albans from New York, looking at a map of commuter lines into London when Charlotte was pregnant with our daughter, having discovered that a return to the capital itself was impossible after five years away because house prices were bananas. Our son had arrived in May, a mewling miracle who refused to sleep. We needed more space, so we were building with the foolhardy optimism of the inexperienced.

In a stroke of luck, we rented the property opposite. I was beginning to realize it also meant we faced a constant reminder of the financial risks we'd taken and the vagaries of builders, who'd torn everything down with gusto then stopped showing up. I'd carved out a small space to work in a ground-floor room stuffed with boxes and spare furniture, a mix of our battered IKEA and French-polished relics of the old lady whose house we'd borrowed. That Sunday afternoon I tried to stop staring at the construction site and catch up on some work. Opening my email, there was something forwarded by Nigel Hanson, the in-house lawyer, subject: '*FT*, hedge funds and criminal dealings'. At first glance it looked like another typo-ridden conspiracy theory from the green-ink brigade,* but reading on I felt a chill. 'I believe your organization should be aware of some of the dealings happening between your journalists and criminal elements of the international hedge fund scene.' The sender had attached emails that 'provide conclusive evidence of such collaboration in the case of Wirecard AG, a German company listed on the Frankfurt stock exchange'.

Scrolling straight to the bottom, I was stunned to see three pictures of messages to and from hedge fund managers. They weren't screenshots, they were photographs of a screen. One was between the head of J-Capital Research, which had published the report on Wirecard's empty offices, and someone at the hedge fund Blue Ridge, discussing what I'd written about Wirecard. I could tell the last one was real. It was right there in my inbox from the corporate investigator, Yousef Majali, sent after our breakfast on the day the Zatarra Report came out. It was to me and his paymaster in New York, signed off with a joke that now looked spectacularly ill advised. 'Please let me know when you publish something – or just before!'

Someone had been hacked. Was it me? More was promised: 'I'm happy to provide you with further evidence about the linkage between some of your journalists and the dark underbelly of the hedge fund world. I will compile a few more emails for you. xxx' Were those kisses from the person trying to frame me for insider trading?

My daughter toddled in to show off a drawing of a picnic. Lifting her on to my lap, I was hit by a sense of invasion, of paranoia. Could I trust the computer I was looking at, or my phone? Was someone listening in now, peering at us through the webcam? The makeshift office had a picture window that left us in full view of the empty cul-de-sac. Instead of feeling open, it now seemed exposed. I snapped the laptop shut. Borrowing my wife's mobile, I called Murphy. He was rattled as well. 'This is just nuts. We're dealing with professional hardcore black ops here.' There was no need to panic, he said. We'd

---

* Before all-caps emails, green biro was the colour of choice for crackpots writing to newspapers.

regroup in the office, when we could talk face to face, as we clearly had to rethink security. We had totally underestimated what we were up against.

Three days later a Reuters investigation dropped, exposing Simon Dowson's paperwork factory in County Durham. More than 400 locals in Consett were directors for a huge range of poker companies, get-rich-quick schemes, websites offering colon cleansers, health foods and much more. 'We were all on the dole and it was free money,' one retired supermarket shelf-stacker told the Reuters reporter, Alasdair Pal. It was a minor sensation, leading the BBC news all day and prompting questions in Parliament about the gaps and grey areas in the system that allowed millions of pounds to flow through UK companies used as 'tools of deception'. The UK Insolvency Service had investigated and shut down a handful of companies in the network, finding large sums in bank accounts for businesses which declared minimal corporate activity, but little more was done. Some of the Consett companies closed and no one was sanctioned. It was a terrific exposé of the lax British system of corporate regulation, except for one glaring omission: Reuters had buckled under legal pressure and taken Wirecard's name out of the story. The news agency cast Dowson as the mastermind of the operation. As he, not unreasonably, put it: 'You're telling me, who left school with four GCSEs, that if a licensed and regulated German bank comes to you and says this is how we're going to do it, I'm the one who's supposed to say hang on a minute, that's not right? You're having a laugh aren't you.'

There was no wider follow-up. I was still wary of poking the beast because of the Zatarra screw-up and the lingering threat of a libel suit. If another outlet wanted to name Wirecard, its lawyers would no doubt ask why their reporters should take a risk which Reuters didn't want to.

The silence was slowly driving Matt Earl mad.

Earl also lived in a cul-de-sac, halfway around the M25 from me, in Surrey. The brick houses were detached, the drives large and the great outdoors nearby. The neighbours were friendly and opposite the open end of the street was a decent pub. It was the sort of safe, comfortable area with good schools favoured by London professionals. He was still working from home, planning the launch of a short selling business, but he intended to do it as far away from the erratic Perring as possible. The longer he'd spent with the oddball, the stranger his behaviour came to seem. At one point he'd heard Perring talking into his phone as if having a conversation in Chinese. Earl was no expert linguist, but it didn't sound like the real thing. In July Perring happened to be on holiday in Turkey when there was a coup attempt against the Erdoğan government. He wasn't anywhere near the action, but Earl told him to be careful anyway. Perring had replied that he knew all about the coup – his friend Ian Hollins was sending a helicopter to get him out of there.

Perring's approach to money was also hard to square with his bold claims of stock market acumen. He'd told Roddy that whenever he had a good month trading stocks he purchased a new house, giving him an expansive property portfolio. Perring also spent the summer of 2016 telling people that he'd made a killing from the Brexit referendum. He'd identified the true support of the country for leaving Europe with the help of Dave the IT guy who, Perring claimed, was a master of advanced techniques to mine sentiment revealed from comments on Facebook. Yet as autumn arrived, Perring and Earl fell out over money. One day Perring popped up on a Skype chat claiming Earl owed him about £100,000 for research costs. Earl was nonplussed. So far as he was concerned, he had done the bulk of the research, Roddy had contributed much of the rest and anyway most of the company filings he'd found were free. The expenses he could think of didn't come close to a five-figure sum, let alone six figures.

Earl watched Perring tap out drivel for a while then settle on internet hosting costs as the big-ticket item. He claimed to have spent tens of thousands in a matter of days as he and the IT guy, Dave, tried to keep Zatarra's website alive in the face of the DDoS attack. Earl asked for receipts, but Perring didn't have them, claiming to have paid Amazon Web Services in cash by buying as many as fifty prepaid credit cards at a time from Sainsbury's. Earl was surprised to see Perring invite the mysterious Ian Hollins to join the conversation. He watched in rising astonishment as Perring and his 'friend' berated him in the manner of a Punch and Judy show.

'What do you mean he hasn't paid you, he sounds like a real dirtbag.'

'Yeah, that's exactly what I said, Ian.'

Earl's jaw dropped. This guy is out of his mind, he thought.* Yet Earl wasn't thinking straight either. Wirecard got inside people's heads. Otherwise rational and profit-motivated short sellers found they couldn't let it go. The way it shucked off every criticism and fact was too infuriating. Earl tried two separate gambits. First he published anonymously again, trying to rescue the work of Zatarra. Posing as a corporate investigator, on Monday, 5 December he sent everyone with a known interest in Wirecard yet another anonymous email. 'I have been left with no alternative but to disclose the following information into the public domain. Having originally been tasked with disproving the work in February 2016 relating to Wirecard, I have serious concerns for depositors, the lack of regulatory action and fear everyone has been lied to.' Attached were links to four VisMas files (as in Visa-Mastercard) written in a cautious technical style which Earl imagined might be more credible to analysts and regulators than the histrionic tone of Zatarra. To the small group of people who read the original Zatarra Report in its entirety, this new work was baffling. I even wondered if Wirecard was behind it, a tactic to put everything in the public domain in the dullest way possible to move on. The VisMas files sank without a trace.

The next morning Earl published a blog about Wirecard under his own name, aimed squarely at Markus Braun. Using Bloomberg data, Earl estimated that Wirecard's head honcho had, since 2008, sold around €24m worth of stock and purchased €46m for a net spend of about €22m. Braun was well paid but not *that* well paid, so Earl asked where had the money come from? It was part bluff. Surely no one would be foolish enough to draw attention to themselves if they were behind Zatarra.

Not long after the blog post went live, Earl got a call from Perring.

* The quotes reflect Earl's recollection of the Skype chat. Perring said Ian Hollins was a pseudonym used to protect his friend's identity.

He was frantic, babbling, so shaken he was hard to understand. Perring said he'd just been confronted by two thugs. He had dropped his daughter at school in Lincoln then walked back to his vehicle, on the edge of a supermarket car park. As he got in, two men appeared from opposite directions. One jumped into the passenger seat next to him, grabbing the car keys, while the other climbed into the back, perching awkwardly on the child's car seat. As Perring told it the men were heavy-set, speaking in thick Eastern European accents with an edge of menace. One of them had a GoPro out and was filming him. He said they demanded to know if he was behind Zatarra, who he was working for. They knew where he lived, and showed him pictures of his children. Perring told Earl he denied everything and was given two days to make a choice: broken legs, or £100,000 for revealing his co-conspirators. Earl was alarmed, but also suspicious. There was that figure again. It seemed to him Perring was implying a price for his silence. 'Go to the police,' Earl said.

That morning I was sitting in the middle of the markets team when I took a similar call from Perring. By the time it finished I had five reporters looking at me wanting an explanation. 'That was a source. He's just been threatened. The heavies said they'd hacked his computer and they mentioned me. They've hacked my laptop as well.' I was in shock, I couldn't quite believe it. Lionel Barber was travelling, so I briefed Paul Murphy and Nigel Hanson about the escalation, then went to talk to the *FT*'s cybersecurity team for more advice. After the hacker's email we'd decided to wait for more before acting. In the cold light of day, Murphy and I reasoned that my inbox hadn't been exposed; there surely would have been other emails highlighted if it had. The photographs of the emails taken on a computer screen also suggested it could be the work of a snooper who briefly got access to someone's laptop, rather than a hacker. With Perring's new warning we decided to replace all of our *FT* phones and computers, while the IT team searched the access logs for anything suspicious.

Back at my desk there was a message to call the Lincolnshire police. The officer investigating was trying to get his head around the idea that Perring might be of interest to thugs because he'd written something about a German bank, but he seemed to be taking it seriously. I checked back in with Perring, who added a new detail. He said a phone of his had recently gone missing. He thought he'd misplaced it, but he was beginning to suspect a burglary. Had I noticed anything suspicious at home?

Freaking out, I left early. By the time I got back to St Albans it was getting dark. The garden of our rented house backed on to a field used by dog walkers. Considering its security for the first time, I noticed that the decrepit wire fence had trees on either side and posed little impediment to an intruder. The interior of the house hadn't been touched since the 1980s, with patterned shag carpets, thick-textured wallpaper and a vivid-pink bathroom. Our back door was wood and glass with an old lock; it was not the type of mechanism praised by sellers of household insurance. I resolved to use the bolt at night as well. Then I realized I'd never paid any attention to the living room. As it was winter, and the room was overflowing with excess furniture, we hadn't used the patio door. To my horror, it slid right open. If it had been locked when we moved in, it wasn't now. Had someone been inside? There was a key, but it didn't seem to do anything. Grabbing a torch, I crossed the road to the carcass of our own home and found a sturdy piece of timber. Cut to length it fitted snugly into the door track, jamming it closed. Charlotte came home, handing me a bundle with our six-month-old son inside, wondering what I was doing. 'I'm just checking everything's secure, to be on the safe side.'

As I told her about Perring, concern flashed across her face. 'Are you in any danger? Are *we* in any danger?' I tried to sound more confident than I felt. Menacing a journalist would be more trouble than it's worth, a sure-fire way to attract the authorities, I said. We focused on getting the kids to bed, then I turned my attention to the electronics. My old MacBook went in a drawer, it couldn't be trusted; the cybersecurity team warned that if it was compromised malicious code could be hidden anywhere, in a favourite photo or file. I spent an hour resetting the Wi-Fi router and changing its settings, jotting all the elaborate new passwords in the back of a guide to hiking in the Swiss Alps, an aspirational purchase finally finding a use after years of gathering dust. On the advice of Sam Jones, the *FT*'s security correspondent, I put the router's plug on a timer. Switching the internet off at night would give any would-be hackers a smaller window of opportunity. Finally I went to bed. Charlotte and I were both exhausted by broken nights, but I couldn't sleep. I'd put a hammer under the bed within reach, just in case. My tired brain was whirring, alert for every sound. Every time I closed my eyes I had visions of a home invasion.

By the time I woke, Matt Earl and Fraser Perring were outed. Photos of each man were published on Twitter, above the ominous title 'Zatarra RIP'. Perring's photo was from Facebook, but Earl's was a hidden camera snap from his doorstep months before, judging by the bloom of his cherished geraniums. The photos of emails we'd seen in November were there, along with a collection of text messages, emails and Skype conversations confected into a grand conspiracy: 'Zatarra is a story of greed, of self-pity and frustration, of men full of ambition but little ability to build, only to destroy. It is the story of men who could not accept that they were mistaken and that what they were doing was wrong. But Zatarra is also a story of corrupt journalists eager to make a name for themselves, eager to make some money on the side, disappointed with their lives and desperate for any story, no matter whether true or not.' I was corruptly working with hedge funds, along with the Reuters journalist Alasdair Pal, it said. It looked like the 'Bat Phone' Perring used had been hacked, as well as some of Perring's other devices or online accounts; there were long rambling messages between him and 'Ian Hollins'.

Earl was horrified. The email had immediately gone round the trading floors, and he knew what people would think: crikey, this person must be criminal. Perring's tale of thugs suddenly didn't seem quite so tall after all, particularly when Earl looked out of his front window that Wednesday morning and saw a black Mercedes coupé parked in the cul-de-sac, an unfamiliar sight among the family SUVs. A couple of large men were walking around. They got in the car and just sat there, facing Earl's house. It could have been a coincidence, and the car eventually left, but Earl was nervous. He was due in the City that day for a meeting at the law firm Mishcon de Reya to discuss his new business, so he asked the children's nanny for a lift to the train station. After he was dropped off Earl realized he'd forgotten his wallet. He turned round to flag her back down, only to see the black coupé behind him. He froze. There was only one person in the car now, and the only direction he could go was straight past Earl. For a moment their eyes locked, the man trying to act normal as he rolled slowly by. He clearly didn't know where he was going because he drove into the car park, a dead end. The Mercedes reached it and stopped, engine running. Earl made a snap decision. He walked into the station, then quickly ran along the platform hoping for a better look while protected by the fence. Adrenaline surging, he fumbled for his phone, trying to switch it to take video, but it was too late. The car turned round, reversing in a cavalier arc, and roared off.

Earl called the nanny back; he had to get home and regroup. As they turned into his close he saw a green car parked outside the local pub. Inside was someone holding a long-lens camera. Really freaking out, but trying to act calm for the benefit of the nanny, as soon as they were inside he locked the door. Earl's first call was to his lawyer, to cancel the meeting and ask for advice. The lawyer told him to call the police, and that the private security guy the firm used for these situations would be in touch within ten minutes.

'Do you feel safe, is there anyone outside?' the policeman asked. Earl's nerves were jangled, but his English desire not to appear ridiculous by making a fuss was kicking in. At that precise moment he was safe, and the street outside was quiet. There was no sign of either car. The officer made a note to treat further calls as urgent and promised to have a patrol circle past. Next, Earl spoke to the private security guy, who asked similar questions and offered to have someone there in forty minutes. Earl called his wife Emma at work, who went through the same cycle of panic. Was she safe, were the children? Neither knew what to make of it. They had both thought Perring was making it up. Earl was clearly under surveillance, but so far no one had tried to bundle him into the boot of a car. Would they? They decided a bodyguard was an overreaction. For now they'd call the school to put passwords in place for collecting the kids, and try to stay calm.

Later that evening Earl called his hedge fund friend Roddy, who could hear the tension in Earl's voice. Peering out into the darkness, fog in the air, Earl could make out a car in the same spot as earlier in the pub car park. Was it the same one? Roddy decided to drive over and check it out, but by the time he got there the car was gone. On the way home he passed the entrance to a golf club, a semicircle of tarmac next to the road which was usually empty. Two cars were stopped, one of them a black Mercedes coupé, and through the mist Roddy glimpsed men standing between the vehicles talking. It was so out of the ordinary that after a few hundred metres he decided to go back for another look. By the time he got there the cars had vanished.

Thursday, Earl didn't go out. He was too tense to sleep, or to eat properly. He kept a baseball bat by the bed. As Friday passed he began to relax a little. In the evening Emma had tucked the kids in and was about to go to one of the neighbour's for a drink when she saw a car approach fast. It pulled up outside their house and two large men got out. 'Matt!' she screamed.

Heart racing, blood thumping in his ears, Earl clattered down the stairs and peered through the peephole in the front door. The rational portion of his brain said the chances of being killed or having his legs broken was really very small, but it was struggling to convince the terrified animal parts. He put the flimsy security chain on the door, as if it would do anything, and opened it a crack.

'Are you Matthew Earl?' said a man looming in the porch. Behind him lurked a henchman the shape of an overfed butcher.

'Who are you?' Earl replied.

'My name is Ben Hamilton, I work for a company called Kroll. I'm here to bring you a letter quite urgently.' A delicate voice. For a man of his size Hamilton was surprisingly high-pitched.

'Regarding what?' Earl snapped.

'Regarding Zatarra,' he said, his tone rising, as if it was a question.

Primed for a fight, Earl was monosyllabic, hunched, peering around the door. 'For what reason?'

'That's explained in the letter. I've come just in case you want to talk to us afterwards, after you've read the letter. Can I give it to you?' Hamilton was polite to the point of creepiness.

'I'll take the letter, yeah.' A pause. Earl grunted 'OK', trying to end the conversation.

Hamilton kept going as he handed it over. 'We work with a law firm called Jones Day, we're working on behalf of Wirecard.'

'Why?'

'We're investigating the possibility there's been some market manipulation.'

'When?'

'In the publication of something called Zatarra.'

'OK, right.'

'Can you talk to us about it, Matthew?' Hamilton asked gently, as if coaxing a reluctant child.

'No,' Earl replied, almost laughing at the suggestion, shaking his head.

'You've got quite an interest in Wirecard, though, haven't you,' Hamilton said, more confident now, stating not asking.

'I've written about it on my blog, yes,' said Matt, taking refuge in a partial truth.

'Have you se-seen the Zatarra Leaks documents in the past few days?' Hamilton asked, stuttering for a moment, his former fluency deserting him as he broached the subject of the hacked emails.

It hit a nerve. 'I'm going to call the police.'

'You're welcome to,' came the reply through the closing door. Hamilton and the doughball loitered while Earl tore open the letter, some of its more alarming words jumping out as he scanned it: defamation, collusion, conspiracy, market manipulation. Jesus Christ, what have I got myself into here, Earl thought. He called his lawyer, who was reassuringly direct: 'Tell them to fuck off, they're just fishing.'

Earl, fortified, reopened the door. 'I've got nothing to say to you, will you please leave.' The Kroll postmen, earning their firm several hundred pounds for each hour of doorstep intimidation billed, showed no inclination to depart. Earl left them to it. That broken legs were off the agenda was little comfort. He'd thought the world would care about a gigantic criminal enterprise. Instead he'd brought the resources of an unscrupulous financial institution down upon his own head.

In the weeks that followed, Earl's appetite deserted him and he rapidly lost weight. He avoided going out. He took to drawing the curtains long before dusk and had a security engineer come to check the system at home. 'Did you know this alarm line was cut?' he said. 'Hey are you OK?' The blood had drained from Earl's face. 'Yeah, it looks like the painters and decorators must have caught it by accident.'

Online he was under siege. Every few hours a new email arrived containing a trap. Hackers were using him as the lab rat for fiendish psychological experiments. Some were obvious, copies of messages from LinkedIn or Google designed to take him to replica login pages. Others were carefully curated, with pictures and information collected from the social media accounts of Earl's friends and family. Fake news articles arrived with headlines about Markus Braun announcing an investigation into Zatarra. The hackers played a game with porn, gay and straight, pretending to have subscribed Earl to niche services. It meant he had to keep his kids away from his devices – another task to add to the draining vigilance intruding into his suburban life. Even if some of the emails were obvious forgeries, every one was a little reminder that he wasn't forgotten. The constant paranoia was also frustrating. Earl was trying to build a new business knowing that anywhere he went might prompt more photos, a visit could cast a prospective client into the net of conspiracy. A black car in the rear-view mirror sparked a flash of emotion, a few seconds of fear and anger followed by self-ridicule; it was just a parent on the school run. Earl didn't see the coupé again, but one afternoon a neighbour mentioned something odd. Out for a walk, the man's dog had rootled at an object in the grass that morning. It looked like a small camera in the ground pointed towards Earl's house. The dog owner hadn't thought to pick it up and when he went back to show Earl it was gone. Whoever placed it there had already swooped in to cover their tracks.

I was conscious enough about my own paranoia not to mention it to anyone while I quietly lined my hat with tinfoil. Our cul-de-sac was capped by a large hedge. Driving in at night, I'd scan it in the headlights for the reflection of a lens in the leaves. The builders had miraculously reappeared and walls were going up. Each morning before work I crossed the road with a tray of tea. Deep down I wasn't really expecting there to be men conspicuously sat in a car on a stake-out, but I looked all the same.

At work, meanwhile, I was haunted by my careless rush to write about the Zatarra Report. Schillings were on to the 'leak' as well. A fresh letter arrived from Wirecard's media lawyers. Had the editor, Lionel Barber, seen the evidence available online that showed the whole Zatarra affair to be a criminal conspiracy? And was Dan McCrum being investigated by the *FT* for corruption?

Those were uncomfortable days. I collected all the correspondence with those involved and sat through a review of what I'd said and done, twice. First with Hanson, then with Lionel Barber himself in the editor's lair. 'Why didn't you email this Majali character right back and set him straight?' Barber said, stabbing the page with a finger. I'd called him instead, I explained weakly, not then conscious of email's role as a permanent record, a well of evidence to damn the careless.

It was painfully obvious I was spending time with the editor for all the wrong reasons. I was in the middle of a bizarre story but couldn't find a way to write it. When I added it all up there were some hackers whose identity and motives were unknown, a private detective delivering a letter, and a story of intimidation from someone I was beginning to realize had capacity for exaggeration. The two separate theories about Wirecard were also hard to square. If it was a money laundering machine, then what was the point of faking profits with dodgy dealmaking? Both theories had been given a thorough airing. I was supposed to be leading a team of market reporters in search of sizzling scoops about debt raisings and IPOs, or the intrigues of investment bankers. Wirecard was shady, but I had to let it go. It was just a personal obsession, a lingering hangover from my previous beat. I'd been moonlighting, badly, and needed to knuckle down to the day job.

16

Black Truffles

2017 – Singapore
Wirecard share price €46, market capitalization €5.7bn

SINGAPORE IS A NOWHERE place. Discreetly authoritarian, a melting pot of Malaysian, Indonesian, Chinese and Indian immigrants, it's an unthreatening home for global business. The city's financial district could pass for a leafier, more humid version of New York, gleaming skyscrapers interwoven with tropical greenery. Where Manhattan welcomes visitors with the Statue of Liberty, the capital-A Architecture dominating Singapore's approach is the Marina Bay Sands casino complex; a luxury ocean liner lifted heavenwards by three towers of glass. An infinity pool at the fifty-seventh floor gives the exclusive penthouse restaurant, Spago, the feeling of floating on air. To a man such as Henry O'Sullivan, it was irresistible. He took friends, family, business partners and hangers-on. Dom Peringon and caviar to whet the appetite, then steaks and spectacular wine. As head of Goomo, Colin was used to going to Spago after board meetings for the travel business with O'Sullivan, but in February 2017 he was surprised to see the restaurant empty, with a banquet table at its centre laid for about a dozen. They had the palace to themselves and Colin marvelled at the feast, a plate of black truffles like lumps of coal passed around as seasoning, tender steaks the thickness of phone books. Bottles of Opus One and other Napa Valley greats were uncorked with abandon while O'Sullivan held court in a salmon-pink blazer, Kiton shirt barely buttoned. His status as a treasured patron was confirmed when Wolfgang Puck, the Austrian celebrity chef and restaurateur behind Spago, appeared to personally serve the guests. Enjoying himself immensely as the evening unfolded, Colin turned to Marsalek and asked what it was all about: was the night some sort of special occasion? Marsalek laughed. 'Because it's Tuesday.'

O'Sullivan was firmly settled in Singapore, living the good life. His home held an aquarium for hammerhead sharks. He kept a white Rolls-Royce, an ostentatious expense given Singapore's punitive car duties, and flew by private jet. Even Marsalek seemed jealous of his office at Senjo, a fintech company where O'Sullivan spent much of his time. Senjo was found on the fifty-sixth floor of One Raffles Place, and O'Sullivan's control was understood, if not clearly documented. His was the largest office, with an expansive view of the bay and a lavish interior. A striking chest of drawers, one half French regency, the other Scandi-minimal, was one designer touch. The same firm outfitted the Goomo office in the style of a boutique hotel, a sumptuous blue overall with accents of brass and gold. The designer also hung chandeliers in the compact space used by Epsilon Investments, a Singapore holding company controlled by the woman whose name also appeared on paperwork as the largest official investor in the Mauritius fund 1A. A bling touch was to enclose Epsilon's small private boardroom in mirrored partition walls, like the VIP room at a strip club, while inside was faux-wood-panel wallpaper.*

When O'Sullivan found someone he trusted, he used them again and again. Senjo had some admin staff, but a frequent presence in the office was the person who kept all the official filings straight: 'Shan', as everybody knew R. Shanmugaratnam, a bald, slightly rotund man with a long face. Shan set up companies and supplied directors to serve O'Sullivan and Marsalek's web of interests. For instance, the two men discussed backing an electric rickshaw company, SmartE, using the Mauritius fund, and it was Shan who incorporated the

---

* The Singaporean woman also controlled two UK stockbrokers, Novum and Daniel Stewart, the latter run by a shooting buddy of O'Sullivan's. Colin believed that O'Sullivan in fact controlled the two brokers.

Singapore entity which eventually invested. No introvert, he was also involved with a small, narrow pub, the Hedgehog, which specialized in 'bar-top dancing', where young women in short skirts mimed pop songs. It was another friendly place where O'Sullivan's boisterousness was tolerated.

By this point in their bromance, Marsalek and O'Sullivan's backscratching was continuous. For a time they both grew out bushy beards, Marsalek's giving him the appearance of a Chechen freedom fighter, his friends joked. They both told people they had stakes in Libyan cement factories. Goomo funded Marsalek's villa in Munich. Marsalek helped arrange a €7m line of credit for O'Sullivan at Wirecard Bank. Yet while they partied as if the good times would never end, trouble was brewing. A whistleblower was on to them.

In May 2016, an employee of Ernst & Young sent a letter to the audit firm's headquarters in Stuttgart, alleging that 'Wirecard Germany senior management' directly or indirectly held stakes in the 1A fund. It was a serious allegation: that executives were putting money in their own pockets by selling assets to Wirecard, and one which threatened to highlight the huge profits made by 1A in the deal. The concerned accountant also said that someone at Hermes in Chennai had attempted a clumsy bribe to persuade EY to sign off on manipulated sales numbers. So Wirecard didn't just face the usual credulous team from EY for its annual audit. The firm had now assigned its crack fraud team to take a look. Codename 'Project Ring', in early 2017 these forensic auditors were demanding documents and answers. Their inquiry threatened to unravel not just Marsalek and O'Sullivan's Indian scheme. In the aftermath of the Zatarra Report, many investors were still wary. If EY refused to sign off on the group accounts then the share price, Marsalek's high life and the reputation of Germany's most exciting tech company would all come crashing down. All that stood in the way of disaster was Marsalek's secret weapon: a thirty-year-old Indonesian bookkeeper called Edo Kurniawan.

Edo was eager to please and keen to get ahead. He'd joined Wirecard in Singapore as a lowly member of the finance team in October 2015. He wasn't the brightest, nor was his English perfect, but he was a problem solver who took pride in cleaning up other people's messes. He soon moved to Munich with his wife, and was quickly indoctrinated into the culture. He took a competitive approach to Oktoberfest, finishing seven great steins and proudly marking the achievement (and the scale of the hangover it produced) by swearing off beer for life. He was just as competitive at work, putting in long hours, where he was determined to fit in. When the India deal was announced in October 2015 the valuation was obviously ridiculous. Kurniawan and a member of the M&A team involved in the due diligence, Matthias Helms, joked about it on a Skype chat. 'I wish I could sell a company to Wirecard,' said Helms.

The conversation turned to the oversight they could expect from Ernst & Young once the deal was done. Helms said the CFO, Burkhard Ley, was already on the case.

'Burkhard "co-ordinated" with EY Munich that there will be a change and that the new partner in India will come to Munich to meet us . . . and get brainwashed,' he wrote.*

'Hahahaha!' Kurniawan replied. He had grasped the Wirecard way. In no circumstances was the company to admit that any of the assets on its balance sheet were worth less than it paid for them, 'even in the event of natural disaster', he said.

Helms agreed: 'You got it, Edo. Totally qualified to join the Munich team :-)'

Asia was Marsalek's area of responsibility, and he had cultivated Kurniawan. First in small ways, asking him to collect post in Singapore, then on progressively more important issues and projects. The younger man had in turn earned Marsalek's trust as a safe pair of hands and, like many who fell into the executive's orbit, he tried to copy his style of sharp suits and snappy dressing. By early 2017 he was marked out for promotion and showing his dedication by jetting back and forth across the globe while his heavily pregnant wife

---

* A lawyer for Ley said at no time did he attempt to influence the decisions of the auditors, with whom his relationship was consistent with professional, objective and, above all, legal dealings. He said Ley had no recollection of meeting an EY partner from India.

waited at home: to Chennai; the US, where Wirecard was buying the prepaid card operations of Citigroup; and Singapore, where Kurniawan joked there was no need to pay for a hotel given the amount of time he spent in the office. He was massaging numbers, finding ways to tweak profits or fill holes all over Asia. As Ernst & Young's fraud specialists probed, Kurniawan used this frantic activity as an excuse. He was far too busy to supply the documents requested by EY's Project Ring.

It wasn't working. At the start of March Marsalek got a warning from someone at Ernst & Young; the firm had doubts about India and might withhold the audit confirmation there. Relations were deteriorating with The Boys at Hermes, Ramu and Palani, so Marsalek lined them up as the fall guys. 'We should treat it as if we believe it was a misunderstanding or some India weirdness,' he messaged Kurniawan, adding that he had a call scheduled with Ramu 'where I will basically fire him 😓'.

Kurniawan failed to placate Ernst & Young. After three months of delay and prevarication, their fraud squad demanded documents and data by the end of the week. In the usually polite world of audit, it was fighting talk. Seeing the stern email, Marsalek followed up: 'Hi Edo, do you have this under control? This seems quite worrying. Cheers, Jan.'

A week later, the matter was becoming serious. The group audit had to be completed by the start of April, but Ernst & Young had a string of outstanding questions about the Indian business. As well as the relationship with Goomo, and a general lack of paperwork in India, the auditors were querying a €7m sale of software added to the Indian revenues at the last minute. Ginned up by Marsalek, the buyer was said to be a Pakistani business whose address was a post office box in Dubai. As the clock ticked down Kurniawan worked all hours, barely pausing for the birth of his son; company legend had him sending emails from the delivery room. Wirecard meeting rooms in HQ were named after cities, and on 30 March Kurniawan was summoned to 'Paris' to join a conflab with Marsalek, Burkhard Ley and both teams from Ernst & Young, friendly and fraud-focused. Dashing to catch a plane to Singapore the next day, Kurniawan shot a message to his pal in the finance team: 'I just sent the report to EY fraud. Stomach ache.'

Still Ernst & Young came back with a now familiar list of demands. Kurniawan exhausted himself on the other side of the world to produce material to satisfy them. For two days he barely slept, when all of a sudden the impasse cleared. The bleary-eyed Kurniawan had stayed in the Singapore office so late he'd missed a flight to Vietnam. He could scarcely believe EY's decision: 'They really play with our feelings. Out of sudden we can recognize the revenue now. That's really super weird', he typed to his friend in Munich.

In the end it came down to a matter of good faith. Wirecard provided statements from senior executives explaining what was going on in their business. Marsalek drafted a text which said the company was confident that millions of euros owed to it would be paid. The managers at Hermes were also asked to sign statements attesting to the solidity of the figures given to Ernst & Young. It was the auditing equivalent of a firm handshake. EY took the measure of the men and decided to trust them. The accounts were signed.

Kurniawan soon got his reward, a promotion and a transfer. At the age of thirty-two, the new father was to head up Wirecard's finance team for the Asia Pacific, back in Singapore. He was to report directly to Stephan von Erffa, the deputy CFO, and was firmly in the Marsalek circle. As for the Austrian, with the all-clear from Ernst & Young it was back to business. Henry O'Sullivan wanted to expand his empire, with the help of a loan from Wirecard Bank. According to the presentation Marsalek handed to his colleagues describing the deal, Senjo processed more than €20bn of payments every year, worked with more than 100 different banks, and was regulated in Luxembourg and Lithuania. It wanted to buy Kalixa, a loss-making European payment processor that was being spun out of the gambling conglomerate GVC. In return for a slice of Kalixa's payments processing business, including premium clients like Arsenal Football Club and Burger King, Wirecard lent Senjo €25m of the €29m purchase price. Perhaps as an inside joke, there was a small indication of where the money would go: illustrating 'Senjo at a glance' was a black and white photo of the Marina Bay Sands by night, twinkling lights hinting at the festivities as Spago floated on air in luxurious defiance of gravity.

17

Defenestrated

2017 – London
Wirecard share price €43, market capitalization €5.4bn

THE ANNIVERSARY OF THE Zatarra attack was bittersweet for me. There was no libel suit, meaning I could breathe a deep sigh of relief. Then the German financial watchdog, BaFin, finally popped up to announce the results of a year-long investigation. The allegations of money laundering, the evidence of the Consett paperwork factory and the questions about Wirecard's accounting: nothing. Instead, the Frankfurt authorities recommended a criminal investigation into market manipulation of the Wirecard share price. Public prosecutors in Munich were asked to bring the perpetrators to justice.

One of the few investment banks to remain sceptical was Macquarie, the Australian upstart. Its analyst, Bob Liao, invited me to talk to a dozen fund managers over a sandwich lunch, and I tried to explain once again my suspicion that there was a big hole in Wirecard's balance sheet. The room was split between true believers and cynics, including the short seller Leo Perry. As we all chatted he tried to prod the audience in the right direction, asking questions to underscore the issues with the accounting. But Zatarra had muddied the water. If anything, the idea that Wirecard operated in legal grey areas helped to explain why it was so unusually profitable. I could see Perry grimace as the debate circled in that direction, dwelling on the remarkable growth Wirecard continued to report. Sales in 2016 as a whole had topped €1bn, from processing €62bn worth of payments. Profits were up by a third, to €307m (Ebitda). Even the group's cash flow was suddenly starting to improve, and yet more growth was promised. Perry mentioned that he struggled to find examples of Wirecard customers out there in the wild, but it fell on deaf ears. One man in particular seemed scathing of the various attacks: Antoine Badel of Alken Asset Management. Up to that point I'd assumed the investors were refusing to properly engage with the arguments, that it was a matter of catching their attention. Yet Badel knew about Consett, that a senior Wirecard salesperson had been involved with the whole scheme of shell companies and dummy directors exposed by Reuters. He muttered that he hadn't got a good explanation about that relationship from the company, as if it was a minor point to clarify rather than the skittering of a large cockroach. It was obvious to me then that Wirecard was a lost cause. Dreams of the future far outweighed any niggling concerns about where the profits came from. These men didn't see it as their job to second-guess auditors and the police. They were there to pick winners, and Wirecard was winning.

I was not. Instead of chasing stories I was pursuing builders, suppliers and contractors. It was slowly dawning on me that the project to build our new home was going to take much longer than the six months we'd arranged to live in the rented house. We were going to have to move back into the building site. Desperate to at least have a staircase in place first, one morning before work I went out to a workshop on the edge of St Albans equipped with giant electronic lathes. The air was rich with sawdust and every surface was piled high with wood ready for joining. The owner sucked his teeth, talking about the intense demand for spindles and his employees' insistence on taking holidays. I said we'd really appreciate not having to carry a baby and toddler up a ladder and he promised to see what he could do. On the dash back home, I was approaching traffic when I hit the brakes and the pedal sank straight to the floor with no resistance. Pumping manically for a moment with no effect, I shoved the car into a lower gear, bumped it along the kerb and yanked the handbrake, coming to a stop inches from a postman's van. The mechanic who came to look at it soon identified the problem: brake fluid leaking out from an ageing part that had to be replaced. Meanwhile I'd cancelled my meetings for the morning and was late for work, again.

In May I was invited for coffee by Patrick Jenkins, a senior editor who gently explained that Lionel Barber was shaking up the markets team with a defenestration: mine. I was off to fill a vacancy in the Lex team. So much for my once bright career prospects. I wasn't just going in the wrong direction, I was being sent back to where I'd started a decade earlier.

Blindsided, I tried to plead my case with the editor. It didn't go well. 'What front-page stories have you produced recently?' Lionel Barber asked in a fierce examination of my time on the markets desk. It was not a long list. It turned out he had an elephantine memory as well. Years earlier I'd taken him to meet a famous hedge fund manager in New York and, so far as he was concerned, I'd missed the story. Did I even have what it takes to be a reporter? I asked for more time, a second chance, desperate for a glimmer of light. Barber relented. He said it was unlikely, but I'd have a chance to change his mind.

When Matt Earl learned that he and Fraser Perring faced prosecution for writing the Zatarra Report, it took weeks to sink in. He kept expecting BaFin to say it had made some catastrophic mistake. How on earth can they have looked into the allegations and concluded that we're the criminals here, he thought. (The equivalent authorities in the UK seemed to have agreed with Earl. When BaFin asked that the houses of suspects who had traded Wirecard be raided, the reply was that typically some significant evidence was required first.)

Once he was through denial and anger, Earl became extremely concerned. He didn't know if he could travel, or if there was a warrant out for his arrest. He discovered that under the German system suspects can sometimes review their criminal case file before they are charged. So he appointed a local lawyer to request it, and six weeks later the case against him came through. There wasn't much to it. Most of the pages were simply suspicious transaction reports listing who had traded Wirecard stock around publication. Then there was some legal correspondence, and BaFin's report. Earl's German lawyer summarized the case against him. The watchdog hadn't found anything objectively untrue in the Zatarra Report. Instead it argued that it was written in a manner designed to mislead. All those footnotes Roddy insisted be included so that readers could see the evidence for themselves: no reasonable reader could be expected to follow them all. The attempt to link Burkhard Ley to the collapse of Kirch Media was unfair and misleading. Aside from that, it boiled down to a similar technicality to that used to convict the newsletter writer Tobias Bosler after the 2008 attack on Wirecard: Zatarra's report warned readers to assume its authors *may* have placed short bets against Wirecard, rather than explicitly stating that they had.

The case was weak, and Earl wanted to fight it. Two weeks after receiving the file he went to the office of his lawyer at Mishcon de Reya to discuss options. To begin with he was combative, but then over the speakerphone his German counsel, Timo, laid out the options in crisp English.

'Well if you choose to fight it you'll have to come to Germany. They will probably arrest you and you'll have to go to jail as you would be considered a flight risk. It'll take a year for it to come to court.' He then explained that the case could get to the penultimate day, at which point if prosecutors faced defeat they might withdraw it. 'You'll have lost a million euros of legal fees you won't get back, and a year of your life.'

Earl's throat was dry, his shoulders sagged as the fire of defiance was snuffed out. Perhaps it was the accent, but the lawyer was so direct and forthright he sounded almost cheerful. There was another option, he said. He had spoken to the prosecutors. He thought they wanted to drop the case but needed a face-saving option. 'I think if Mr Earl makes a donation to charity the file will be closed. It can't be reopened after that.'

It was a shakedown. 'OK, if I want to fight this I lose €1m and have a year in jail whatever happens. So what are they looking for in terms of a donation?' he said, bracing for the worst.

'Oh, I think they'll probably look for something like 50,000 to 60,000 euros. But I'll get them down,' the lawyer said, as if he were haggling for a used Porsche.

'Er, right. How does that work? Do you send them an email?' Earl asked.

'Oh no, no, no, no, nothing in writing,' the lawyer replied at this naive suggestion. 'We will have a telephone conversation. They will say a figure. I'll come back with a figure. And then we will agree on that. You will make a donation to the charity and provide evidence of that gift, and then they will drop the case.'

Earl's London lawyer had a mad look on her face. Neither of them could quite believe what they were hearing. It might be a common occurrence in Germany, but a secret deal with prosecutors sounded like something out of a banana republic. Earl knew he had to take it; the opportunity for a blank slate was too valuable for him and his business. Plus the lawyer was as good as his word, bargaining the amount down to just €35,000, paid to a food bank. In July the letter arrived. He was in the clear.

While I was casting around for stories to save my job, Paul Murphy tried to come to the rescue with a bold proposal to move to Mozambique. He'd go there for six months, working online. That meant I could rejoin Alphaville to keep an eye on the team in London. I'd escape Lex, while Murphy and his wife Kate spent some time in Moz, which had recently been whacked by a tropical cyclone. They'd help with recovery efforts, while also getting their own building project back on track. (After the hurricane, the Murphys discovered their local partner in the project wasn't the God-fearing family man they thought. He'd ridden out the storm in the area's only five-star hotel with a nineteen-year-old girlfriend, playing sugar daddy with Murphy's cash while the contractors went unpaid.)

To Murphy's great surprise, Lionel Barber was fine with him going for six months. He thought sometimes journalists had to be indulged, and that they paid you back if they did. He recognized the hack in Murphy, that spikiness and the instinct to expose, the nose for a story.

The intervention didn't save my skin. Barber had made his mind up: there was a McCrum-sized hole in the Lex team. However, the tone of our second meeting was different. He was reflective, this time the sofas in his office were for therapy, and it was a relief to be put out of my misery. What was the right job afterwards, he wondered? Maybe something digging into companies. It was a lifeline; perhaps I wasn't sunk after all.

A week later Murphy found out the price of going to Mozambique. Barber knew he had an itch, that after a decade on and off Alphaville he needed something new. At fifty-four, Murphy could feel time pressing on and he wanted the next big thing, whatever it was. We'd even discussed spinning Alphaville out of the *FT*, launching it as a separate start-up with some of the venture capital gushing around the world. Barber had a different idea. Just as his allotted time was coming to an end in 2015, Pearson sold the *FT* to Nikkei, a Japanese newspaper group owned by its employees. The takeover gave him a few extra years in the editor's chair, and he had the trust of those in charge. It was a rare situation which provided the time and space to take some risks for stories that would hurt those exposed. He called Murphy back in to make him an offer he couldn't refuse. 'Paul, I'd like you to run the investigations team.'

The clean audit from Ernst & Young in April 2017 was a rallying call for investors, so that summer most of the short sellers were licking their wounds, forced to abandon their bets against Wirecard by the relentless rise in the share price. One of them was Oliver Cobb at the hedge fund Greenvale Capital. He was good-natured and enthusiastic, but Cobb's mind was a pinboard of conspiracy theories, all pictures and red string, meaning he couldn't help but get tangled up in Wirecard. He caught the bug after the Zatarra Report, chasing down loose ends and characters at the fringes, but eventually Greenvale's founder, Bruce Emery, told Cobb to put his efforts into some moneymaking positions for the firm instead. So a few months later they were both surprised when a broker offered to bring Wirecard's CFO, Burkhard Ley, to visit the cramped offices of their small fund overlooking Oxford Street, London's once-glamorous shopping drag. Cobb and Emery were even more surprised when Ley arrived. He marched in with the PR woman, Iris Stoeckl, and announced why he was there: 'I just wanted to look our most aggressive shorts in the face and ask what's going on?'

Not much was learned from the short and combative exchange which followed, but Cobb had other things on his mind, as he was about to get married and fly to Mauritius for a welcome break. Two days after his return an email arrived with the subject: 'Amelie Cobb has shared HoNeYmOoN . . . <3 with you'. The phishing email was packed with romantic pictures plundered from his wife's Instagram account, a violation that filled Cobb with rage. It was the first of many. For six months Greenvale's staff were bombarded by the hackers, forcing Greenvale to rebuild its entire IT system from scratch twice, after a second consultant criticized the thoroughness of the first. On one sweep of the office for bugs a technician removed a yellow brick from the wall to investigate an unknown power source and the hole became a permanent monument to their fruitless campaign.

In public, meanwhile, Wirecard was finding its moment. There was something in the air, a whiff of optimism. Markus Braun's utopianism was becoming the default pose of every executive who could claim their business used technology. Companies were no longer merely serving customers in the hope of a buck or two, they were disruptors reshaping society. Everything was up for grabs and no industry was safe from reimagination. The sums available to start-ups had been transformed, along with the language. Private companies valued at a billion dollars or more were now 'Unicorns', and chasing these magical creatures was an industry. SoftBank, a Japanese conglomerate, announced the launch of a $100bn Vision Fund to throw at private companies like the taxi group Uber and the office space provider WeWork based on fantasies of world domination.

In the stock market, Wirecard caught the eye. Its numbers were great, but more than that it was global, it was at the forefront of payments processing. In March it had announced a second deal with Citigroup designed to make Wirecard a household name across Asia. It would take over payments processing for 20,000 merchants spread over eleven countries in Asia and the Pacific, from India all the way to New Zealand. Investors grabbed the backs of envelopes, jotted down the number of people in the world, the value of things they might buy online in the future, then compared that gazillion-dollar figure to the tiny portion of commerce Wirecard processed: the potential, at least in theory, was mind-blowing. To Germans, here was a home-grown technology company. The only other software group which rivalled those in Silicon Valley was SAP, which specialized in complex systems for manufacturers. In the summer of 2017 Wirecard wasn't just in the clear, it was the future, and by October its share price had doubled to more than €80, valuing the company at €10bn.

For short sellers who bet that the price of a stock is going to fall, a share price which doubles is a major problem. For instance, say you had €100 and used €2 to buy Commerzbank stock. When the share price halves, you'll lose €1 and be left with a €1 problem. Each further loss is a smaller and smaller part of your now €99 investment portfolio. By comparison, let's say you short €2 of Wirecard stock and the share price goes up 50 per cent: you have also lost €1, but now you have a €3 problem and whoever monitors risk on your trading desk is shouting at you to stop being an idiot and to cut your losses. One by one, most of those who had circled Wirecard cut their losses and moved on.

Not everyone gave up. One told me that he couldn't let it go entirely, that if it was still going strong in the future he'd dedicate his retirement to exposing it. Eduardo Marques at Valiant Capital adjusted the size of his short, but he stuck at it. Wirecard's Indian deal ate away at him. He trawled the long lists of every foreign direct investment into India. Marques could see that everything in India was somehow linked to Senjo in Singapore, and he even had a working theory. The excess cash earned by the Mauritius fund 1A was a cookie jar. It could be used to make investments in companies which would then buy services from Wirecard. At the end of October 2017, he laid everything out in a presentation which he circulated to other investors, and which found its way to some journalists.

I was working on the story in the New Year when I was scooped by Roddy Boyd at the Southern Investigative Reporting Foundation. His story was the 'Great Indian Shareholder Robbery', and in absolute terms it was a smash hit, knocking €1.5bn off Wirecard's market capitalization in a few days – more than the Zatarra Report managed.

But by this time Wirecard was almost three times larger; the share price dropped from €109 to €99. It was a blip.*

Yet a few weeks later, something strange happened. Murphy grabbed a quick, dry lunch with one of his regular contacts at Signor Sassi, a splashy Italian in Knightsbridge which served the Harrods crowd. The walls were covered with photos of movie star customers, and the chatter and bustle gave it a pleasant background din as the pair tucked into lobster linguine. After they'd caught up on the usual gossip about takeover bids, Wirecard came up.

'You do know they will pay you good money to stop writing about them,' the market contact said. Murphy smiled, dismissing the idea. 'No, I'm serious, they will pay you proper money,' he insisted. 'I've heard $10m thrown about. Go and talk to Gary. He'll help you.'

Intrigued by this latest twist, Murphy went to see the Fabric owner Gary Kilbey in a bar near the club to find out what was going on. Gary's son Tom was a former professional footballer who'd appeared on the reality TV show *The Only Way Is Essex*. Kilbey Jr had run into Jan Marsalek's old friend Sina Taleb at a party in LA, who suggested resurrecting the idea of bringing Paul Murphy and Marsalek together to bury the hatchet. The Wirecard man came over for lunch with both Kilbeys at Estiatorio Milos, a white-tablecloth dining room in St James's which flew in fresh fish from Greece, and they were dazzled by Marsalek, who made a convincing case that all of the company's problems were in the past. In the course of that meal Marsalek asked if Murphy or I would take a large 'charitable donation' to go away. Kilbey senior said he didn't think so, but Marsalek was still extremely keen to meet us, ready to fly over at a moment's notice.

'Let's do it,' Murphy said.

Back at the office, we tried to work out what had prompted the overture. CEO Markus Braun had celebrated Christmas by borrowing €150m from Deutsche Bank, secured against the value of his

---

* Boyd's story did have one effect: reading it in India, a person with first-hand knowledge of Wirecard's India deal was jolted into action. They logged on to BaFin's online whistleblowing portal and provided details of the suspect transactions, hoping to spur the German regulator into action.

stock. The way the share price was going, he'd soon be a billionaire. If the offer of a bribe was real, it suggested a level of resources and will we'd never encountered before. Who couldn't be bought for $10m? It also smelled like a trap, a sting to demonstrate that an *FT* journalist was corrupt, but if Marsalek was that cavalier it was an opportunity to catch him. We'd have to monitor it covertly.

The Murphy-Marsalek lunch was arranged with surprising speed. On Friday, 6 February 2018 Murphy and Gary Kilbey arrived at Cut, a steakhouse in the hotel 45 Park Lane, Wolfgang Puck's first restaurant in Europe. A series of Damien Hirst lithographs hung on the walls and the room was flooded with light from picture windows overlooking Hyde Park. Eye-popping prices kept the crowds away, so a playlist of American soft rock helped the ambience along. Murphy found Marsalek already at the table, his snug blue suit and military buzz cut instantly recognizable from Wirecard's corporate photos. He jumped up, flashing a million-dollar smile. Here was the gracious host, delighted to meet the famous Paul Murphy at last and to have the opportunity to talk a little. The table was round, of dark wood, with five heavy leather chairs. Tom Kilbey, fashionably scruffy, Murphy already knew. The mysterious Sina Taleb was there as well. Bigger than Marsalek, with a mane of black hair and a deep tan, he had the healthy glow of the seriously rich and was vague about why he was there or what he did for a living.

Murphy was sweating. He had to create a situation where Marsalek could offer a bribe without walking into the trap of asking for one. We hadn't planned to send him in alone, but there'd been a last-minute change of venue. As he walked through the doors at Cut, he'd only had a chance to text '45' to the *FT* back-up team mistakenly positioned up the road at the Dorchester Grill. He had no idea if they'd know where he'd gone.

The lunch party exchanged pleasantries as they briefly considered menus which offered a choice of Wagyu beef from five countries. Marsalek was poised, back ramrod-straight with shoulders relaxed, quietly dominating the conversation. He had expressive hands but, possibly because he was on his guard, he used one at a time. While gesticulating with his right, the left sat in his lap. When he switched to emphasizing a point with the left, he kept the base of his other palm pressed against the edge of the table, as if holding himself in position. When he laughed, his whole chest was involved. Marsalek's central theme was how Wirecard was misunderstood. Yes it had processed payments for porn and gambling, but that was in the past. It had to do a better job of communicating how it had changed. The company was sensitive to uneducated criticism due to the attacks it had faced before.

As waiting staff fussed around them to lay out the first course, Murphy caught a glimpse of three 'ladies at lunch' being shown to a nearby table and stifled a sigh of relief. It was Cynthia O'Murchu and Sarah O'Connor from the *FT* investigations team, and Camila Hodgson, then a trainee reporter. The three women gossiped and argued over what to drink, giving every sign of ignoring their surroundings while carefully placing a handbag over the back of a chair. Inside was a hidden camera, aimed at Marsalek.

The closest Marsalek came to offering a bribe was to argue that journalists could be bought easily. He wouldn't go into details, just claimed to have first-hand experience. Perhaps that was supposed to be Murphy's cue, but dirty dealings never seemed likely with the other three men at the table. While they spoke little, only jumping in occasionally to let Marsalek eat, Murphy was always conscious of his audience. What Marsalek did say was that, knowingly or not, I was working with short sellers to damage Wirecard's share price. The unknowing part he conceded, because he was told that Murphy and I 'lived very normal lives'. It was an admission, albeit indirect, that someone was running a spying operation against us. 'Maybe friends of mine did it,' Marsalek said. And he explained, almost candidly, why this was needed: a misinformed or malicious *FT* story represented an 'existential threat' to Wirecard, which, like any financial institution, had to retain the trust of those it did business with. 'If we lose our correspondent banking relationships, the business would go down almost overnight,' he said.

It was a lunch of sparkling water and Diet Cokes, and it wasn't long. Marsalek had done most of the talking, and he was determined to have the last word. To pay the bill, he pulled out a novelty credit card cast in solid gold.

Afterwards, Murphy reconvened with the *FT* team in a nearby hotel, disappointed. At another table there had been a man dining alone, and they suspected that the *FT*'s amateur black ops may have been spotted by Marsalek's professionals. More than ever, we were convinced there was something very wrong about this company, but we had nothing to show for it.

Three months later, in May 2018, Murphy tried again. This time he met Marsalek alone, for a late lunch at The Lanesborough. The restaurant was almost empty, save for the two of them and a pianist elegantly tinkling. Murphy was wired for sound, but Marsalek behaved in a way which made his speech hard to catch; he positioned himself facing at an angle to Murphy and spoke in a murmur. Such countermeasures were a bad sign, so Murphy reasoned he might as well get something useful out of it and switched to cultivating Marsalek as a source. They bonded a little over a glass of white wine and discussion of Marsalek's bad back; he said he'd slipped a disc, and was considering all sorts of treatments, including immune therapy. It wasn't helped by his constant travel, Marsalek said. (He claimed to mostly fly commercial, although in the weeks that followed he offered Murphy help with a story about lax security at a UK airfield which attracted Russian private jets – Marsalek said he could put an *FT* reporter on a Gulfstream in Moscow, if he wanted. Murphy declined, as that level of co-operation was a little too close for comfort.) Marsalek also talked about some of his private investments. He was looking at backing a reformed Cambridge Analytica, the scandal-hit political consultancy which had been caught harvesting Facebook data on a massive scale. Marsalek had also put $7m into a fundraising by Telegram, the group behind the encrypted messaging app, and encouraged Murphy to write about the project. (The US authorities later forced Telegram to return the $1.2bn it raised in total from investors.)

Murphy and Marsalek parted on good terms, hatchet buried. Murphy assured him there was no *FT* vendetta against Wirecard, with a warning that if new evidence emerged we would report it. 'I'd expect nothing less,' Marsalek said with a smile.

Gary and Tom Kilbey had brokered the lunch and were waiting for Marsalek in the hotel bar. He joined them in good spirits and they celebrated détente with a series of large gin and tonics. The question of the fee for their public relations efforts was settled: a six-figure sum each for the father and son. As the evening wore on, Marsalek talked about his interests, his fascinations with technology and security, name-dropping as he went. He'd met Elon Musk, he said, and was a firm believer in Tesla: 'Buy that stock and tuck it away,' he advised them.

Marsalek's idea of relaxation was a little different to the Kilbeys'. 'My leisure time is more work in Libya.' He talked about his stake in three cement plants which once belonged to an Austrian conglomerate, but were sold after the country descended into chaos. He seemed to enjoy thrilling the two men, telling them about an attack on one of the plants by Isis. He'd watched on a monitor as the assault was blown to smithereens in an airstrike. As he talked there was a glint in his eye, but to Kilbey Sr it didn't seem like a tall tale. With all the gin, and getting Murphy onside, Marsalek seemed to think he was invulnerable.

18

The Reluctant Whistleblower

September 2017 – Singapore
Wirecard share price €76, market capitalization €9.5bn

Pav Gill was, before anything else, a product of his mother's determination. Born in Singapore to Sikh immigrants, she first fell victim to an arranged marriage then defied it, kicking out her drunk husband and raising her son alone in Singapore's public housing while working as a banker. Sometimes she had to take him on business trips with her, or send him to relatives in England, but she always prioritized his education, pushing him to thrive in the city-state's best schools and to secure a place at its elite law college. Gill inherited that hard-working and determined streak, along with a striking head of prematurely silver hair, and he forged a career as an expert in financial services at Magic Circle law firms. He'd worked for a time in Dubai, but was back in Singapore at a start-up when he was headhunted to become Wirecard's first legal counsel for the Asia Pacific. The company flew him to Munich, and his new boss took him for a beer and a ride on a ferris wheel at Oktoberfest. He was to be the legal team's eyes and ears in Singapore. Gill was pleased and impressed, happy to be working for such a large and rapidly expanding financial institution. Wirecard was everywhere in Singapore, its credit card readers on shop counters, restaurant tables and in taxi cabs, and its big deal with Citigroup was supposed to give it a similar presence all across Asia. Gill had been told there was a bit of a job to do, to put procedures and policies in place somewhere which still had a start-up culture, and he was looking forward to it.

When he actually arrived in Wirecard's Singapore office above Asia Square, Gill found he was sharing a room with another just-hired lawyer, Royston Ng. A fastidious Singaporean who favoured bow ties and braces, Ng was a former prosecutor and magistrate working for the team in charge of the Citi deal. His job was to deal with regulators, applying for all the licences Wirecard needed to actually take over payments processing from Citi in each of the eleven countries. As they got to work Gill found everybody friendly enough, but there was a culture clash. The Singaporeans Wirecard was hiring to professionalize its operation had a big-company mindset. Ng had spent time at the US behemoth General Electric, for instance, which made a science of management. Wirecard was run less as a go-getting start-up and more like a small business controlled by the entrepreneurs who'd sold their firm to Wirecard years earlier and for some reason stuck around. Money always seemed to be tight, not just in Singapore but at various country offices which were busy doing their own thing. The purse strings in Asia, meanwhile, were controlled by Edo Kurniawan. Gill found that the chubby young Indonesian was outwardly friendly and cheerful, but he had an unusual amount of responsibility for a thirty-two-year-old whose English wasn't up to scratch. He flew around a lot for an accountant, and complained about how often he had to go back to Munich to see Jan Marsalek and Burkhard Ley, the CFO who was about to retire. It was a humblebrag to underscore his influence, but Kurniawan was also in a constant state of agitation. Sat next to him on a flight home from Vientiane in Laos one day, Gill marvelled at the relentless work rate as Kurniawan ploughed through email after email at a furious pace, and suggested he take a break. The Indonesian said he didn't have time, but took a moment to vent.

'I do so much for this company, I still don't get treated well enough. I don't know if they appreciate it, I spend my time going to India fixing up so many of their problems. I'm on a flight every week; I go to Indonesia, the Philippines. They just shout: do this, do that,' Kurniawan complained.

Gill didn't know it then, but Kurniawan wasn't joking about his effectiveness. The young man had a knack for one of his most important jobs: charming the auditors at Ernst & Young. In December the lead audit partner from EY Germany, Andreas Loetscher, flew into Chennai for a two-day site visit at Hermes to better understand what was going on. Afterwards he wrote to Kurniawan to thank him for the 'preparation, discussions, explanations and entertainment', while a colleague requested 'local cuisine' for their trip to the Wirecard office in Philadelphia the following week. The ever-present Kurniawan made it to there as well, taking the auditors to a tourist trap where the waiting staff dressed as pilgrims. Whether it was the food or the company, the EY men once again flew home happy.

One incident in Singapore had caused Ng to raise an eyebrow. The lawyer was applying for a licence to issue prepaid cards in Hong Kong, but the accounts provided by the finance department showed the unit was loss-making. There was no way the regulator would wave the application through if its finances weren't sound. Kurniawan's response was to ask what number Ng needed. A new set of accounts soon arrived; the Hong Kong business was profitable after all. It was just a ripple – any large business can shift profits around if it needs to – and at Christmas Gill took another trip to Munich for the Christmas party, enjoying the sprawling event. Markus Braun positioned himself to one side with the PR team, while Jan Marsalek had an almost rock-star status, surrounded by a throng of Wirecard employees hanging on his every word. Gill felt drawn in, posing for a photo with this corporate celebrity. His luck was on the up.

In the spring of 2018 a member of Kurniawan's team asked to talk to Pav Gill, away from the office. They met for a coffee early on a Monday, and she was nervous. It had taken her a long time to get to this moment. She didn't want to blow the whistle, and she was scared for her job, but she felt she had no choice. Once she started talking, unburdening herself, Gill scribbled down notes, not quite able to believe what he was hearing.

At the start of the year Wirecard had been in the process of moving to new offices in a building favoured by other tech companies. The large floor was not yet fully occupied, boxes still littered the place. Kurniawan called half a dozen people into a meeting room. He picked up a whiteboard pen and began to teach them how to cook the books.

What Kurniawan sketched out was a practice known as 'round tripping'. A lump of money would leave the bank Wirecard owned in Germany destined for the subsidiary in Hong Kong which was applying for the payments licence. But it would stay there only momentarily; just long enough to satisfy regulators that the business was well funded. Next the cash would depart to sit briefly in the books of an external 'partner', from where it would travel back to Wirecard in India. In each country the individual legs of the trip would look to local auditors like legitimate business. In Hong Kong the partner was a supplier being paid, while in India it was a valued Wirecard customer. In reality, the money would move in a circle.

As Kurniawan explained how the scheme would work, he mentioned that the reason for all the subterfuge was to help cover up a mess in India. A spat was brewing with the Ramasamy brothers there, but getting rid of The Boys hadn't been as easy as Marsalek expected. They still owned a big chunk of a business Wirecard needed to use in Chennai and were restricting use of an overdraft.

For two months the whistleblower had watched with rising alarm as the plan went into practice. She handed Gill a sheaf of documents, and the lawyer combed through them. To begin with he thought that the whole thing had to be some sort of misunderstanding. Why go to such lengths when the money involved was so small, just €2m? It didn't make any sense.

Gill trusted Ng, and together the two Wirecard newcomers quietly investigated. They soon had other reasons to suspect Kurniawan and those around him. They discovered Wirecard Singapore was more than a year late in filing audited accounts for 2016 due to a disagreement with the local arm of Ernst & Young. Meanwhile, in the Philippines a Wirecard business didn't have enough cash to pay a tax bill, so Kurniawan had instigated another round of suspect manoeuvres to find the money. Gill reported all of this up to Wirecard's head of compliance in Munich, Daniel Steinhoff, who in April landed in Singapore to hear the details himself. A full investigation was needed, the first on Steinhoff's watch. As compliance was an after-thought at Wirecard, there was no manual for how he was supposed to proceed; Steinhoff improvised. On the recommendation of Royston Ng, he commissioned a team of expert investigators, former prosecutors at the big Asian law firm Rajah & Tann, for 'Project Tiger'. It would be their job to assess what had happened, and whether Wirecard faced any legal repercussions. To do that Rajah & Tann needed evidence, so the German lawyer ordered Wirecard's IT team to 'mirror' the email inboxes of Kurniawan and two accomplices. Soon the Singaporean lawyers were reading Kurniawan's emails.

What they found was damning. Pav Gill could watch a series of frauds unfold. In one email a member of the finance team sent himself the logo for a company. In the next he attached an invoice bearing that logo for payment by Wirecard, an amateurish forgery. Gill soon identified a string of suspect transactions. Documents were backdated, contracts were signed for software without any involvement of the Wirecard sales or technology teams. The amounts for each weren't huge, but the book-cooking operation had been going on for years.

At the start of May, Project Tiger took on a new urgency. Gill's whistleblower continued to feed him information, and she alerted him to a new round tripping scheme. This time the money would be routed to India via Kuala Lumpur, with Wirecard supposedly paying €2m for a market research study on payments in Malaysia. The head of the business there told Gill he knew nothing about it. With €2m about to walk out the door, everything accelerated. Rajah & Tann pulled together a thirty-one-page report on their interim findings, which laid out the alleged crimes in gory detail. Wirecard's executive board had to be told, so Royston Ng summarized everything in a PowerPoint presentation. He dispatched it to Munich, and the two Singaporean lawyers waited for the company to spring into action.

It was a critical moment for Wirecard. A groundswell of enthusiasm was carrying Markus Braun towards a goal which had been laughable when he first mentioned it all those years ago, but now had the air of inevitability: membership of Germany's DAX Index. It was the country's most select corporate club, representing the thirty most valuable public companies. Joining it would make Wirecard an automatic investment for pension funds, charitable foundations and private savers the world over. Overnight it would catapult Braun into the ranks of a tiny global elite, one of the corporate leaders shaping the future with their exploits. He had just become a billionaire and was starting to act the part as well.

Braun had always controlled Wirecard's public relations behind the scenes, obsessing over press releases. At times it seemed to some staff that was all he did, and they knew better than to approach him when the stock price was falling. As Wirecard's growing size attracted the spotlight, Braun stepped into it wearing a black turtleneck jumper in the style of Steve Jobs. (As he retained his black jacket, the effect was more awkward cousin than heir to the visionary Apple founder.) Braun had also added a few empty phrases to his quiver. He was a 'pathological optimist', he told investors, who lapped up the rhetoric. That Monday in May Wirecard was worth €15bn, its share price €118, but the figure was rising daily and there was an irresistible arc to its ascendance. If it was to enter the DAX, then another member of that club would have to be ejected. A likely candidate was Commerzbank, the staid old financial institution. What better sign of Germany's modern economy could there be than such a farewell to the old and an ushering-in of the new?

Pav Gill had expected the report on Project Tiger to spark a storm of activity, a sharp intervention to stop the €2m going out, then suspensions pending a full investigation. Instead, Project Tiger was taken out of his hands. The Munich legal team were to oversee it, with assistance from Jan Marsalek, as he was in charge of Asia. Royston Ng threw a fit. At the very least Marsalek was a person of interest, a witness to some of the dodgy dealings, whether his involvement was witting or not. Ng's objections were squashed with a sharp rebuke from Munich.

Gill and Ng shared their unease with Daniel Steinhoff over Telegram, on a shared chat they'd used to discuss the investigation.

'What's going on?' Ng wrote.

Gill piled in as well. 'I don't understand how a few people commit several extremely serious financial crimes and then go on with impunity.'

Steinhoff, who was on holiday in Bali, had more of an insight into how the senior executives interacted:

'I think Jan understands very well what it's about, but they don't shit in each other's bed.'

Ng was worried about liability. So far as he was concerned all of them had a responsibility to report the suspicious transactions to the appropriate authorities.

'As a former prosecutor, I say it very clearly: we will be prosecuted personally if we don't do anything.'

Gill's thoughts turned to Shakespeare:

'Nowadays it seems easier to do something wrong than right. Reminds me of the beginning of *Macbeth* – "Fair is foul, and foul is fair".'

Almost immediately Gill noticed a change in behaviour on the finance team. Kurniawan started to lock his office, while his cronies gave the lawyers the cold shoulder. The whistleblower became terrified there was a hunt under way for the mole and refused to do any more. In June Rajah & Tann came in to conduct interviews, and the suspects admitted everything. Kurniawan was almost arrogant, telling the lawyers to talk to Marsalek, that he had approved everything. In August the law firm sent an updated set of findings direct to Munich, but still nothing happened. Kurniawan and his gang carried on regardless. Gill tried to throw himself into his work, but by September his position was untenable. He was offered a choice: resign or be fired. He chose to go quietly, but Wirecard didn't walk him out of the door there and then. Deciding he needed an insurance policy, Gill took copies of the Project Tiger email archives, seventy gigabytes worth of data: the mirrored files in which the true face of Wirecard was reflected.

At home with his mother, unemployed, Pav Gill tried to find another job. Royston Ng urged him to go to the Singapore authorities, to report what had happened, but Gill was despondent. He thought that if he went to the police it would all sound fanciful and put him in the line of fire. He'd seen all the forged documents; what was to stop someone at Wirecard faking something about him. He also imagined difficult questions. *Oh, you have the proof? Do tell us exactly how you came to be in possession of this material, Mr Gill . . .*

He applied for positions, only for them to fall through at the last moment; he suspected a bad reference. Invited to one interview, it became an interrogation; instead of his job history and qualifications, it focused again and again on why he left Wirecard and what he'd done there, as if it were a test to see if he'd break confidentiality. Neighbours reported strange men taking an interest in the apartment Gill shared with his mother. They both began to suspect he was being followed, seeing the same few faces again and again when he left the house. His mother went on a picnic with friends and noticed a man sitting awkwardly close to them, straining an ear to their conversation. Gill wondered if they were incompetent, or the visibility was the point. Was it a message? He tried not to let it get to him, and even went for drinks with a couple of Wirecard fixers at Broadside, a German-themed bar. Over a few beers they explained what they were there to do.

'Yeah it's very common, in these sorts of situations. It's our job to speak to the person and find out what they want. If they have material with them, we find out if there's a way – if the material is incriminating in some way, for instance – we can come to some sort of financial arrangement.' The man left the clumsy suggestion hanging in the air. Gill sipped his lager while considering the matter. He knew he should end the conversation, but he was rather enjoying the food and the refreshments, while an idle part of him wondered what the number would be. After weighing it up, he shrugged. 'No. I don't have anything like that.'

In the end it was Gill's mother who took matters into her own hands. To her, every story about Wirecard's success was an affront. That summer the share price had spiralled up to as much as €192, a market capitalization touching €24bn, making it far more valuable than Deutsche Bank. Commerzbank was ejected from the DAX in September, while Braun used the media attention for even more outlandish predictions. Wirecard would grow even faster over the next ten years as society went cashless. By 2025 he forecast the company would process more than €700bn of payments each year.

Gill's mother was disgusted that such a high-flying company wouldn't act against criminals in its own ranks. While Gill searched job listings, she sat on the sofa trying to find ways to expose Wirecard. She began to approach journalists, and on Saturday, 13 October she sent me a pseudonymous email offering 'some highly sensitive information that can expose an international financial company that has been conducting corrupt activities the last many years'. She didn't name the company, just that the story was 'highly sensitive and dangerous in nature' and that she had to be sure I could be trusted to protect my sources.

When Gill found out, he felt sick to his stomach. 'Oh my God, Mum, what have you done now?'

19

Notes from the Bunker

October 2018 – Singapore
Wirecard share price €165, market capitalization €20.4bn

THE FURAMA CITY CENTRE was a serviceable business hotel in Singapore's Chinatown. An escalator at the entrance delivered guests into a large lobby on the first floor, an asymmetrical atrium ringed by jutting internal balconies. The odd angles, beige surfaces and absence of natural light gave it the feel of a starship imagined in the 1970s. The only windows were at the far end of a buffet restaurant off to one side. Next to it in the lobby was a seating area walled by a long white curtain, behind which staff disappeared to fetch coffee and drinks. It was the spot Pav Gill had chosen for our first meeting at 10 a.m. sharp. He was casual in a polo shirt, fidgety with a sort of nervous determination as we got to know each other. He was a couple of years younger than me, with soft features and grey hair that made his age hard to place. Gill's eyes were tired, and he kept playing with things on the table, picking up a pen or a packet of sugar and passing it back and forth between his hands. There were flashes of contempt for the clowns who had wronged him. 'Edo is this guy who can't even string a sentence together in English. Dude, what the fuck is he doing running the finance department. I just don't get it.' He was also extremely patient. Every time we started talking about different aspects of what happened I'd get bogged down in names, countries and businesses. We had to start from the very beginning. I fetched paper from the front desk, and he sketched out org charts and diagrams of suspect transactions as I filled a notebook trying to keep pace with this tutorial on the inner workings of Wirecard.

At lunchtime we were joined by Gill's mother, who insisted on going by her *nom-de-guerre* of 'Evelyn'. She was in her late fifties and short, with shoulder-length silver hair and a sparkle in her eyes. We shifted a few metres to a restaurant table, and she took over for a while, directing my attention to some of the acceptable local dishes on the eclectic menu. I ventured chicken with sambal while she opted for congee, a rice porridge, blaming a lack of energy for the bland choice. Her opinions were chiselled in rock. 'My favourite bankers were always the German bankers, they were always very nice, very professional and efficient, nothing like the French.' She was protective: 'Markus Braun, he is not a good guy. I do not trust him, you see. This is my only boy. You can't let anything happen to him, you understand.' At the same time, she was a cheerleader for her son. 'You know, my dear, stupid Wirecard is in trouble. They messed with the wrong guy,' she said, emphasizing the point with an infectious laugh. I said if it came to a choice between protecting Gill and publishing the story, then we wouldn't, but at that moment the threat seemed remote and abstract. We were chatting away, waiting for the food, when someone appeared at the table and clapped him on the shoulder.

'Pav, hi, fancy seeing you here! How are you doing?'

So much for an out-of-the-way location. Gill awkwardly ignored my presence and introduced this friend to his mother: it was the head of the team from Rajah & Tann, one of the ex-prosecutors who had worked on Project Tiger for Wirecard. I mutely slid my reporter's notebook off the table into my lap, trying to be inconspicuous. When the man left, Gill was cavalier. 'Don't worry, I'm sure he wouldn't care that I'm talking to a journalist, he'd probably be happy.' I wasn't so sure, but if lunch with his mother was a test, I seemed to have passed. By the time the two of us called a halt, having switched from coffee to beer during ten hours in the lobby, my head was spinning. Gill had dozens of little stories, each of which on its own was scarcely believable. For instance, Wirecard's entire business was supposed to be moving money around electronically. Yet he'd discovered that

Kurniawan's team at one point discussed withdrawing several thousand dollars from the bank in cash and physically taking it to a money-changing kiosk in Raffles Place to get a better exchange rate. It was the sort of thing a small business might do, not a giant international financial institution.

On my second day in Singapore we were joined by Stefania Palma, Italian, diminutive, with wavy black hair, a kick-ass reporter who'd been with the *FT* for a few months. I knew her from the occasional game of football with other hacks on Friday lunchtimes in London. An expert in Mandarin, her previous job had been Asia editor at *The Banker*, a venerable monthly based on another floor of the *FT* building at Southwark Bridge. At twenty-eight she'd been thrown in at the deep end, sent to Singapore just in time to cover the summit between Donald Trump and North Korea's Kim Jong-un, and had hardly drawn breath since. It was Palma who initially met Gill and Evelyn at Changi airport on her way to a conference in Sydney. She'd sussed them out in a four-hour stint, her first experience of dealing with whistleblowers, before sprinting through departures dragging a suitcase. She'd barely had time to let me know they were the real deal before take-off, leaving me with an agonizing day in London waiting for details. Reporting with her, she had the disarming knack of clutching her head while muttering '*Alora, alora,*' as if lost. 'Wait, stop, really, are you serious? Explain that to me again,' she'd say as she subtly extracted details and tested what she was being told.

Gill, Palma and I spent that second day out in the open, in the plaza underneath Wirecard's old building, which was still occupied by its partner, Citigroup. He was starting to relax, enjoying the thrill of proximity to his subject. It seemed as if the burden of what he knew was lifting – passed to us. We sat near a fountain on the aluminium chairs and tables scattered about, relying on the burble of the water and the bustle of the streets to cover our conversation. That evening in an empty hotel bar Gill showed us his Telegram chats, another revelation. For a regulated financial institution to let its staff conduct official business on an encrypted messaging app was unheard of. At Wirecard it was expected: it was one of the few apps staff could download to their 'sandboxed' company phones.

For our final morning Stefania and I suggested somewhere properly out of the way, where we could use a laptop without being overlooked. I was anxious to get my hands on the evidence. We settled on Beanstro, a black-walled café in the cavernous shopping mall underneath the Marina Bay Sands, the hotel topped by Spago and the boat. The entire complex was deserted and anonymous, a marble and gold temple to luxury brands; placeless signifiers of wealth. We took a table in a corner with Gill and Evelyn, going back over what we'd learned, gently trying to coax Gill into handing over the goods. It was the final step, and he was understandably conflicted; he wanted to be rid of it, but was also wary that it might carry traces of his identity. We discussed security measures, settling on the codename 'Harry'. Once we took a copy Gill planned to give the stash to his grandmother on a USB stick to keep safe, a piece of technology she'd never use; the code for that was 'Panjiri', a Punjabi name for the densely calorific dish given to mothers after childbirth. Assuming the worst, about both Wirecard's hacking capabilities and Singapore state surveillance, I was equipped with a pile of temporary equipment: an old iPhone that had been completely wiped and I'd only use for the trip; a thin Chromebook if I needed to log on to email, with strict instructions to never use hotel Wi-Fi; and a hefty air-gapped laptop with all its wireless connections disabled, for reviewing and encrypting any documents I might get. The data dump was so large we ordered lunch while the transfer took place. I picked at an omelette as the computer whirred under the table, its faint humming the only sound of a digital avalanche.

To save £170 of *FT* money I had to take a 1,000-mile detour to change in Brunei. When the pre-departure prayer rang through the cabin for the long leg back to Heathrow, I finally started to relax. Carrying the precious cargo brought back teenage memories of when I used to help my mother ferry the day's takings from our family's newsagent to the bank; thick piles of notes bound with elastic bands, stuffed inside a shopping bag. Walking through town I would act casual, enjoying the secret while holding on with white knuckles. What I had tucked beside my feet on the plane was far more precious, I was sure, and I hoped that somewhere in there I would find the answer to the question which had nagged at me the whole time in Singapore: why? Why all the petty schemes for such small amounts?

All that was put aside when I finally got back to St Albans on Saturday lunchtime. I walked into the kitchen to find Charlotte decorating a giant cake with a bonfire of orange icing and chocolate flakes. In no time the house was filled with five-year-olds. My job was outside in the back garden with a neighbour. With just our phone torches and a bucket of sand for emergencies, we scuttled around lighting fountains, roman candles and a row of rockets propped for launch in empty Cava bottles. You flick the lighter, hold it to the touchpaper, and hope to God it doesn't burn the house down or explode in your face . . .

While Stefania knocked on doors in Singapore and Kuala Lumpur, I spent six weeks trying to get inside the mind of Edo Kurniawan. I had his entire inbox, from the day he started at Wirecard in 2014 to when a copy of the archive was taken for Project Tiger in 2018. I could scroll through his calendar, his chats with colleagues, the reminders he sent himself. His gripes, his admin, the reprimands he dished out; it was all there. He was obviously a workaholic who juggled a huge array of tasks and duties, with hints of problems scattered everywhere. Each year I could watch the audit unfold, a frantic race to get the numbers in line. Wirecard's businesses in Asia seemed to be constantly short of cash, forcing Kurniawan to scrape around for funds. There were references to internal rivalries, half-conversations and dead ends. I worked in a room about two metres square, and as I followed threads through the emails I printed the interesting ones out on an old laser printer. It was secure, because it wasn't connected to the *FT* network and left no tiny 'microdots', a sort of invisible manufacturer's stamp on each page which identified the machine.* It was also slow and kept overheating with the effort as I built up piles of

---

* The colour laser printers common in offices typically leave microdots, and the technology has been widespread since at least the mid-2000s. Reports suggest that manufacturers were encouraged to use microdots by the US Secret Service in the 1980s due to fears that wider access to high-grade printers would encourage counterfeiting of banknotes.

paper for different subjects. Some days it would be frustrating: just as the messages got juicy Kurniawan and the others would pick up the phone, or switch to Telegram. On others I would dance around the tiny room cheering the latest piece of evidence. Everything Wirecard's own lawyers had found was right there: contracts without customers, amateurishly forged invoices. What drove me on was Jan Marsalek. He was always at the edges, sometimes dishing out orders but more often his instructions were relayed second-hand, or a mystery would be explained simply by his involvement; that it was of one of 'Jan's companies'. I was determined to put Marsalek in the frame, to expose this man I'd never met or spoken to who had battled us from the shadows for years.

Stefania Palma, meanwhile, had rustled up a new whistleblower. This 'Jack' had been baffled by what he'd seen in Singapore. Wirecard's business there was running out of cash for day-to-day operations, so he'd tried to bring in a professional collection agency to pursue a few of the customers who hadn't paid their debts in years. Several million dollars were at stake, but Kurniawan hadn't allowed it. Just like with Gill, Jack's description of the workings of the finance team was so far removed from the image of a global technology company that it was hard to believe. As he told it, there was a group of young women in the accounts team who spent their days manually creating invoices in Microsoft Word for small dollar amounts and sending them out. No one seemed to care whether or not the customers paid.

On 5 January 2019, the air in Singapore was heavy. Evelyn was on the open walkway outside her apartment. She decided to go inside to cool off and her hand was on the handle to open her front door when her strength failed. She dropped to the floor, unable to move. A few seconds later and she would have been trapped inside, alone. Instead, a neighbour discovered her lying there and she was rushed to hospital with a suspected stroke. In the tests and scans which followed came more bad news. The doctors saw a mass on her lung: a tumour. It was operable, but going under the knife soon after a stroke would be a risky business. Looking for a clot in the brain, they found something else, an anomaly. Evelyn was given the likely prognosis: brain cancer, stage four. Gill's world was collapsing around him. In the hospital room together they began to make funeral plans. Evelyn had refused to mope; she saw setbacks as a matter of fate, something to be made the best of. Trying to hide his grief, Gill joked that at least he would have an inheritance and somewhere to live.

In London, I couldn't face the idea that this wonderful woman might not live to see her son vindicated; we had to get the story out. I also promised to do something for Gill. He wanted packets of documents to go to regulators in several countries, as well as the people running Visa, Mastercard, Citigroup and Ernst & Young. If they arrived postmarked Singapore, it would point straight back to him. I would send them instead. Strictly speaking, I wasn't supposed to be handing out super-sensitive legal documents; that was one of the reasons the laptop and files went in the safe each night. Wearing latex gloves, I printed out about 100 pages of documents for each packet: the Rajah & Tann interim report and a selection of supporting evidence which seemed relevant to each jurisdiction. A meticulous lawyer like Gill would probably have itemized and described the contents. Under the gun to get the story finished, I opted for brief cover notes instead. The letter to Hubert Barth, the managing partner of EY Germany, simply said:

Dear Mr Barth

Wirecard has been lying to your audit partners for years. Please see the attached dossier of evidence for its extensive accounting fraud.

I trust you will take appropriate steps.

A whistleblower

A courier firm wouldn't work – it would involve too much traceable paperwork. I calculated the international postage for each packet, then went to a post office near London Bridge station to buy the stamps I needed, a baseball cap pulled down over my face. When it was my turn, the agent behind the counter asked for the parcels. My scribbled list of the weights and countries was no use. He could only print out labels, and for that he'd need each package placed on his scale, with the destination address to tap into his system. That would be far too easy to trace for my liking. Stymied, I was leaving when the next teller along, an older man, waved me over. 'We're not really supposed to do this any more. They don't like us selling stamps now, for some reason, I'm surprised we still have these around to be honest,' he said, as he opened what I'd been looking for, a battered old binder holding sheets of stamps in all the denominations. He carefully measured out a small pile for each total on my list, along with a page of blue airmail stickers, and I handed over £60 in cash. Back in my bunker at the *FT*, I soon had a pile of dossiers a foot high plastered in stamps and ready to go. I could only fit half in my rucksack, so it took two trips to red post boxes in other parts of the city. There was a small thrill as I set them on their way, and I wondered if it would work, whether they'd reach their intended destinations across the world and if any would find their way to the desk of an official or executive with the power to investigate. Still, even if they didn't, the story was finally shaping up and all the signs were we'd get the all-clear from the editor that week.

Except, that Friday evening came the disaster in Lionel Barber's office, when the QC blocked the story due to the risk of an injunction. Evelyn was still in hospital, but she was well enough to be furious. Gill, his patience exhausted, threatened to take the story to someone else if I couldn't find a way to land it. 'Tell the *FT* to grow some fucking balls.'

20

Manipulated

30 January 2019 – London
Wirecard share price €167, market capitalization €21bn

T HE CENTRE OF THE *Financial Times* newsroom was an oval of desks surrounding the news editor, a maestro conducting all around him. Hung above that hub were several large TV screens displaying the various rolling news channels, sound off except for natural disasters and impromptu Donald Trump news conferences. Radiating outwards were the various desks required to put out a website; pictures, graphics, stats, IT, video, breaking news; a small army of sub-editors who published stories, stitched the paper together and were the last line of defence against garbled and inaccurate copy. In January 2019 preparations for the move to a new building by St Paul's Cathedral were under way, and the floor had an air of decay about it. The carpet was dirty and worn, mouse sightings were common and some of the ceiling tiles were battered and askew. Most surfaces were covered with old newspapers, mementoes, coffee cups and piles of notebooks.

Amid it all, I was about to publish the biggest story of my life. The investigations team had half a dozen seats in a corner by the entrance to the U-bend, a position which made it a dangerous spot for a 'drive-by': the sudden appearance of the editor, Lionel Barber, with a passing word of encouragement or instruction. 'Anything yet?' he asked, emerging from the corridor of power and pausing just long enough to catch me anxiously killing time on Twitter.

'Nothing so far.' Clocks showed five time zones; an hour to go, six since I'd spoken to Edo Kurniawan in Singapore and fired questions at Wirecard HQ. I half expected to see Nigel Hanson bearing down on us with a summons from Schillings to injunct the story. My stomach was churning. I had a crumpled tie in my desk drawer, just in case. 'You hit publish, then you almost throw up,' Paul Murphy said of these moments.

We planned to publish while the stock market was open and trading, as a big move in the share price would amplify the attention by forcing the news agencies to explain what was going on. I'd picked red trousers that morning, a small bit of bravado for the battle ahead. It was lunchtime, but I couldn't eat. Murphy's strategy was to head over the river for an early crab sandwich and glass of wine at Sweetings. He'd scarcely been gone half an hour when he swept back in, red-faced. 'We've got a fucking leak.'

Throwing his coat down, he quickly explained what had happened. Perched on a bar stool on Sweetings, he'd taken a call from Gary Kilbey, the nightclub owner. He'd heard that a Wirecard story was coming. 'Everybody's talking about it, it's all round the market. Word is there's a story coming at 1 p.m., it must be your lawyers or something.'

Murphy told him the rumour was rubbish, abandoned his sandwich and rushed back to the office. How could we have a leak? I'd gone to ground for three months. The story wasn't even in the *FT* system yet.

As soon as we stopped to think, the source was obvious: 1 p.m. was the deadline given to Wirecard. It was diabolical, Marsalek had set bandits loose all over London and was going to blame us.

Murphy pulled up the Wirecard share price on his Reuters terminal and we stared at it as if we could divine evidence of insider trading from its path across the screen; it had been in the red all morning after the company released some headline financial figures earlier that day, holding steady in the low €160s. For the last thirty minutes the price had ticked slowly but surely downwards, and as the deadline approached we watched it drop below €160: signs of selling pressure. At 1 p.m. the price held on the low of the day for a minute, then started to rise again. It could be nothing, just swirls in the ether. At five past Schillings sent a holding email, not an injunction. We offered them just another forty-five minutes more to comment, effectively saying, 'You better believe we're serious.' Whether it was a conscious minor aggression or the result of frantic typing, Schillings' letter arrived another five minutes after that extended deadline. Murphy printed and handed out a few copies as Lionel Barber strode out of the U-bend. 'There's nothing here,' he said, turning over the pages as if looking for more. So far as Wirecard was concerned, Kurniawan's conduct was fine, we had a malicious source peddling misinformation, and I was corrupt. We'd already discussed the leak. It took a few minutes at the desk with Nigel Hanson to include the gist of their response. Barber gave the command: 'Get it published.'

In modern stock markets the robots react to headlines first, and this one included the words 'falsification of accounts'. The stock dropped by a quarter, wiping €5bn off Wirecard's market capitalization.

I ignored the hedge funds and analysts lighting up my phone. A string of fire emojis from Pav Gill was more compelling. I rang him in Singapore to discover it was a double celebration. Evelyn was home, discharged from hospital that day. She would have to return in six weeks for an operation on her lung, but that was treatable. I was delighted to hear that additional scans of her skull had ruled out brain cancer after all; her doctors attributed the mystery seizure to stress, and now it was the turn of Wirecard's staff to feel the pressure. After feeling under siege from Wirecard ourselves for months, we all enjoyed the thought of the chaos inside their offices in Singapore and Munich, and I assured Gill that the whistleblower dossiers had been sent. Evelyn, relieved but determined as ever, wanted to know if there were more stories to come. I told her I'd keep working, but it depended on how Wirecard chose to respond.

Back at my desk I saw the share price was rallying, and was delighted to learn the reason. Wirecard was pushing back hard. It had put out a statement calling the *FT* article 'false, inaccurate, misleading and defamatory'. Murphy sat opposite me, and I stood up to see him over the screens. 'Our story lacks any substance and is completely meaningless,' I said with a grin.

'They're criminals. They just don't know how to behave like a normal company,' he replied.

Markus Braun and Jan Marsalek didn't have the imagination to change their approach. Had they blamed a few bad apples in Singapore and promised to clean house, we might have declared victory and moved on. Instead, the blanket denial meant the details we had held back were now trump cards we could play at our leisure; even the most blinkered High Court judge would be able to see that the company was lying. A few anonymous Twitter-bots burst into life. 'McCrums a criminal . . . Dannyboy McCRIM is GOING TO JAIL!!' It was funny, the kind of squawking from the margins I was used to. Let them sing, I thought, the truth will be out soon enough.

On Thursday, I had a spring in my step. I was admiring the *FT*'s front-page picture of Edo Kurniawan when a news editor shouted over, 'Have you seen Commerzbank? It's an absolute disgrace.' I thought it had to be a hoax. It looked like a piece of research from the investment bank, but it said the Wirecard story was 'fake news', that I was a 'serial offender', and investors should buy the stock: 'We are actually more concerned about [the] obvious active participation of the *FT* in market manipulation than about the allegations to the company.' I rang the analyst, Heike Pauls, to let her know there was a joke flying around with her name on it and she punctured my naivety. The market manipulation was obvious, Pauls said, remaining vague about her reasons but resolute in her suspicion. 'If it walks like a duck, it usually is a duck,' she said, and hung up. That was weird. Then the stock market regulator in Frankfurt joined in. A spokesperson for BaFin told Reuters it was investigating whether the crash in the share price involved market manipulation.

Did their packet of incriminating documents get lost in the post?

I had a story to write. Murphy was hitting the phones, trying to find out who had gone short on the leak, pushing back on the idea that it came from us. He was on to a trader at a French bank: 'You think you can go around the market saying this. Tell me, how do you spell your surname exactly?' Leaving him to it, I got to work on the next big reveal.

Late that afternoon, Sam Jones appeared back at the investigations desk. He was the laconic charmer on the team with intelligence agency contacts and an expertise in Russian literature. 'Hi, I think you better have a look at this,' he said, handing me his phone.

Walking back from the gym, he'd noticed an odd couple on the Thames Path in his way. Something seemed off, like they were performing distinct but separate tasks. A balding man in tracksuit and trainers underneath a long black formal winter coat was peering at the *FT* office through binoculars while he fiddled with an electronic device mounted on a sturdy tripod. He waved a hand in front of it for a second, checking it was firing. Jones recognized the set-up: it was a laser microphone. Aimed at a window, it would pick up every word of conversation inside. It was dusk, and figures in the *FT*'s first-floor conference room were brightly lit up as they discussed what would be published the following day. A few windows along was Barber's office. Behind the man was a woman wrapped up against the cold in a furry pink parka who seemed to be keeping lookout. 'There's a couple of cut-price spies over there trying to listen in,' he said, as I flicked through his pics. 'They're not being very subtle about it.'

Our first thought was for better, printable photos. Chris Batson, a no-nonsense Londoner on the picture desk, grabbed his camera and set off. Then we realized we'd better tell someone senior. Murphy and Barber weren't around. By this point we'd drawn a small crowd of reporters. We had to alert the deputy editor, Roula Khalaf, but her office was right on the river as well.

'Pssst.' Khalaf was behind her desk. She looked up, baffled to see us gesticulating outside her door. For a moment there was a game of charades as we simultaneously tried to wave her over, warn her about the window, and signal that someone was listening in. Once she was extracted, we all retreated back around the U-bend and Jones quickly filled her in.

Khalaf was a highly experienced editor and reporter who had ranged from exposing the Wolf of Wall Street in New York to burning shoe leather on the streets of Iraq, but a bungling spy operation on the streets of London was a first for her as well. 'What should we do? Has anyone alerted security?' Crammed into the corridor, everyone began urgently whispering at once.

'We should call the police.'

'Call 999? And say what – hello officer, I'd like to report a spy operation.'

'There's a man acting suspiciously by the river.'

'That makes it sound like a terrorist threat.'

'We could run a story.'

'How do we know he's a spy for sure? What if it's some weird hobby: amateur surveyor arrested in *FT* panic over laser pointer.'

'The day after Wirecard? Come on.'

The head of the security team arrived in the middle of this. He drew himself up to his considerable height and settled the matter. 'I'll go and 'ave a word.' However, the snapper had already scared them off. He'd taken a few sly pictures of the odd couple, then papped them with the flash bulb going. There was a brief, frank exchange of views, then the spies scarpered, taking their fancy tripod with them.

Our next card was played on Friday, revealing gory details of the law firm's investigation into Edo Kurniawan. The stock market reaction was brutal, because two things were obvious to investors who were paying attention: Wirecard had lied, and the *FT* had more up its sleeve. From €169 per share on Wednesday morning, the price traded below €100. We knocked more than €8bn off the market value of the company, a signal the German authorities couldn't ignore. Commerzbank folded as well, retracting Heike Paul's 'Fake News' analyst report. That night Charlotte and I toasted the end of a frantic week with a bottle of Aldi Cava in the kitchen. She was flat out as well running her PR firm, Harper Gray, and we laughed at the clown spies, whoever they were. We still put our phones in another room to talk about it, but right then the black ops we'd feared for so long didn't feel quite so scary. After months of work it also felt terrific to finally have something concrete in print, something real about this weird company I'd bored friends and neighbours with for years.

'LIE!' I scribbled in big letters as I listened to Markus Braun and his new sidekick CFO, Alexander von Knoop, steady the ship. On Monday, 4 February they held a conference call to address the Singapore investigation with analysts and investors. It was a classic of the genre: calm, reasonable, filled with dry descriptions of process. The numbers involved were small, Braun said, related to only €13m of problematic contracts, and everything had been investigated in a way which 'shows perfect compliance'. Pav Gill and I swapped outraged messages at the chutzpah. He was so annoyed he joined Twitter anonymously to try and talk sense into the world. Braun cast the Project Tiger investigation as a minor disagreement between staff. 'Where there are human beings, there are sometimes emotions,' he said. Von Knoop, possibly more wary given that he'd been CFO for little more than a year, clung to inoffensive facts like describing how the compliance team worked. The usual fans lapped it up. It was a buying opportunity, advised Commerzbank's Heike Pauls: 'The dust will settle quickly.'

Helpfully, Braun claimed there was no impact whatsoever on Wirecard's business, a useful quote to throw back at them if they did ever sue, said Nigel Hanson. However, Hanson was the only lawyer we had and he was unnerved when Herbert Smith Freehills, a juggernaut in complex international litigation, replaced Schillings as the London-based law firm bombarding us with legal threats. Barber disagreed. 'You know what, something's wrong, I bet. Schillings would have stayed with them.'

'We know they're desperate because they're trying to drag Charlotte into it,' said Paul Murphy. The tortuous new angle from Wirecard and its army of online supporters was that the *FT* was enabling my personal vendetta: years earlier my wife Charlotte ran the communications for a venture capital firm which had invested in a rival payments company. We'd spent years managing potential conflicts and this wasn't one of them. (When we lived in New York and she advised on mergers, I was kept in the dark for sanity as much as anything; there are few things worse than headline news you can't tell. The most extreme was when Charlotte said she had to travel for the weekend and was specifically instructed not to tell me where she was going, because the Midwest city held only two companies of note and the takeover target would be obvious.) The sock puppets ran with it anyway. 'Why are my mentions filled with people saying I work for Adyen?' Charlotte said, looking up from her laptop. A weak lie but another line crossed; Wirecard was going after the person I loved.

*

Singapore was the first to act. Friday, 8 February was the day after the Chinese New Year holiday and staff stood around dumbstruck as ten cops from the white-collar crime division barged in and demanded phones, laptops and notebooks. They interviewed senior staff and carted away boxes of documents. Edo Kurniawan had long since vanished, leaving a pedestal of drawers underneath his desk locked tight. Unable to open it, the police wheeled it out as well. Singapore had decisively moved to investigate, and it seemed like they wanted to brag about it.

An employee tipped us off about the raid, and Stefania Palma was surprised to get an on-the-record confirmation from the usually taciturn police department. Wirecard's reality distortion field was in operation, meanwhile; its staff in Singapore simply had a prearranged chat with officers to help them with their inquiries, it claimed, but the share price suggested Markus Braun was no longer getting the benefit of the doubt. It had crept as high as €136 after the billionaire CEO's reassuring chat with investors. With the police at their door in Singapore it crashed to €86, and Braun wasn't a billionaire any more. On a drive-by even Barber admitted he'd caught the bug; he found himself obsessively checking the share price as well.

In theory, reporting isn't supposed to be antagonistic, a matter of us versus them. American newspapers in particular, which historically faced less competition than in the rough and tumble of Fleet Street, adopted a dispassionate pose of neutrality as if every choice of word, focus or presentation didn't involve implicit and explicit decisions. Fairness to the subject is probably a better aim, and as well as the threat of legal action the *FT* had various rules and standards to ensure it; even if I was convinced the company was lying, I still had to give them an opportunity to comment and share that position with readers. Being reasonable and rigorous was supposed to bolster the strength of what we printed.

What we were all starting to realize was that Germany didn't see it that way. The country's equivalent of the *FT* was *Handelsblatt*, a business-focused broadsheet which took itself extremely seriously. It served Wirecard's purpose to portray what was happening as a fight with the *FT*, and *Handelsblatt* seemed happy to sit on the sidelines munching popcorn. Our reporting was another of the attacks which kept detracting from Wirecard's delightful business figures, apparently. The cost of my rush of blood with the Zatarra Report was clear: it was more of the same from that guy who wasn't credible.

A former *FT* colleague, Daniel Schäfer, was now a senior business editor at *Handelsblatt*, so Paul Murphy slipped him a copy of the key document, the Rajah & Tann Report. The result was an extensive interview with Markus Braun, where *Handelsblatt* published details of the internal investigation then played stenographer as he explained away the whole affair. Murphy was exasperated. 'He told me people there don't like the foreign press attacking German companies. It's just bizarre.' Without public pressure, the authorities seemed in no hurry to act. Prosecutors in Munich let it be known that they saw insufficient evidence of Germans committing German crimes to do anything.

The insular coverage wound up Lionel Barber as well. He'd studied German at Oxford (reading Kafka in the original, that sort of thing) and lived over there for a couple of years. He called Mathias Döpfner, a friend and former newspaper editor who ran the publishing group Axel Springer, to vent. 'I can't believe how we're being attacked, imputing that we're colluding with market manipulators. Does anybody think for a minute we would take the risk of writing something without believing it was true?'

Döpfner sympathized, and offered Barber advice. 'Be careful not to turn this into an Anglo-Saxon capitalist assault. Don't make it personal.' It was too late for that, judging by our fan mail. One emailer said he'd lost €60,000 from our 'attacks'. He suggested: 'If you have a private issue with Wirecard CEO Mr Braun, you should invite him to a sword duel, instead of hurting so many innocent people.'

Still, the saying is that *stories get stories*. I was starting to hear from other former employees of Wirecard. One described dysfunction in Munich, and the offhand extravagance of Jan Marsalek. The new source said that on a sales trip to northern Italy he and a senior Wirecard employee stayed in a cheap airport hotel. Marsalek invited the intimidated junior for lunch at his own lodgings, a five-star lakeside pile that served a few salad leaves artfully arranged for €60 a plate. Possibly inspired by the expansive view of the water, the Austrian mentioned he was thinking about buying his girlfriend a boat for her birthday. Seizing this conversational opening, the younger man launched into a recitation about the wonders of Amazon and its amazing range of products. He thought they would probably stock inflatable dinghies. Had Jan looked there? No, Marsalek said, that wasn't quite what he had in mind. He didn't think the online retailer had got round to outfitting yachts just yet.

Other tips were weirder, more intimidating. Someone on the far side of the world shared a couple of emails she'd received by accident. She used ProtonMail, an encrypted email service, and in February 2018 was mistakenly copied into correspondence from a 'Ray', introducing his 'dear uncles' to Jan Marsalek as 'family to me and a brother in arms to us'. The 'uncles' were a celebrity former CIA spy called Gary Berntsen, who had battled Al-Qaeda in Afghanistan, and a former US ambassador to Uruguay, Martin Silverstein.* Marsalek wanted help with a political project. 'I'll let him fill you in but basically he's trying to move the Austrian embassy to Jerusalem and I had told him about your success with Guatemala,' 'Ray' wrote. Signing off, he encouraged the trio to 'also pay some attention to financial opportunities while you all play your game of thrones'.

Guatemala was one of the few countries to have followed the lead of Donald Trump and switched its official diplomatic base in Israel from Tel Aviv to Jerusalem, the divided city expected to one day serve as the capital of any future Palestinian state. Pushing for other countries to move their embassies into one of the world's most politically sensitive locations, where Israel maintained an illegal occupation, was a cause célèbre of far-right politicians around the world, including Austria, as Marsalek explained in his response. He claimed to have a close relationship with the leadership of the far-right nationalist Freedom Party (FPÖ), which had just entered into a coalition government with the mainstream centre-right party. Describing the FPÖ's 'unfortunate history of affiliation with ultra-right-wing organizations and individuals and a strained relationship with parts of

---

* Silverstein said he never received the email and didn't recognize the address.

Austria's Jewish community', he said its leadership 'looked favourably on moving the Austrian embassy to Jerusalem as part of a broader initiative to reshape EU foreign policy'. Marsalek was seeking informal channels to explore the US position on the subject.

What sort of friends did Marsalek have? Was Wirecard politically connected, protected even? Another tip of unknown origin alleged discussion of a project to move money out of Syria, a war zone where the government faced international sanctions, via Vienna. Murphy quietly pulled me aside. We needed to have a chat somewhere away from any electronics where we definitely couldn't be overheard. We went and found an empty internal room. Slightly shamefaced, he admitted he'd kept something to himself.

'I didn't want to distract you from the main story or freak you out. There's a Russian angle here. Marsalek has the recipe for nerve gas, Novichok.'

I looked at Murphy as if he'd just said Marsalek had faked the moon landings.

'What the actual fuck are you talking about?'

The previous year, two Russian assassins had attempted to poison a former spy in Salisbury with one of the world's deadliest nerve agents hidden inside a perfume bottle. Their intended victim survived, but the discarded container killed a woman in a nearby town after her boyfriend fished the expensive-looking bottle out of a bin as a present. Murphy explained that the Organization for the Prohibition of Chemical Weapons conducted an investigation, producing a highly classified report on the affair. Jan Marsalek had somehow got his hands on the top-secret documents, including the Russian objections to the British version of events. Murphy knew about it because in the summer of 2018 Marsalek had touted the files around London to bandit speculators, trying to impress them with his Secret Service links.

I had to sit down. This wasn't funny any more.

There'd been times when I felt vulnerable before. Those imaginations of home invasion had lasted weeks after Fraser Perring's tale of menaces in Lincoln. I knew it was bonkers, but I'd lie there in the dark while my brain ran scenarios of men in balaclavas inside the house, and after Murphy's revelation the insomnia was back. This time my commute was when the real fear crept in. A BuzzFeed investigation had reported a Russian assassination programme in London: fourteen deaths where the British police ruled out foul play but US intelligence suspected the hand of the Russian state or mafia. I kept far from the edge of train platforms, but at St Albans it was on the bike ride home in the dark when every trailing car felt like a threat. I couldn't vary the route much so I chose one where I mostly picked through slow traffic or cut through side streets, keeping an irregular schedule and trying to quell that voice which said wouldn't it be convenient if I was hit by a truck.

Ten days after the Singapore police raided Wirecard's office, the German authorities finally responded by protecting Wirecard. In Frankfurt, BaFin announced a two-month ban against short selling of the company's shares, citing the group's 'importance for the economy'. It was the regulator's most powerful weapon, a ban on speculation only previously used during the depths of the 2008 financial crisis when eleven banks were at risk of collapse. The broader European Securities and Markets Authority piped up as well, declaring the ban proportionate and appropriate as 'the current circumstances related to Wirecard are adverse events or developments which constitute a serious threat to market confidence in Germany.'

Nasty speculators were the problem, along with corrupt journalists. *Frankfurter Allgemeine* broke the news that I was under criminal investigation for market manipulation. A spokesperson told the newspaper that 'we have a specific criminal complaint from an investor'. I was starting to get used to operating on the wrong side of the looking glass, but it was disorientating all the same. I found myself standing at the shoulder of an editor as he played with the copy, inserting the *FT* spokesperson's robust denial into a story about how the newspaper was itself under investigation. 'Are you *sure* you didn't let anything slip?' he asked for the second time, attempting to tread the line between collegiality and duty. It was a bad dream. What on earth was going on?

21

Bearing Witness

30 January 2019 – Smithfields, London
Wirecard share price €169, market capitalization €21bn

Here's what happened that Wednesday when we were about to publish. Gary Kilbey was in his office above Fabric. It was a pocket of light and normality overlooking the street, another world from the industrial space of the nightclub deep below. Kilbey's business partner was there, along with Kilbey's son-in-law Daniel Harris, who helped out around the club. Just after noon a broker came in with some hot gossip about a couple of well-known traders and a spread betting account which he hoped Kilbey, with his connection to Murphy, might be able to verify. 'They're shorting the absolute bollocks off Wirecard. There's an *FT* story coming at 1 p.m. today.'

Kilbey promptly interrupted Paul Murphy's crab sandwich, hoping for some sort of confirmation. 'Are you doing a story on Wirecard, 'cause if you are you've got a fucking leak.' Murphy denied it and Kilbey didn't trade. Later, Murphy called back for more details. The spread betting account was called 'Bank of Oman' and held at Sigma Trading. It was said to be used by multiple people, and at the time was on a hot streak of five or six winners in a row. One of the traders who used the account was the Turkish businessman who had tried to connect Jan Marsalek with Carson Block. (The man would later tell Murphy he was short in anticipation of Wirecard's figures published that day, and his position was smaller than usual.)

Gary's son Tom Kilbey, the former footballer, arrived at Fabric in the afternoon. He'd stayed in regular Telegram contact with Marsalek, who was stringing him along with promises to invest in his music business. The Austrian was delighted to hear of events inside the nightclub, and wanted to know if the gossiping broker who tipped off Gary would sign an affidavit testifying to what had occurred. 'Don't you fucking get me anywhere near it,' was the considered reply.

The son-in-law piped up. 'I don't mind making that statement. It's true, that's what happened.'

The next day Wirecard's lawyers lodged a complaint with the Munich public prosecutor's office, informing them that the company had 'strong evidence' that the *FT* article was leaked to a circle of investors before it was published.

However, by now Daniel Harris had second thoughts. He'd had brushes with the law before. In a 2017 trial at the Old Bailey he was accused by police of running a drug gang which distributed sealed bags of cocaine emblazoned with the Union Jack via dealers on mopeds pretending to be trainee Black Cab drivers learning the 'Knowledge'. A jury acquitted Harris of the most serious charges, but he received a two-year prison sentence for concealing £116,000 of the drug gang's cash under his daughter's bed inside Asda carrier bags. (The detail was unlikely to deter Marsalek, as Wirecard regularly used carrier bags from the German chains Aldi and Lidl to transport six-figure sums in and out of HQ, starting at least as early as 2012. Because Wirecard Bank had no branches, a large safe was installed in Aschheim to hold cash, with substantial sums frequently going in and out. On one occasion Marsalek asked his assistant to take €300,000 for Ray Akhavan, the porn baron, to the airport for collection. On another, €500,000 arrived when the safe was full, so Wirecard staff hid the notes around the office.)

Daniel Harris called his father-in-law for advice. Should he sign the statement? 'Not unless Wirecard is going to pay you, and I don't think they're going to pay you for that, how could they?'

Valentine's Day was a Thursday. Wirecard's lawyer handed prosecutors a witness statement attributed to Harris. It did disclose that his brother-in-law, Tom Kilbey, had worked for Wirecard, but there was no mention of the conviction. Instead it described Harris as a specialist spread better with a background in asset management. It said that the broker was told by a friend that a *FT* story was coming at 1 p.m. At the bottom there was no signature. Daniel Harris had not gone through with it. Armed with this 'evidence', on Monday morning BaFin announced the short selling ban.

Suit crisp, poise confident, Jan Marsalek walked into the office of the Munich public prosecutor just after noon on Thursday, 21 February. He was flanked by Franz Enderle, one of the most famous corporate lawyers in Germany. A weighty presence next to the slim Marsalek, a sexagenarian with thick eyebrows and a bow tie, he was renowned as a relentless advocate at one of Germany's most fearsome firms, Bub Gauweiler. Much of that reputation stemmed from a marathon pursuit of Deutsche Bank, whose CEO in 2002 made an offhand remark on television that no one in finance was willing to lend money to Leo Kirch, a magnate whose business empire was in trouble. The banker was right: Kirch Media duly failed, cursing Deutsche for sending it over the edge. The relentless Enderle pursued Deutsche through the courts for more than a decade, until it finally agreed to pay a €925m settlement to Kirch's heirs. The commercial litigator might have been an odd choice to take to a meeting with prosecutors, but then Marsalek was not there as a suspect. He was a witness, with a tale to tell.

Waiting to hear it was Hildegard Bäumler-Hösl, a woman in her mid-fifties with a guarded manner and a neat bob of brown hair. She was one of the most experienced prosecutors in the country and the head of the department. Hers was the decision about whom to pursue with the full weight of the law. Another prosecutor, who was in charge of the case against the *FT*, was there as well. There were brief formalities, explanations about the process, then they sat and listened carefully as Marsalek explained the matter at hand: his main field of activity at Wirecard was sales, but since the publication of the Zatarra Report in 2016 he had worked to ingratiate himself into the network of speculators targeting the company. He called it *Feindaufklärung* – enemy reconnaissance.

Marsalek said he had obtained information from these contacts, which had been of some help, but this had led to offers about which he was not happy. For a moment he was coy, an upstanding business-man in unfamiliar territory, then he gathered himself to address the point directly: to put it in concrete terms, there was an attempt at blackmail.

The extortion artist was someone called 'Ali', who liked to race Ferraris. Marsalek said he was introduced by a friend in London at around the time of the Zatarra attack. After the latest series of *FT* articles Ali got in touch again, via the same friend, with a warning and an offer: a negative story about Wirecard from Bloomberg was coming, but Ali could stop it, even have the news agency write critical commentary about the *FT* reports instead, for a price.

Over a series of calls, one of which Marsalek claimed to have recorded, Ali had laid out the urgency of the situation. There were competing offers available to the supposedly corrupt Bloomberg employees. They were also being offered cash by traders, and by employees of the *FT*, to gin up negative coverage about Wirecard. If the company wanted to get involved, Ali proposed disguising the payments as sponsorship of his racing team, which he would then use to make the bribes. Marsalek pulled out his phone and help-fully emailed the £2.25m invoice he'd received for this purpose to Bäumler-Hösl.

The eagle-eyed prosecutor at least spotted a hole in Marsalek's tall story. If he'd only received it that month, why was it dated 28 May 2018?

Marsalek waved this inconsistency away. He hadn't noticed, or really looked very closely at it before. When the other prosecutor pressed him on details of the scheme, he didn't quite have those at his fingertips either; he wasn't sure whether it was the *FT*, dodgy traders, or some combination thereof which was offering the rival lump sums to Bloomberg. Indeed, Marsalek himself was suspicious. He thought that the part about the journalists receiving cash was an attempt to put Wirecard under pressure so that it would offer as much as pos-sible. He said the latest status of the 'negotiations' – indicating his reluctant part in the charade with air quotes – stood at £4m for influencing the reporting and a further £1.75m for information on the traders involved.

Was Bäumler-Hösl convinced by this picture of a corrupt London financial scene where millions were changing hands over the words in a news story? She asked if the negotiations were still ongoing.

Marsalek described a game of *the cheque is in the post* with Ali. He said he'd insinuated that the £2.25m had been sent, and was receiving almost hourly Telegram messages complaining that the money hadn't arrived. He told her he thought he could stall for another week if he had to, demonstrating his knowledge of the international payments system. Marsalek explained that a sterling payment would go through the SWIFT network, so he could claim that a correspondent bank had frozen the transaction and requested more documentation.

Asked for more about Ali, Marsalek offered a glimpse of the bandit world. He said that, to the best of his knowledge, there was a small circle of people actively involved in insider trading. They knew each other and shared the information floating around. Why, he himself had heard two days in advance that HSBC would publish disappointing figures that week. Marsalek said he assumed Ali knew one or two people in this crowd well, and that ultimately his influence wasn't a matter of charisma or personality; it came down to cold, hard cash.

It was a careful performance from Marsalek. Here he was, the resourceful victim, doing his best to battle a strange and unusual enemy in a spirit of co-operation with the authorities. The danger was that Bäumler-Hösl might dwell on his connections to the circle of traders in London manipulating the Wirecard share price, so he came prepared with a villain. Claiming to have been fed the information by an acquaintance who worked for a foreign state, he pinned the leak of the Project Tiger investigation on Royston Ng, the former magistrate who worked with Pav Gill in Singapore. This Ng had just resigned, Marsalek said, and Wirecard suspected that he was one of the *FT*'s sources. Supposedly the lawyer had flown from Singapore to London on a flight paid for by a Mark Westcott, a co-founder of a London investment firm called ShadowFall Research. As it happened, the other founder of ShadowFall was Matt Earl, the man behind Zatarra. Marsalek didn't say any more because he didn't have to, his gift-wrapped conspiracy theory was obvious: the attack on Wirecard was nothing more than a redo of 2016 by the usual suspects. He was typically charming as he finished up. It was possible that mistakes had been made, but the source of the information had always proved to be extremely reliable in the past. That was all he could say about the facts of the case. If there were any further questions on these or other matters, he was at the disposal of the investigating authorities at any time they required.

The prosecutors were left with an unenviable choice. They could swallow the line that journalists at two of the world's most respected media organizations were corrupt; that coverage was bought and sold; and that a group of speculators for some reason kept targeting this one German company for nefarious reasons. If not, the alternative was that executives at one of Europe's largest and most celebrated technology companies were lying to their faces, not to mention conspiring to defraud some of the country's most renowned banks and investment houses.

It took three days for the thinking of prosecutors to find its way into *Handelsblatt*. 'New attack against Wirecard planned', the headline thundered. The story explained that the short selling ban was triggered by information provided to prosecutors by the company, and quoted Bäumler-Hösl herself: 'We received serious information from Wirecard that a new short attack is planned and that a lot of money is being used to influence media reporting,' she said.

22

Manila Envelope

February 2019 – Manila
Wirecard share price €115, market capitalization €14bn

THE PHILIPPINES IS NOT a safe place to be a journalist. In 2009 a convoy in support of a local politician was travelling through a southern province to file election papers. Warned of an attack, the candidate sent female family members and supporters in her stead, along with thirty local reporters, believing that such a large group would be left alone. They were not. Armed men ambushed the convoy, took them to a remote hillside and opened fire; fifty-seven bodies were dumped in a mass grave, in what the Committee to Protect Journalists has said is the deadliest incident for the press it has ever recorded. Since that massacre another eighteen journalists have been killed in a country where the strongman president, Rodrigo Duterte, came to power in 2016 urging the murder of drug addicts and dealers.

Stefania Palma had reported from Manila before, and she knew that for this trip she shouldn't go alone. We wanted her to knock on the door of Wirecard's business partners, and we didn't know what or whom she would find when she did. She flew in late on Sunday, 24 February, staying at a hotel in the main business district that another correspondent said was reliable and secure. Early the next morning she met her escort, a woman, young like Palma, a 'fixer' who spoke the language and knew how to get things done; Jilson, a rangy photographer in his early twenties with a battered bag of lenses; and the driver, an unknown quantity. First they battled through the notorious traffic, a haphazard crush of cars, trucks, buses and vans, to escape the city. Nothing about what she was doing was easy. She was anxious about every aspect and feeling the pressure to do well; the Philippines was such an important piece of the puzzle, and she didn't want to go back to Singapore without getting the story. She tried to give the fixer a broad outline, conscious that the man at the wheel could hear every word. The address they were heading to was supposed to be the location of an international payment processing business; it was connected to a German company the *FT* was interested in.

After three hours on the road, fields of rice stretched away into the distance on all sides. They came to the edge of a city, Cabanatuan, and the car stopped on a paved residential lane outside a neat walled villa. The walls were orange, topped with sharp iron railings painted white. Stefania Palma recognized it from the Google Street View photo which had prompted the trip. One of the companies which 'Jack', the whistleblower, had wanted to chase for unpaid bills was called ConePay; it had owed Wirecard Singapore a few million dollars in commission payments for years. ConePay's website looked the part but didn't name a single human and its contact address was in the middle of nowhere.

Palma knocked on the metal gates. Her biggest fear was that no one would answer, in which case the whole day would have been wasted. There was also the possibility of disturbing gangsters. The internal explanation Wirecard staff were told about these special partners was that they processed payments which were too unsavoury to be handled directly. Instead Wirecard referred such clients to its friends, in return for a lucrative commission on every transaction. What sort of payments those might be we weren't sure, but there were disturbing rumours given that the Philippines was a known sex tourism destination where the legal age of consent was just twelve. John Hempton, the Australian hedge fund manager, had told me about the 'Member for Manila', a Queensland MP who in 2018 was investigated by the Federal Police for his frequent trips to the Philippine capital. The probe found no evidence of illegality but raised concern that the MP remained an ongoing risk of being compromised. The scuttlebutt passed on to Hempton by the son of the Australian prime minister was that many of the credit card payments examined by the authorities in that probe were alleged to have been processed by Wirecard.

The door to the compound was opened by a teenage boy. Stefania Palma stepped into a courtyard shaded by palm trees where a couple of middle-aged men were using electric clippers to trim the fur of a white poodle on top of a glass table. A fluffy brown Pomeranian yapped at their ankles. Several washing lines were hung with clothes and sheets. A motorbike was parked under a covered porch at the front of the house, and the whole scene was untidy with the paraphernalia of family life. The appearance of a white woman in their midst was clearly the most interesting thing to happen that morning. A couple of toddlers stopped and stared. Palma was quickly surrounded by about a dozen people of various ages who spoke minimal English. An old man came out of the house and the small crowd parted to let him through. He was mellow, happy to have a conversation with this strange visitor as the fixer interpreted her questions. He was neither particularly interested nor upset. The answers were all no. He'd never heard of any payments company. The patriarch was a retired seaman, he owned the house and his family had lived there for half a century. Palma began to despair that this was a dead end. Then one of the watching daughters went inside for a moment and came back with a white envelope. 'Oh yes, I'd forgotten about that. It arrived and we had no idea what it was for,' the old man said, passing it to Palma.

She froze. The envelope was addressed to ConePay International. For a second she felt like she was going to scream and pass out at the same time. 'Can I open it?' The man shrugged. To him it was just a random piece of junk mail, not a priceless piece of evidence.

With shaking hands, Palma carefully tore it open and pulled out the contents; it was a Wirecard Bank statement showing accounts in multiple currencies with no money in them. It was a damning piece of evidence. Both Wirecard and the payments company used this address as if it were the headquarters of a real business, one which owed Wirecard millions of euros. But there was no sign of it, it never paid its bills, and there was no money in its bank accounts. ConePay was a Potemkin village.

Trying to keep her cool, Palma asked if she could take photos. 'I don't care, do whatever you like,' the man said. As soon as she stepped back outside the gates Palma sent me the photos, so she didn't have the only copies. It was 4 a.m. in London, too early to talk. The fixer suggested trying the barangay hall, the local government office where any company in the district would have to register for a permit to operate. The office was open but empty, so they sat down to wait on a bench. Eventually someone wandered in. He wasn't the clerk, but the official only lived two doors down, he said; they should try there. The fixer knocked and was told she would be along shortly. They waited some more in the shade. The air was hot and still, and stray dogs roamed the quiet street. After an hour or so the smiling bureaucrat moseyed in. There was no record of a ConePay; nothing, in fact, which might be a payments or technology company. 'Most commercial businesses we have are small shops, like the stores over there,' she said, indicating a stand on the corner which sold tissues and other essentials. 'The biggest business we have here is the gas station.' Stefania Palma and her team piled back into the car. Everything pointed in the same direction: Wirecard's income from ConePay wasn't real because ConePay didn't exist. As she was approaching the outskirts of Manila her phone rang, and she answered it with laughter: 'Oh my God, Dan, you are not going to believe this . . .'

In London I'd been distracted by a German-Italian horse breeder from San Marino offering up a whistleblower. She presented herself as working for an Israeli research firm which specialized in finding, tracing and vetting corporate insiders. She said her man could explain how Wirecard processed dodgy payments in the past, but cleaned up its act; Jan Marsalek's old line. As soon as she mentioned the whistleblower's name I knew exactly who he was: a British former Wirecard employee who was embroiled in a heroin-trafficking scandal in the 1990s. After three years in a Thai jail he was acquitted on the trafficking charge, but his companion, who claimed he had promised her cash for hiding three ounces of smack inside her body, received a twenty-five-year sentence. After that brush with the law he'd gone into the reputable world of payment processing. From the emails I could see that Edo Kurniawan, Wirecard's Singapore book-cooker, regularly approved the man's consulting fees. It didn't smell right.

I went back to my files in the bunker and made another discovery. The man whose footprints I followed around Bahrain was involved: Christopher Bauer. He had two different payments companies which operated from the same address in a Manila shopping centre. One owed Wirecard Singapore commission payments worth €3m at the end of 2016. The other was PayEasy, and it owed Wirecard €123m, serious money. Stefania Palma's next job was clear: she had to track down Christopher Bauer.

Christopher Bauer's bright-yellow tour buses were a regular sight on the streets of Manila. The centre of operations for Froehlich Tours was in a courtyard between two office buildings connected to a shopping mall. It also served as the office for PayEasy, his international payments company. Decals for both covered the windows, and inside more logos were plastered everywhere. On the wall was a bulletin board with notices to staff. Next to a warning for employees not to use loud ringtones was a memo signed by Bauer and his wife about a change in payroll date. Beside the board was a framed football shirt worn by Thomas Dooley, a famous German-American soccer player who had coached the Philippine national team. There were signs of activity, with bus drivers coming in and out. When Stefania Palma asked to speak to Bauer, the receptionist stonewalled. He rarely came in, she said, and eventually gave Stefania another address, assuring her that 'Mr Bauer is there all the time.'

At the end of a dirt road of sheds and fenced lots Palma found a covered bus depot, full of yellow coaches, where the dirt of Manila was hosed off. Inside was a bare office space. The only occupants were a couple of guys in old, tattered shirts, dispatchers who kept track of the buses. She asked if Christopher Bauer was around.

'No,' said one of the men with a measure of contempt. 'He's never here. I haven't seen Mr Bauer in, I don't know how long.' As they spoke a stray dog wandered in, a gristly brown mongrel which sniffed at the ground behind Palma. Unaware, she turned into it and the mutt erupted, lunging at her and the photographer. There were ten seconds of incredibly loud commotion as the two men jumped on the furiously barking dog to drag it away. Heart racing, Palma shook her head at the absurdity of it. All our worries about gangsters and she'd almost got herself savaged by a dog.

She had better luck above another shopping mall. The lift decanted her and the fixer directly into the reception area of a company which sold buses. 'Who's in charge here, I need to speak to them please,' Palma asked the women at the front desk. Stonewalled again, she resolved to sit and wait. All of a sudden an older man in a suit and tie came out of an office, heading for the lift. He looked important, so Palma grabbed the fixer and they rushed in after him.

'Hold the door please! Hi, hi, sorry, thanks, are you the CEO by any chance?'

'Yes?' he said, raising his eyebrows.

'Perfect!' cried Palma. She explained who she was and peppered him with questions. 'Are you familiar with a company called PayEasy?'

The businessman was surprised, but said they could talk on the way to his car. By the time they got to the kerb she had what she needed. He had no idea what his company's logo was doing on the PayEasy website. It didn't use any sort of payment processor at all.

Palma's days in Manila fell into a pattern. They piled into the car in the morning and spent hours in traffic trying to get to various addresses I'd given her to check out. They used the time to research online, and in one of those traffic jams they found the Facebook pages for Bauer's wife and daughter. The website was wildly popular in the Philippines and a lot of profiles were fully public. She could see which school the daughter went to, which presented an opportunity and a quandary: by waiting outside, she might catch one of the Bauers arriving to collect their child. Could she do that? Time was running out and she got hold of me at breakfast, getting my own daughter ready for school. I briefly considered how I'd feel if I was doorstepped there. I wouldn't be happy, but then we wanted to ask Bauer about his involvement in what looked like serious fraud. He wasn't going to be happy. I said to go for it, but only talk to the adults.

The school was fronted by a large, open parking lot. As the kids filtered out, the pair kept trying to spot the right one from the Facebook photos. The fixer grabbed Stefania Palma's elbow.

'There, I think that's her.' She had seconds to decide what to do as the girl walked towards a car.

'Wait, it's just a driver,' Palma said, with a mixture of disappointment and relief. The Bauers weren't there.

'OK, shall we follow?' the fixer asked.

It was the sort of can-do attitude which was proving incredibly useful, but Palma said no, that was the line. Trailing a child through the city was a step too far.

As the week progressed, Palma's nerves frayed. Her presence was obvious. She was prodding at a sleeping beast, and at some point it was going to wake up. During the day she had the others with her. At night in the hotel alone, writing up her notes, any noise from the outside would make her glance at the door and bring memories of her hostile-environment training flooding back. Most of the week was in a classroom, but on the last day they moved outdoors to thick woods. The premise was they were ten war reporters trying to cross the border from Syria into Turkey. Dressed in helmets and flak jackets, they packed into rickety jeeps. In the middle of a narrow track thirty actors burst from the undergrowth brandishing real-looking weapons. They roughly dragged the class out of the vehicles, took their shoes off them, hooded their heads and forced them into stress positions with demands to identify their leader. Palma was pulled deeper into the woods by herself, made to put on an orange jumpsuit and record a confession video while a man stood over her brandishing a large machete; and that was just the start of the six-hour practical. One useful piece of advice was that a small wedge pushed under a door was an effective way to secure it from the inside. Or it would have been useful if she had remembered to bring one. Instead she piled a few belongings in the way. It wouldn't stop a determined intruder, but the noise would at least wake her up.

Prodding the beast finally prompted a phone call. 'Why are you coming to my offices, questioning my staff?' Christopher Bauer demanded, flustered and angry. Palma said she was interested in his payment companies, whether they paid their bills to Wirecard. Bauer tried to distance himself as he had when I asked him about Ashazi in Bahrain. He was just an investor, he wasn't running PayEasy. Shouting down the phone, he said he wasn't about to hand out the names of the people who were in charge just so that Palma could bother them with her ridiculous questions. It was the last piece we needed, and it was time for her to get out of town.

'Has anyone seen Nigel?'

It was Paul Murphy. A month after Stefania Palma's trip we were about to publish the smoking-gun photos of the fake business she got in the Philippines, and our lawyer was missing. I was up on the second floor of the *FT* building, standing at the Big Read desk helping to tweak the captions on the pics, when Murphy came to find us. 'I hope you've got a plan B,' he said cheerfully to Geoff Dyer, the editor responsible for the flagship feature piece the newspaper published each day. 'Wirecard's suing us.'

'What, really? I hadn't seen anything,' Dyer said. I'd left my phone downstairs, a drawback of the constant security paranoia.

'They haven't responded yet. It's a spoiler, before the story hits. The press office is getting calls,' Murphy explained.

We left Geoff hanging and nipped back downstairs to find that we were making press history in Germany. Wirecard had announced it was suing the *FT* for misuse of business secrets, and intended to seek compensation for shareholders, a novel bit of legal manoeuvring. Given that the drop in the company's value ran into billions, that would be quite the bill for damages, several times what Nikkei paid to buy us a few years before. I should ask Nigel Hanson how much the insurance would cover, I thought as I scanned my emails. One caught my eye. 'Oh shit. Suicide.' Murphy jumped out of his seat. 'Sorry! Body on the tracks. Nigel's stuck on the West Coast Main Line somewhere outside Reading. He's not going to be here for hours.'

Wirecard left us guessing what the lawsuit was about. Legally, it was hard to think of a justification, but tactically it was a masterstroke. The company filed papers in Munich, then sat on the news till the right moment, which was to undercut our big story about the

Philippines. When it appeared the next morning, Friday, 29 March, the German papers were full of stories about the legal action. The share price dropped another 10 per cent, back down to €112, but well within the recent range. Our smoking gun was an incremental titbit; we weren't changing our minds. As it was Friday afternoon, Murphy and I slipped out for a glass in the cellar of a Borough Market wine bar. 'We're in hand-to-hand combat here,' he said. 'You're going to have to drive a stake through its heart.' The encouragement was great, the question was how. What was it going to take?

Stefania Palma's beat had taken her to Jakarta for the chaos of a presidential election set for 17 April. She jumped into a scooter taxi, blinking back the tiredness as she tried to make it to the latest impromptu campaign event. The previous night she'd watched 100,000 people cram into a stadium for a heavily Islamic rally till 3 a.m. Now she had to get to the private residence of a former general with a scary reputation. She made it in time, and fought her way into the throng of press crushed against the gates, which only opened at the last moment. With 260 million people about to go to the polls, the general was losing and his floodlit speech seemed unlikely to change the tide. Afterwards Palma decided she had had more than enough colour, and grabbed some dinner with a friend from *The Economist* at the first restaurant they saw. It was well after midnight when they finished and stepped outside on to the pavement. Palma glanced at her phone to check in with the news desk and saw a chain of emails between various editors discussing the draft of a story: 'BaFin files criminal complaint against two FT journalists.'

The German regulator had told prosecutors to investigate her, me and ten unnamed speculators for market manipulation. She called me, conscious that she was standing next to another journalist, yet also with a barrage of questions she wanted answered: who, what, how, why, really? I started to explain but then caught myself. 'Wait, hold on a second. Nobody told you?' I burst out laughing, it was so farcical. The world was topsy-turvy. *Der Spiegel*, a German paper, had broken the news that afternoon: Palma and I were the criminals.

23

SoftBank to the Rescue

April 2019 – Munich
Wirecard share price €108, market capitalization €13bn

W EEKENDS WERE FOR VIENNA. Markus Braun spent them with his wife and daughter, plus a little socializing in the aristocratic scene where he was a big fish in a small pond; dinner at Fabios, an achingly fashionable white-tablecloth Italian, or allowing others to pay their respects at the Vienna Opera Ball. There were grand events in a castle thrown by his friend Alexander Schütz, a Viennese money manager who oversaw the Atlas supporting Germany's financial system, Deutsche Bank, as a member of its supervisory board. In this crowd, the impression flourished that Braun had a second fortune salted away because he understood technology and so was early into the big tech stocks like Apple and Google. He threw a little money at politics, backing the centre-right Austrian People's Party, whose government was propped up by the far-right FPÖ. In the summer of 2017, Braun appeared at a campaign event with Chancellor Sebastian Kurz, and he travelled in influential circles as a member of a think tank linked to the party and as a captain of industry, invited to intimate private dinners with the Austrian premier and his wife. So Braun's friends had no doubts when it came to the storm of controversy swirling around his head.

'I read in the *FT* what a naughty boy you are ;-)' Schütz wrote in a February 2019 email mainly concerned with their holiday plans in the

South of France that summer. Both men liked the French Riviera, where Braun kept a modernist home of concrete and straight lines outside St-Tropez. But he also liked to rent a boat suitable for the friends, children, nannies and security which vacation required. The *Lady S*, a sixty-nine-metre floating palace with five decks and nineteen crew dedicated to keeping a dozen guests in perfect comfort, was a favourite charter, but it had been sold to an Asian buyer that winter and with all the fuss Braun had yet to nail down his plans. Schütz remained hopeful of a rendezvous. He had bought shares in Wirecard the previous week, he said. 'Do this newspaper in!! :-),' he urged.

A tree-lined avenue of elegant nineteenth-century apartment buildings in Bogenhausen, a well-to-do part of Munich, was Braun's home in the work week. His was painted a pale yellow, with stone steps and a red carpet that ran from the door to the top of the building. The neighbours who passed him on the stairs realized they weren't important enough to warrant his interest and that he'd happily be rid of them; Braun said to one he would buy them all out if he could. He knocked together two apartments into one mansion that spanned a full floor, and purchased a third on a storey below. On a good day his commute to Aschheim was a mere fifteen minutes by chauffeur-driven Maybach, a black ultra-luxury Mercedes. It was a familiar sight in the neighbourhood, and one evening in early April, about a week after the *FT* story about the Philippines was published, an onlooker was surprised to see five men waiting for Braun to return home. They were heavy-set, in cheap suits, and he did not invite them in. Instead they had a serious conversation in the street which lasted some time. The neighbour took the men for law enforcement by their appearance, but the Munich prosecutors denied all knowledge when asked about it by journalists.

At headquarters Braun focused on public relations, judging by his email traffic, tweaking press releases and demanding fresh material for his Twitter feed. That April, however, he had a much more important task: convincing some of the world's most powerful investors that he didn't want or need their money. He had been approached by Soft-Bank, the Japanese conglomerate whose €100bn Vision Fund had transformed technology investing mainly by raising the table stakes for everyone involved. It doled out billions to chosen companies like WeWork, encouraging them to use the money to smash the competition. A former Deutsche Bank trader called Akshay Naheta, now an investor at SoftBank, smelled an opportunity at Wirecard. His bet was that whatever the accounting issues, the stock was cheap. Backing from SoftBank would rehabilitate Wirecard's reputation overnight. Plus, if the SoftBank family of companies all used Wirecard for their payments processing, that flood of new business would wash away any problems. With SoftBank support, Wirecard could go on a buying spree, rolling up rivals into one giant company. Naheta and the other Deutsche Bank refugees who ran the Vision Fund from an Edwardian townhouse in Mayfair were also experts at structuring complex trades. These financial wizards could throw $1bn at Wirecard while taking very little actual financial risk.

To broker the deal Akshay Naheta turned to Christian Angermayer, a business wunderkind with a mixed record and a very successful knack of attaching himself to voguey trends. For a while it was Africa, where he befriended the president of Rwanda, then Bitcoin and psychedelics. In 2015 he tried 'shrooming in the Caribbean (where it was legal) and the lifetime teetotaller returned evangelical. He backed a company researching psilocybin-based treatments for depression, and another focused on speculative science to extend 'healthy ageing'. He also dabbled in Hollywood as a movie producer. A charming and handsome networker, Angermayer also went to the parties of his very good friend Alexander Schütz, whom he helped put on the board of Deutsche Bank in 2017.

SoftBank's Akshay Naheta was soon in touch with Wirecard's Markus Braun, and the outline of a deal came into view. SoftBank would lend Wirecard €900m (then equivalent to $1bn) in the form of a convertible bond, a type of debt which could be exchanged later for Wirecard stock. The proposed financial terms were so one-sided it would effectively be a gift to SoftBank for their support, so shareholders would have to approve it at the annual meeting that summer. In conversations about the deal Braun repeatedly said versions of the same thing: 'The cash I don't need, the SoftBank brand is nice, the business is what I want.'

Christian Angermayer, meanwhile, was granted a modest finder's fee: 1.25 per cent of the €900m, which came to €11m. All that was needed was for Ernst & Young to approve Wirecard's accounts, now that attention had been drawn to a secret at the heart of its business.

The apartment which Oliver Bellenhaus called home was an oasis of clean Scandinavian minimalism about a third of the way up the world's tallest building, the Burj Khalifa, which soared into the clouds above the sprawl of Dubai. It was a refined life of separation away from the rest of Wirecard that seemed to suit all concerned, as others in the company preferred to keep Bellenhaus, his politics and his business at a distance.

Of the politics, there were multiple signs. He insisted on *clean* food, typically from an Asian restaurant, that met his germaphobe standards of hygiene. Bellenhaus was like Donald Trump in that he swiftly sanitized after a handshake and showed an expansive view of what, and who, was dirty. After a flight, particularly to or from Dubai, colleagues would watch him throw away the polo shirt he'd worn for the trip, now irretrievably contaminated by the shared air of the journey. At a conference in London, the Wirecard salesman Martin Osterloh stood with Bellenhaus during a networking break, a plate of cookies between them on one of those small, high tables used to encourage interaction. Hundreds of people from the gaming world were mingling over coffee, and a fellow attendee, a black man, strolled up with a smile. 'Do you mind if I have one of those?'

'Two euros!' said Bellenhaus. The men chuckled at the lame icebreaker. Bellenhaus followed up, pointing to a chocolate cookie. 'But these ones are cheaper. They're only one euro.'

Perhaps too surprised to vent in a professional environment, the man took one and laughed it off.

'Oliver, you'll be spending the night in jail if he talks to the police,' Osterloh warned after the man had gone, to a shrug.

Bellenhaus denied being a racist. Osterloh and others at Wirecard seemed to attribute such behaviour not to bigotry but to a delight in crossing lines, such as when Bellenhaus mused in meetings with companies from Tel Aviv: 'Germans and the Israelis, we are so much alike in many ways.' Some colleagues said that it was humanity in general Bellenhaus disliked, describing a compassionate friend who gave money to support orang-utans and gorillas.

In more private settings, when Bellenhaus seemed to think he had a receptive audience, he was frank. Discussing the region's politics with an Arab-Israeli, he said that his grandfather was a Nazi, and if it was good enough for him . . .

The business which Bellenhaus ran was also something the rest of the company preferred not to examine closely. Colleagues would joke in mock horror that they didn't want to know what he was doing. CardSystems Middle East had come a long way since his card whispering days. The blank white cash cards of Click2Pay were long gone. Instead Bellenhaus managed Wirecard's relationship with a few key partners, a part of its operations known internally as 'Third-Party Acquiring'. It was the no-questions-asked business model Marsalek had first tried to establish a decade earlier with Simon Smaul in Dublin; a separate outside partner who processed payments for the highest-risk clients, sending a fat commission on each transaction back to Wirecard as a thank you.

Christopher Bauer's PayEasy in Manila was such a partner, along with Henry O'Sullivan's Senjo in Singapore. The third and most important of the trio was Al Alam Solutions, based nineteen floors up in a Dubai replica of New York's iconic Chrysler Building. The Al Alam office had about enough room for a dozen people and a wine fridge, in the words of an Australian Wirecard manager, Dashiell Lipscomb. He ran Wirecard's other business in Dubai, a back-office hub full of Indian technicians which was the company's engine room. For a while, when Lipscomb ran out of space, Al Alam put up a few Wirecard employees. He asked Bellenhaus about this partner, and the German said the structure was a fig leaf to distance Wirecard from the payments. The employees there were 'monkeys in suits' who did what they were told.

In early 2019, interest was growing inside and outside Wirecard about how exactly that relationship worked, and what Bellenhaus was doing with these partners, because the numbers were too big to ignore. In 2018 CardSystems booked about €600m of commission from partners, of which about €300m was profit – more than half the earnings generated by the entire group. Only a handful of staff were directly involved; it was Jan Marsalek's domain. It raised the question of what exactly the other 6,000 Wirecard employees were needed for, if they could mint a fortune with such little support. There were also practical questions: how did Wirecard monitor the payment volumes and check it wasn't stiffed on the commissions? What obligations did it have to these partners, and what would happen if one of them went bust? Wirecard's internal audit team in Munich tried to launch an examination of Third-Party Acquiring in January 2019, but Bellenhaus shot it down, claiming a lack of resources and the onerous workload of dealing with Ernst & Young. There was no point in duplicating the work of the external audit, he said.

Ernst & Young was the full extent of the oversight, because there was no local audit firm preparing the figures for CardSystems. Wirecard just put the figures together in Munich, bypassing its own Dubai-based finance team, and handed them to EY. In the past the auditors had taken an interest in Al Alam Solutions, giving its office in Dubai a once-over and finding it full of people. In March 2019 a delegation flew there again to talk to Bellenhaus, interested in some of the merchants CardSystems supported and the way they were screened for issues like money laundering red flags. The concerns EY had were taken seriously: in consultation with Marsalek, Bellenhaus promised to make changes in the next accounting period, and introduce a special project to improve the quality of the data.

Ernst & Young was taking extra care this year. Due to all the publicity around Wirecard there were various additional parts of EY taking an interest in the audit, including senior figures in the US. There was also the impact of the anonymous package of documents which had arrived in February. Once it was forensically examined for fingerprints, the dossier raised a series of issues that pointed to an organized book cooking operation in Singapore.

What helped Jan Marsalek address these questions was Ernst & Young's starting position – chest-deep in the quicksand. The firm's partners had signed off on Wirecard's accounts for the best part of a decade, in spite of warnings from inside and out, meaning EY's reputation was on the line. The same could also be said for the EY partner in charge of the audit, Martin Dahmen, a twenty-year-veteran accountant with blue eyes and a sweep of light-brown hair. It was his first time in overall charge, but he'd been part of the EY team at Wirecard for years, building up and applying a highly specialized knowledge about its business model and finances. If anyone outside the company really believed they understood its inner workings, it was surely him. After all, the accounts of a group with operations in more than forty countries serving 250,000 customers are a highly stylized artificial construct. Dahmen didn't start from scratch. EY began with the previous year's figures as a reference point. The big decisions, all those questions of interpretation and principle such as when to recognize a sale or a cost, had already been taken. The partners in the Third-Party Acquiring business like Al Alam and Senjo were treated as extensions of Wirecard's own business, for instance, mere subcontractors doing what they were told.

Singapore was different. The issues were new, and Ernst & Young's own team there had been arguing about the accounts for years. The lawyers at Rajah & Tann were supposed to be finishing the job they started with Project Tiger. The solution Marsalek applied to this problem was to make sure that everyone was wearing a blindfold; no one could be allowed to step back and view the whole elephant.

For the Rajah & Tann probe, that meant limiting the flow of information. A consulting group called Control Risks was commissioned to look at the accounting issues raised by the original R&T investigation. Its consultants were spoon-fed information before passing their conclusions up the chain to R&T; based on snapshots of the elephant's left leg and trunk, the beast appeared to be healthy.* The former prosecutors appear to have done their best, and concluded that various Singapore laws were broken, but they had no evidence to conclude significant revisions were needed to the accounts; based on the description of the photographs provided there appeared to be

---

* Control Risks said it was bound by client confidentiality, and that were its reports to be examined as part of the judicial process, the integrity and usefulness of its work would stand up to scrutiny.

some small dents in a tusk, and it was not possible to form an opinion on the ears and tail.

Ernst & Young was trickier this year, and Marsalek was also interviewed by members of the supervisory board, but again no one took responsibility to tear off the blindfold. EY's job was to tick boxes. The issues raised in Singapore and the package were broken down into a long list of individual questions which appear to have been addressed in isolation. To do that Marsalek hired yet more lawyers.

He began to work with Kritin Sundaram, an associate at Fieldfisher in London.* Marsalek seemed to trust him because he'd previously advised Wirecard on some of the issues from dealing with The Boys in India. Fieldfisher conducted yet more interviews and examined more material provided by Wirecard. At the very last moment, on 23 April, Ernst & Young was given an extensive letter from Fieldfisher addressing most of its outstanding points 'based on interviews and the documents provided'. Based on Marsalek's selection, it was another up-close postcard of grey and wrinkled skin. Martin Dahmen and Andreas Budde of EY signed the accounts.

SoftBank's decision to throw $1bn at Wirecard and engage in strategic co-operation with the group was announced the next day, a vote of confidence which temporarily buoyed the share price as high as €142. It was followed by Wirecard's full results on 25 April. CNBC carried an interview with Markus Braun via video link in Munich, a gold-coloured earpiece protruding from one ear. Instead of the black turtleneck was a white shirt open at the collar and he looked clammy, his thinning hair a little longer than normal. He blinked incessantly as he gave a number-heavy recitation of Wirecard's financial results: revenues for 2018 were €2bn, its Ebitda €560m, both up more than a third on 2017's performance. 'So I think we are very enthusiastic, and begin the year in a very strong and robust way,' he concluded.

The anchor, an American woman, cut to the chase with the urgent tone of early morning news. 'Let's begin with the accounting allegations, because many investors are still trying to ascertain where the revenues are coming from. There's been a fresh report from the *FT* in

---

* Sundaram declined to comment, citing client confidentiality.

the past twenty-four hours and they are talking about half of your worldwide revenue and almost all of your reported profits coming from three opaque partner companies in recent years. This is what the *FT* is claiming. What do you say to that, about the sources of revenue and profit?'

'Yeah. I think there are three points in this latest report. There was one point that a subsidiary wasn't audited. There was this point that three partners do the majority of profits. And there was a third element about an employee also working for a partner. All three are not true,' Braun said, blinking in overdrive as he touched on the sensitive issues. He brandished Ernst & Young as a shield. 'We want to leave all of this behind, we see this a little bit as market speculation, and all the allegations that were brought forward were part of the audit process, so I think today is really a turning point.'

'But you can't really leave it behind, can you Markus. Good morning to you!' An Englishman on the CNBC desk jumped in. 'Because you are taking the battle to the short sellers and to the *Financial Times*, specifically to Dan McCrum, who is the journalist in question who is pursuing your company,' he said, leaning into the controversy and explaining for viewers how the company was fighting back through the Munich courts. 'The battle is on, isn't it.'

It was the first time in the interview that Braun smiled. 'I concentrate on the innovations and the strong business. I leave all of this to the institutions and to the lawyers,' he said. While he spoke a chyron popped up on screen totting up the recommendations of financial analysts: there were twenty buyers, four holds, and just two who advised their clients to sell.

24

Empty Chairs and Empty Tables

24 April, 2019 – London
Wirecard share price €134, market capitalization €17bn

THE *FINANCIAL TIMES* WAS slowly packing itself up to move. Nikkei had purchased the organization, not the building, and had found us new digs. Stickers marked the cabinets emptied of files from beats long forgotten and large bins were filled with unread business books, optimistically destined for charity. Paul Murphy arrived at the investigations desk in an upbeat mood, dodging the piles of plastic crates strewn about. 'You do realize Soft-in-the-head Bank has just bet a billion dollars that you're wrong.'

Talk about the best-laid plans. I'd aimed to reveal Wirecard's reliance on its three strange partners before the audit was completed. Life, however, had intervened. After months of high-stakes pressure everyone needed a break. Charlotte and I took the kids to Lanzarote, for once only thinking about sun hats and ice creams as we splashed around the pool and idled away the hours between meals at an extravagantly diverse buffet. By the time Murphy and I, the lawyer Nigel Hanson and Lionel Barber were all assembled and able to take the fight back to Wirecard it was too late: the audit was done and Soft-in-the-head Bank had arrived on the scene. The details were hazy, but the bottom line was that a renowned technology investor appeared set to buy 5.6 per cent of Wirecard. Who cared what was in the pink pages of the *FT*? Markus Braun said it was wrong, with a prestigious accounting firm on one shoulder and now SoftBank on the other.

I boxed up my huge collection of Wirecard files and we said farewell to the old place. Barber stood in the centre of the newsroom and gave an emotional speech to the gathered ranks of the *FT* staff, the Nikkei top brass flown in from Tokyo and the cameras of the PR department. Afterwards the more senior editors disappeared to hobnob, while the hacks nipped off to a nearby off-licence and reconvened in the empty cafeteria on the top floor for a proper send-off. Contributions were piled high like a student house party as various bottles of obscure spirits discovered in drawers were emptied. Smoke filled the room, war stories of the glory days were swapped, and we all gossiped about how much longer Barber would be in charge and who would win the race to replace him.

Over the river the new building was a homecoming. Bracken House was purpose-built in the 1950s for the *FT* on the edge of the old financial district, half a mile up from the end of Fleet Street and over the road from St Paul's Cathedral. The paper had moved out in the late 1980s, and for our reoccupation it was comprehensively gutted and refitted; a sign of our own infusion of Japanese cash, as well as the confidence of an organization with a million readers. Inside the floors were open-plan donuts, the hole filled with glass elevators which gave the meeting rooms and offices arrayed around them a goldfish bowl quality. There was a lot of bare concrete and steel and it took a while to get used to the way that a colleague could appear from any direction. Photocopying alcoves were no use for discreet conversation; it was soon discovered the peculiar acoustics broadcast any chat around the bend of a nearby corridor to desks arrayed in the wings. Anticipating the future, the investigation team desk was a few steps away from Hanson for legal questions. We also now had a genuine bunker, hidden deep down on one of the sub-levels, for sensitive work.

Lionel Barber's new office was a grander, larger version of the old one, with black-leather and chrome sofas for his meetings and a long wall of windows. It lacked the covert approach of the old U-bend, so a sort of bus stop structure was erected outside to give those lingering for an audience a degree of privacy. Barber was inside chatting to one of the senior editors when the head of the *FT*'s corporate legal team knocked on the door – an unusual occurrence. Like most newspapers, there was a church and state separation between the commercial and editorial sides of the organization to prevent advertisers or moronic business interests influencing the paper's coverage.

'What's the problem?' asked Barber, surprised at the interruption.

The mild-mannered paper pusher began to explain.

'Well, it's this story in Manila, and the allegations of bribery.'

There'd been a report in a Philippine newspaper, the *Manila Standard*, that one of Wirecard's business partners had filed some sort of criminal 'cyber libel' case with the Cabanatuan city prosecutor's office against Stefania Palma and me. Supposedly the old sailor in the villa had been paid 100,000 pesos ($2,000) to hand Palma fake documents when she turned up unannounced. It didn't make any sense, but that hadn't stopped the pro-Wirecard crowd on Twitter holding it up as fresh evidence of corruption at the *FT*. The other allegations came from Christopher Bauer, who claimed I had tried to bribe government officials into handing over financial records for one of his payment companies and that Palma had threatened staff at his bus company as if she was some sort of mafioso. (It earned her the office nickname Donna Stefania, while I tended to be greeted with cheerful shouts of 'Have you been arrested yet?') The lawyer had unwisely caught Barber off guard and with an audience.

'You are honestly telling me that I'm supposed to take notice of some crap, corrupt Manila newspaper. And you're casting doubt on our reporting. Are you insane?'

The *FT*'s general counsel tried to explain that the provisions of the UK Bribery Act are particularly onerous, with companies facing unlimited fines if caught, and that as a responsible organisation the *FT* had a duty to at least consider all allegations. With everything that had been thrown at the paper from the outside, Barber was not about to stomach quasi-legal worries from inside his own house.

'No way, you're out to lunch, I'm not doing anything. This meeting is over.'

*

Outside the *FT*, others were still battling. Matthew Earl was no longer shorting Wirecard stock, it wasn't worth the aggro, but it wasn't about money any more. In 2016 he'd spoken a few times to the compliance team at Mastercard. They seemed interested and one of the men on the calls, Paul Paolucci, told him Mastercard had dished out heavy fines to Wirecard in the past, but nothing public resulted. After Earl had settled the German criminal case in the summer of 2017 he'd tried the Metropolitan Police in London. He met a superintendent and detective sergeant in the cyber crime unit and ran them through how he thought Wirecard's money laundering operation worked. After three hours the officers' response amounted to: 'Right, OK, urm, yeah.' They didn't have the resources, so would refer it to the FBI.

The American authorities called a year later. In a basement interview room under the heavily fortified offices of the Department of Justice for the Southern District of New York, Earl faced two Federal investigators focused on the hacking of Wirecard critics. He was an expert, because the phishing emails never stopped, just varied in intensity, ingenuity and effort, as if he was being passed around the hacking organization as an unresolved project. Earl sent all of these on to Citizen Lab at the University of Toronto, a group of 'white-hat' academics who studied, and sometimes exposed, online surveillance in all its noxious forms. Earl and I, along with other targets of Wirecard hacking, had agreed to keep quiet about the US investigation in the hope that it would lead to prosecutions of those involved, a promise we began to regret as nothing happened and the battle in Germany intensified.

In 2019, Earl tried for the third time. It didn't help his nerves when a fellow passenger suffered a heart attack, forcing the plane into an abrupt and sharp descent to Munich International. The next morning Earl finally met his German lawyer, Timo, who had chosen a black-velvet jacket and cravat for his trip down from Düsseldorf. It was a Joe Pesci kind of look. Oh Christ, I've got *My Cousin Vinny* as a lawyer, thought Earl, as he told Timo he'd accepted the prosecutors' invitation because he hoped to talk to them about the evidence he'd prepared. 'Oh I don't think they'll be interested in any of that. They'll just want any information you have about the nasty Dan McCrum and that case,' said Timo.

The meeting was in a drab room with the chief prosecutor, Hildegard Bäumler-Hösl, and her underling investigating me, Earl's business partner in Shadowfall Research, plus a detective and an interpreter, whose translation initially gave the proceedings a slow and extremely formal quality. The more junior prosecutor started by asking Earl about his relationship with me. We occasionally had lunch together and talked about markets, Earl said.

'Did you have any foreknowledge of the articles published this year about Wirecard?'

'Dan had disappeared off the face of the earth, I hadn't heard from him for about six months,' Earl said.

The prosecutor switched tack: 'Did you pay for the Wirecard employee Royston Ng to travel to the UK from Singapore?'

'No,' said Earl, finding the question bizarre, but the prosecutor persisted.

'Are you sure?'

'Yes, I think I'd remember,' said Earl, wondering where on earth this was coming from.

There was a pause. The questions seem to have hit a dead end so Earl suggested that, seeing as he'd come all that way, could they talk about the money laundering? Bäumler-Hösl agreed, Earl pulled out his laptop and soon the whole tenor of the room changed as he gave the best rendition of Wirecard's scheme he'd ever managed. He took them step by step, how Wirecard had taken money from US gamblers and passed it to companies in the British Virgin Islands via shell companies in Consett, County Durham. His audience quickly got it and the German detective was soon finishing Earl's sentences. 'Can you guess who owns this company . . .'.

'Fermoya!' the policeman answered with a pleased look, like he'd won a prize. Bäumler-Hösl had warmed up considerably and was leading the questions with interest. The problem of the whole set-up, or its beauty from the perspective of Wirecard, was its cross-jurisdictional nature. No one authority saw the whole thing. But there was potentially a fairly simple fraud at the heart of it: the misreporting of transactions to Visa and Mastercard. Bäumler-Hösl wanted to know the dates, calculating the time which had elapsed.

Earl's examples were mostly outside the statute of limitations, she said.

'Well, this was all much more current when I first tried to interest BaFin in it three years ago,' Earl pointed out. Bäumler-Hösl muttered something darkly to herself, which the translator chose not to pass on.

Eduardo Marques, the Brazilian at the hedge fund Valiant Capital, was very much still short when SoftBank arrived. 'Holy fuck. We are totally fucked,' was his initial reaction. His next was to text everyone he knew in London to find out who was behind the trade, on the assumption they had no idea what they'd got themselves into. He arranged to send a presentation to Akshay Naheta. Based on Marques' long experience of Wirecard, the essential message was simple: it wasn't the amounts or even the details which mattered, it was the practices. Why on earth was Edo Kurniawan not fired? Marques asked the SoftBank man if the company was conducting a full due diligence process and got the answer: 'No, we pride ourselves on our speed.'

While Marques was in town I saw him for a coffee, sitting outside the Caffè Nero by Mansion House where it had all begun with the short seller Leo Perry five years before. The sun was shining and we hung out for a while reflecting on what a crazy few months it had been. 'I dunno, man. At this stage I'd have to catch Markus Braun at a paedo party with Harvey Weinstein for anyone to care,' he said.

Marques had pulled at every single Wirecard thread he could find for years, and he was running out of ideas. But he mentioned something which made my ears prick up. In May 2019, the Federal Trade Commission agreed a settlement with no admission of wrongdoing with Allied Wallet, a Californian and UK payments company, for helping a bunch of con artists defraud $110m from consumers. According to the FTC, the scams included pyramid schemes, as well as a phantom debt collection agency which threatened people with lawsuits over non-existent loans for things like blankets, paint supplies or hiking equipment. Allied Wallet had been accused of creating fake shell companies and dummy websites to hide fraud from banks and the credit card networks. It was run by Ahmad 'Andy' Khawaja, a politically connected American-Lebanese businessman indicted in a separate criminal investigation for helping to conceal the source of millions of dollars of donations to the Hillary Clinton 2016 presidential campaign. Marques had spotted Wirecard's name in one of the related suits.

I knew the name Allied Wallet for a different reason. According to the document trove I'd been puzzling over, it was a valuable customer of Wirecard Bank, and was also involved with the Oliver Bellenhaus operation in Dubai. Yet something odd happened when I asked Allied Wallet for comment; it confirmed a relationship with Wirecard but emphatically denied any knowledge of its partner in the Middle East. 'We have never worked with "Al Alam Solutions" and do not know who/what that is.'

Back at the office, I popped my head over the desk to ask Paul Murphy what he thought. Maybe they didn't want to admit to dealing with Al Alam in Dubai because that was where the really bad stuff happened? He disagreed. 'You can take their statement at face value. They're in clean-up mode. They've just signed a settlement with the US authorities and they're not going to poke them in the eye by lying about their business in print.'

I went back to the Wirecard spreadsheets. There was a surprisingly small number of clients, less than thirty-five, generating all of the huge payments volumes Wirecard was sending to Al Alam. In addition to Allied Wallet, there was a notorious online financial broker. Banc de Binary closed under regulatory pressure in March 2017, but in Wirecard's records nothing changed, the payments carried on for the rest of the year. There were a couple of Irish prepaid card businesses. I pulled up the Irish registry, got a hit. The first was liquidated in 2013. I did a double take; was that right? I quickly put in the next name. It was liquidated the year before.

I gasped, loud enough for Murphy to hear. By now he was used to these outbursts. 'OK Dan, what is it?' I slowly stood up, chuckling to myself. It was so simple. This puzzle I'd spent months poring over; suddenly the answer was blindingly obvious. He looked at me expectantly: 'Come on, don't leave us hanging. Out with it.'

'None of it's real. The customers are fake. There's nothing there.'

25

Gold-plated

17 July, 2019 – London
Wirecard share price €147, market capitalization €18bn

NICK GOLD ALWAYS MADE a strong impression. A fast-talking party animal, he was in terrific shape for someone in his forties, with a deep tan and lustrous black hair. To the tabloids he was a lovable rogue, thanks to his model wife and the whiff of scandal which lingered in his wake. They'd married in Miami Beach, all in white, and she interspersed pictures of their charmed life among the bikini shots shared with her Instagram following. An evening with Gold was a challenge to hold on and keep up, bombarded by his charm, generosity and obscene self-deprecating schtick about what he called his small Jewish penis. He made big money from office supplies, but who wants to talk about stationery? Bars were his thing. His London home had a Moose bar, his house in Cannes a Lion bar, but the draw for the rich men around him was The Box, his Soho cabaret club.

Gold's brushes with controversy included placing bets based on inside information from jockeys riding to lose; in 2012 he and his father were 'excluded' from British horse racing for several years by the authority which oversaw the industry. He was a non-executive director of businesses run by his father that were accused of using dubious tactics to sell table salt to Swedish councils at fantastical prices as special 'ice-melting chemicals'. (Gold said he wasn't involved, had never been to Sweden, and the operation was anyway legitimate.) By day he had the same spread betting affliction as many of the London bandits, taking a scattershot approach to the latest stock market gossip and sharing his account with others. He had plenty of his own cash, peppering his monologues with the prices he'd paid for the objects around him, and he sometimes suffered big reversals; he'd lost millions by being on the wrong side of the betting group Flutter when a bid rumour sent the shares soaring. On the morning of 17 July 2019, he was in his office on the top floor of Clearwater House, around the corner from the Chiltern Firehouse, a trendy spot where Gold held court. The office was a modern steel and glass arrangement, with a black and white designer pool table and a bar stocked with pink champagne and plenty of vodka. Gold was there with his close friend and business partner Jonathan Dennis, a property guy, waiting for another old friend, the premiership football agent Saif Rubie.

Gold had recently bumped into Rubie at a beach bar in Cannes, showing off to beautiful women in bikinis by spraying champagne about. As they caught up in the sunshine Rubie mentioned he'd somehow got connected to a sovereign wealth fund with billions at its disposal. He knew Gold was a prolific and successful trader and wanted to put him together with the money man. If Gold had a good trade, he said, this guy had the resources to back it.

Just after 11.30 Rubie walked into Gold's office accompanied by a Mancunian in a three-piece suit. Gold was in a hurry, said he didn't have long. 'What's your background?'

The visitor explained as he sat down and made himself comfortable. 'Right, well, I'm basically to be a mouthpiece for the people I'm representing. Do a lot of trading in the Far East.' The Mancunian didn't trade himself, he was a facilitator, he said. 'At the moment they're looking at investing 50 million.'

That was Gold's cue. He had a North London accent, with the faint hint of a lisp. 'OK, let me tell you what the scenario is. There's a company in Germany called Wirecard. It's a payments facilitator. It's worth $20bn, and there's been loads of articles in the last few months from the *FT* making certain allegations about the company.' Gold didn't mention his brush with it in the past, when Jan Marsalek was on the trail of Zatarra and had offered Gold a fat sum to stop the short attacks in a meeting at the Mandarin Oriental. Gold said he couldn't, and was one of the few people immune to Marsalek's charms. He'd found him boring, a dry, tea-drinking accountant. Instead Gold talked up his recent trading history, of well-timed short bets: 'I've sold it myself. I sold it before the first article came out, at 180-something, and closed at 120. Then it went to about 80.'

The visitor pulled out a pad, said he wanted to make some notes as Gold continued to describe his trading history, selling after other articles came out. 'It's not illegal, it's not insider trading, short selling a company.' Everything was based on public information, he said, then continued. 'They've got a whistleblower, the *Financial Times*: €240m of revenue in a certain quarter are fraudulent. They're going to announce it tomorrow, probably Friday at the latest.'

Workmen were digging up the pavement outside, and the sound of drilling made Gold's rapid-fire mumbling hard to hear. His guest didn't catch it. 'The stock's as liquid as you like,' Gold repeated, meaning it would be easy to short in size, for someone else at least. 'We can't trade it,' he said, without explaining why. The visitor's mysterious investors shouldn't make trades in Germany either, Gold warned, as they had different rules there. 'It's not worth us going to jail because someone's come along wanting to make money.'

Having framed his reluctance to trade as a matter of the rules, Gold got to the point: he'd like someone else to put the money up. It was the common bandit strategy of teaming up to trade. 'Tomorrow, we believe this stock could go to zero. So we need somebody to take a position with. If we lose, they'll get the money back the next day. If we win, we'll figure out how to get the money down the line,' he said, promising there were other things to do. 'But it's got to be today.'

'Sorry, how d'you know this article's coming out? Have you got, you know, info?'

'The *Financial Times*.'

'Sorry?' The Mancunian wanted more.

'The editor of the *Financial Times*,' Gold said, as if this were totally normal. 'He can tell me. You know, he's allowed to tell me what he's doing and the way he feels about the company. They've questioned

the integrity of the *Financial Times*. Said, you know, the articles written are on the back of short sellers, these articles aren't true.'

Gold's business partner Jonathan Dennis joined in. 'They've
accused the *FT* of market manipulation, issued legal proceedings.
Now the *FT* have got it in their head they're going to destroy them.'

The man paused, as if considering this. 'OK, so you've got another
article coming out tomorrow or the day after.'

Gold hedged. 'I mean, it could be tomorrow, you never know. The
reason it's not really insider trading is that we don't know the full
contents of the article. It could get pulled, delayed, you never know
why these things happen.'

Dennis backed him up. 'That is, categorically, why it's not insider
trading, based on legal advice, because you don't know that at 3.15
on Thursday afternoon it's coming,' he said. 'And second, it's categorically not market manipulation, because market manipulation is
spreading false truths.'

'It's not for us, because we've done it a few times now and the
advice was it's not worth it. It's also a darling of Germany, they've
built it up, so you're taking on them as well,' Gold said, although he
seemed more concerned about fingerprints than genuine legal exposure. What he wanted was a payday using someone else's money to
place the bet. 'So ideally we need to get on in size with you guys and
look how it ends.' He began to talk numbers. Two million was too
small, 50 way too big. Something sensible would be 10, so 5 million
each, to test the water.

The Manc agreed. 'I think that's going to be the way forward, to
test the water, for a first transaction like this. Obviously we'll do our
homework.'

Gold pressed on to seal the deal. 'You haven't got long to do your
research. But all I can tell you is if you get it wrong, the downside is
five euros, it's not going to rally twenty. There's five euros downside
and 140 euros upside. So it's the sort of trade we like. Maybe I get it
wrong and it halves, it doesn't go to zero. The likelihood is a payments processing company, in today's world of compliance you can't
fuck around.' Like the rest of the figures he mentioned, Gold had
only a loose sense of the numbers; he thought SoftBank was putting

in €800m. 'My guy says why do they need €800m?' He went back to his key point. 'They've got documents, they've got invoices, they've got a whole load of stuff and it's coming, it's real. Every minute we sit here talking is another minute we're not trading.'

'I get that. What I'll have to do is I'll have to speak . . . ' He was cut off by Gold asking how long he needed, then Dennis took over.

'Look, the reality is I'm finding it hard to paint a good picture. I'm a property developer by trade, in Canary Wharf, in the Docklands, and I remember when Enron was taking a 1.2m-square-foot tower in Canary Wharf. It was all over the news about signing up, and this was a company that had nuffing.' The Essex accent came out more when he was emphatic. Gold's phone went and he walked out of the room to answer it, feet clacking on the wooden floor.

'Interesting. Obviously I'm going to have to speak to my guys. They've got their own team of researchers, they'll have to do that for them. I'll leave that for them. Have you spoken to anyone else? Just out of interest, my guys will want to know.'

Dennis said they had, 'through contacts that aren't so close, shall we say. Because we don't want it leaking back, which obviously makes it harder . . . It's harder when you're meeting someone for the first time.'

'That's why I flew in.' It was the football agent Rubie. 'I wanted to introduce the two parties and make sure that, er . . .'

Dennis interrupted, speaking quietly, conspiratorially. 'The other thing is our source has more to come. I mean, you can't get a better avenue here.'

'That source from the *Financial Times*, you mean?'

'The head of the investigations team,' Dennis said. He offered up a few more details of what the *FT* had published about Wirecard's issues in Singapore, before circling back to the main point, that it was 'hyper time-sensitive'.

The visitor seemed to have got what he came for. He assured Dennis that his guys in the Far East would be fine on timing. The whole meeting lasted less than fifteen minutes. 'Has Nick gone?' the Manc asked, looking around, and they all started laughing. 'I will state to them it's time-sensitive. I'm sure by the time pound signs ring up, they will move.'

They started to talk about the importance of trust. Rubie joined in. 'That's what I said to Nick. I wanted to introduce you guys.'

Dennis agreed, giving a little insight into how they behaved. If Gold said throw 20 million quid at a trade in a company he'd barely heard of, he would. Only then at three in the morning would he suddenly think, hang on, what have I just done?

The guest sympathized. 'I think everyone's been there.'

A pause. Gold's absence hung in the air. Rubie, the professional middleman, filled the silence by reminding them of his role. 'For me, it was like, can we connect the dots,' he said. They made small talk about the rest of the day; the football agent was flying back to France later.

The facilitator of Far Eastern money was beginning to get restless. 'Are we just waiting for Nick now?'

Dennis went to find him. He was on the terrace, their second meeting room, and would be back in a sec, he said. The man didn't wait. He said his thank yous and goodbyes, and left.

In Munich, it was approaching 1 p.m. Jan Marsalek was sitting in the sun outside one of his favourite restaurants, Käfer-Schänke. A short stroll from his base of operations, Käfer was part restaurant, part luxury delicatessen, the closest thing the city had to Harrods' food hall. Marsalek often ordered Käfer catering out to the Wirecard headquarters, or threw lavish meals in a private room. At that moment, however, he was drinking Coke Zero with his PR guru, a specialist in high-level crisis situations whom I'll call 'Mr Samt'.

Marsalek had his phone in his hand and a look on his face Samt had never seen before, or would again. It was a serene calm, that still moment where the lottery numbers have been read out and the brain is still processing that they match the ticket. 'What if we have evidence that the *FT* is doing things together with short sellers?'

The PR man considered this for a few seconds, surprised. 'That would be a scoop. I can't believe it would be true though.'

'No, it is, we have the proof. What if I have it on tape?'

'Is it audio tape or video tape?' asked Samt, expecting it might be a phone call. But Marsalek said it was a live recording of short sellers coming together and talking about an attack on Wirecard. It was all based on an article in the *FT* which is going to appear, so they can get the money, he said. He was getting excited. The company could make an announcement denouncing the *FT*.

'Don't do that. If you make accusations yourself you'll have every newspaper and magazine against you. It's far wiser to set them fighting each other,' said Samt. He suggested feeding the story to one reputable publication to investigate for itself. He was also concerned about the tendencies of Wirecard's CEO. 'Don't tell Markus, he'll immediately put out a press release or start calling analysts to tell them he has the smoking gun.'

Within hours, questions arrived from the *FT*, appearing to confirm the leak of an imminent story. The questions demonstrated how much had been uncovered: were the customers of Al Alam real? Did Wirecard deny that staff at its Munich head office were involved in an operation to deceive auditors and fake several hundred million euros of revenues? Before he handed everything over to a friendly journalist, Mr Samt wanted to see and hear it all himself, and to meet the Wirecard investor Marsalek claimed had discovered the information. A meeting was set for the following morning, back at Käfer.

Marsalek was ten minutes late when he texted Samt; they would be there in two hours. The PR man went to buy a selection of reading material and settled in. Samt noticed a tall, muscular Arab gentleman at the table next to him. He was wearing a polo shirt, white and red shorts with crisp sneakers and was slumped low in his seat, playing with his phone and occasionally looking around, bored. A couple of hours and a few Coke Zeros later a cab pulled up and Marsalek got out accompanied by the 'investor', Rami El Obeidi. They made an odd couple. The two of them were laughing and joking together like old friends, and both had buzz cuts, although Rami was shorter than Marsalek. With them was an older man with an aquiline nose. He and El Obeidi walked over to the big guy in shorts and exchanged a few words. The big guy looked up and down the street, looked at

Samt, then nodded. Everything was OK. The patient PR man was mystified by the performance; what did they think he might have been doing, setting up a microphone himself?

The men sat down at the table with Marsalek and Samt while the bodyguard positioned himself in a chair between the road and El Obeidi, who introduced himself to Samt and began to explain what had happened as if he were addressing a four-year-old child. He came from a rich family, and they had lost a lot of money from the actions of what he called a short selling gang around Nick Gold. When the opportunity had arisen to get back at this crew, he had hired a private detective to do so. Since then he had been threatened – by men in black-leather jackets, while he was still in London, and then in messages. As his family was in danger he had sent them to the Lebanon, and would be joining them as soon as his business in Munich was concluded. The whole time El Obeidi spoke his older companion stared fiercely at Samt, leaning forward with his chin close to the table.

'I need proof, affidavits, and you should talk to the journalist yourself,' Samt said. What he would do is broker the meeting and ensure that it was treated as deep off-the-record, so that El Obeidi wouldn't be named. He also explained a key ground rule for dealing with journalists: it's essential to set the terms first, rather than try to take words back once the horse has bolted.

Afterwards Samt sprang into action. For the drop, he selected Sönke Iwersen at *Handelsblatt*, the newspaper's head of investigations, who was soon supplied with the tapes, statements of authenticity from the Manchester private detective agency which had recorded them, El Obeidi himself, and the *FT* questions about Wirecard's accounting fraud. It was everything he needed to expose the failing and corrupt *FT*, served up on a plate.

26

Caught in the Trap

18 July, 2019 – London
Wirecard share price €139, market capitalization €17bn

LIONEL BARBER WAS ALL at sea, and it was disconcerting. He took off his reading glasses, leaned back on the sofa and looked up at the ceiling for inspiration, exhaling deeply.

'You're going to have to help me here guys. I've never encountered anything like this.' On the glass coffee table between us were two letters from the law firm Herbert Smith, one to me, and one sent direct to the *FT* legal department accusing us of insider trading with Nick Gold. Wirecard said it had passed a recording on to the criminal authorities in the UK and Germany, and demanded that the *FT* not publish anything until their investigations were complete.

'It's a set-up, it has to be. We know we're not corrupt.' It was my turn to make the case.

Nigel Hanson, the lawyer, was circumspect. 'Yes, and our response has always been to ask them for the evidence. If they have it, we'll have to at least consider it.'

Paul Murphy was in shock. He was the one in the hot seat. Nick Gold was a contact of his, one he hadn't known for long, another nightclub operator from the same bandit social circle as the Kilbeys. 'You know me, Lionel, I'm an open book. I don't know where this has come from. You can go through my finances if you like.'

Barber had regathered his normal authority. 'I trust you, Paul, but

220

this is very serious and I need to talk to the lawyers.' He demanded a robust legal response from Nigel, and a fresh draft of the copy.

As we left his office I cursed our attempt to be clever. I'd spent June on the phone, hounding answers out of mostly baffled or uncommunicative companies about their supposed relationship with Wirecard and its partner Al Alam in Dubai. I'd enlisted a colleague in Tokyo, Leo Lewis, to twist the arms of the Japanese organizations on my list. I'd pieced together clues to identify a Filipino businessman who ran an online variant of gin rummy and thought highly of Wirecard, but had closed the games down when President Duterte won election in 2016. Not one of them knew anything about Al Alam, and only a handful admitted to still working with Wirecard. At the start of July, I was so sure that I'd found the big lie at the heart of the company that I decided to set a trap.

On 2 July I'd sent Wirecard some partial questions about its spreadsheet of customers which didn't exist. The aim was to tempt the company into a bear pit by revealing a small amount of what we knew, and Wirecard walked right into it. Herbert Smith told me, in lawyer-speak, to piss off: 'Our client has already informed you of its position that this document is inauthentic . . . It is therefore unclear why you persist in asking questions of our client based on the same, and we request that you cease doing so.'

Bingo. The company had run out of excuses. Wirecard had stated, through their Silver Circle lawyers, that the spreadsheet I was looking at was fake; but I knew it wasn't because I knew precisely where it had come from. So the plan Murphy and I had cooked up was to present readers with a choice by publishing the actual underlying documents. Then the world could decide: either the spreadsheets were fake, or Wirecard's profits were fraudulent. It was a battle we could win. But we underestimated Jan Marsalek, giving him two weeks to prepare a trap of his own.

The mistake Murphy made, when he sat back down at his desk after the meeting with Lionel, was to think like a reporter instead of a suspect. His instinct was to get to the bottom of it, so he immediately texted Nick Gold: 'Who did you meet in your offices at 9.15 yesterday?'

'A football agent. Why?'

'Well, he recorded you.'

'OMG.'

Gold, predictably, did not take the betrayal lightly. On Saturday a fresh letter arrived from Herbert Smith. As before, the law firm played the part of the waiter carrying the tray, taking no view on whether its client had poisoned the drinks. Wirecard offered a few supposedly incriminatory quotes from Nick Gold, and said it was concerned how he had learned of its complaint to the *FT*. Then *Handelsblatt* joined in with a lurid story about the 'ominous sound recording'. It gleefully parroted Wirecard's accusations of corruption at the *FT*, then followed up in a second piece with more details about the tape recording, telling readers that Gold's information 'matches the questions that the newspaper asked Wirecard'.

I read that sentence three times. Then I picked my jaw off the floor and found the questions I'd sent, and read it again. Everything *Handelsblatt* needed to take Wirecard down was there, and yet the newspaper seemed more concerned to go after us. Indeed, Sönke Iwersen followed up with a triumphant interview to an industry magazine about how the *FT* was a journalistic institution in the twilight.

The general counsel reappeared at Lionel Barber's door. Germany's business newspaper of record was not some tinpot Manila rag. Nikkei and the *FT* board had never questioned Barber about our Wirecard reporting, but he had heard on the grapevine there was some queasiness about the criminal complaint.

On Tuesday morning I was at home when Barber called. He apologized. He had every confidence in my reporting, he trusted me and Murphy, but he was going to call in the law firm RPC to conduct an investigation nonetheless. He said the gold-standard reputation of the *FT* was at stake, and we had to get ahead of Wirecard, to clear the air for us and for the good of the newspaper. He expected the probe would be quick, and then we could strike back.

I understood, I'd even expected it, but all the same I was numb. Barber's voice sounded like it was coming from a distance, the words weren't really registering. I'd been on the brink of triumph, finally exposing the truth. Now I had become the story. My reputation was ruined and the journalistic protection I'd counted on to blunt the paranoid fears of my imagination had evaporated. If something happened, well, who would care; even the *FT* was investigating that criminal McCrum.

'Hang on a second. Before we start, can I just ask if there's anyone in the audience here from Herbert Smith Freehills?' Paul Murphy scanned the crowd in the East End theatre, eyes narrowed against the stage lights. It was a packed house, faces peering down from the ornate balconies, and the bare plaster of the walls was damp from the breath of the crowd in the heatwave gripping London. A tentative hand rose in the stalls. 'Security, if you'd please.' Heads swivelled as Murphy waved over a tall, dark Irishman in a black jacket, who half dragged the woman out of the hall.

'What are you doing? I'm allowed to be here. I have a ticket. This is totally unreasonable. Lawyers are people too . . .' A thud of closing doors cut her off.

'I'm very sorry for that interruption, but if we're going to talk about Wirecard we have to take such precautions.' Two days after the internal investigation was announced, Murphy was having a little fun. We were on stage to talk about the company for the latest experiment from the brain of *FT* Alphaville's editor Izabella Kaminska, a one-off evening of high-concept vaudeville at Wilton's Music Hall. Her team had persuaded the former *Baywatch* actress Pamela Anderson to help sell tickets with a video endorsement. Other entertainment that evening included a sermon from the Reverend Craig Wright, an Australian chancer with a giant bodyguard, who claimed (to snorts of derision from some watching) to be the billionaire inventor of Bitcoin. As Murphy and I ran through our careful script, we were interrupted by shouts from giant puppets, socks with buttons for eyes, projected on to the back of the stage: 'Crummy McCrum is going to jail!'; 'Go for it Markus!'

It felt good to show a small part of the world we weren't hiding away. The location was also a reminder of how the underworld had changed. That afternoon we'd rehearsed with a pint of Guinness in what was once a pub frequented by the murderous Kray Twins. It had no menace any more, although while I was standing at the bar an off-duty postman strolled up, pulled out a book of unused taxi receipts and tore off a wodge for the landlord, taking a pint of lager in return.

A week later Lionel Barber was in Sicily, at the three-day summer camp for billionaires thrown by Google. It was like a whistle had sounded and called all the private jets in the world to heel. The Silicon Valley set were there, enjoying the usual entertainments to flatter their self-image as conscientious and charitable custodians of power. The robber barons heard from Prince Harry on climate change and nodded along to a set from the campaigning Chris Martin of *Coldplay*. As for networking, Barber was a paid-up member of the lycra mafia. He went on his first serious ride since breaking his collarbone, and as it wound up into the Sicilian hills in the blistering heat the views were literally breathtaking. He found himself sweating along-side a Googler and the grey-haired Austrian chairman of Deutsche Bank, Paul Achleitner, who took the opportunity to ask: 'What is it with you and Wirecard?'

The internal investigation was a sore point. 'You know what, these people are crooks and if you have anything whatsoever to do with them you need to be careful. It's a total fraud. I can't believe what we're being accused of, and the German media have been disgusting.'

The third biker intervened. 'What's the problem? All you need to know about Wirecard is that it's a German company run by Austrians.'

Barber pedalled on, determined to have the last word. 'Yeah, it's funny. But it's also a fraud.'

July's optimism about the pace of the investigation became August despair, as we learned that lawyers don't understand journalism, or finance. It wasn't the RPC media team who arrived at Bracken House and started by asking Barber how exactly the newspaper was put together. The *FT* had used the firm for years because it was a defence specialist that fought the likes of Schillings, so we thought they'd have a basic idea of how the sausage was made. Yet they wanted to know the production process, the publishing system, the lines of command. The genie was out of the bottle and very slowly ambling around the building while the clock whirred on his billable hours. Herbert Smith was also doing its best to delay matters on behalf of its client, by arguing about the terms under which it would release a tape that Wirecard had already leaked to the German media. I was told I'd get to see a transcript when I was eventually interviewed, so RPC would get my impressions fresh. That was to be scheduled later, once they'd trawled through my inbox. Barber had at least limited the scope of the inquiry to email, avoiding a fight over the protection of confidential sources had they asked for our phones.

Those were dark weeks as it dragged on, the threat of whatever Wirecard had cooked up hanging over us. I wasn't suspended – Barber had even told us to keep working on the story – but then I wasn't able to publish anything either. In normal times there's a journalistic grumps which comes on at the end of an unproductive day, particularly when no useful words are written. I didn't want to go to the office, which felt aimless, but then I didn't want it to seem like I was hiding either. Twitter was a dumpster of vitriol. I'd play with the kids in the garden and forget for a while, only for my mind to slip into the vortex. 'Daddy, why aren't you listening to me?'

What shook me out of the funk was lunch with Paul Murphy and Fahmi Quadir. She was twenty-eight, a second-generation Bangladeshi immigrant from Long Island, and was fast making a name for herself as a short seller. We left our phones behind as a precaution and went for lunch at J. Sheekey in Covent Garden, a reliable fish joint, as a taste of London class. Quadir had dark eyes, black hair piled up on her head and New York glamour. She was an accidental short seller who'd studied Maths and Biology and was set for academia when she took a corporate intelligence job to earn some cash before grad school. Quadir found she was good at gently prising information about pharmaceutical supply chains out of production managers at factories in Hungary and other out-of-the-way places. But she realized the drug makers buying this intel weren't using the data to avoid supply shortages; instead they raised prices for essential medicines hospitals couldn't do without. She quit, and went to work for a hedge fund instead. In late 2017 she'd quit again and was founding her own fund when she ran into Zatarra's Fraser Perring at a Washington DC get-together organized by the renowned short seller Marc Cohodes, who had retired to raise chickens and horses in wine country but kept his hand in. Perring was in rude health (no cast or crutch in sight). He now presented himself as an expert researcher rather than a trader and was claiming a victory for his new activist short selling brand, Viceroy Research; it had put out an attack report about a South African furniture business called Steinhoff *after* it announced accounting problems. (Parts of the document were copied verbatim, without permission, from work by the London hedge fund Portsea Asset Management written six months earlier.) Quadir thought Perring was a bit strange, but Cohodes cherished unusual characters and seemed to trust him. They stayed in touch, and while Perring also mentioned that his friend 'Ian Hollins' could help Quadir raise money for her new fund, his talk of Wirecard put her on to the scent.

So she'd been watching our battle with the company, and also conducting her own research. In the spring of 2019 she drove to Pennsylvania to knock on Wirecard's door with her fund's researcher. They found a huge office with no security. At the unmanned front desk was a binder full of the names and phone numbers of people said to work there, but only about ten were visible. A salesman came over and Quadir asked about prepaid cards. They sat down and he explained that Wirecard would do its know-your-customer checks on her business. She could then hand out the cards to anyone she liked. They could be loaded with a staggering $150,000 each, and reloaded wherever she wanted; with cash; with another payment card; at an ATM. What the salesman was proposing would be a licence for her to launder money, avoid taxes, run a drug gang – anything cash-rich and attention-shy.

Then came a whistleblower, someone who knew Jan Marsalek and the high-risk processing world well. He picked Quadir to speak to because she published a scathing attack on BaFin when it banned short selling of Wirecard shares, but the reason he wanted to talk was because he was scared. In March 2019, an experienced payments executive called Gary Murphy had driven a quad bike off a cliff in

New Zealand. Rumours were flying around that it wasn't an accident, that Federal investigators were closing in on a money laundering operation with the help of a co-operating witness, and that Gary Murphy had been the rat.* Quadir's whistleblower decided he wanted to be on the right side of history, so had told her all about Jan Marsalek, his Mastercard contact and their friend the porn baron Ray Akhavan.

'Wait, hang on a second, did you say Ray?' A forkful of fish pie dangled on its way to my mouth momentarily forgotten as I interrupted Quadir. A bell was clanging at the back of my brain. I looked at Murphy. 'Ray. Why do I know that name?'

A spark of recognition. 'What, do you mean the CIA uncles? That was Ray, I think.'

Quadir looked back and forth between us. 'The CIA? What? Come on, play fair, what are you talking about?'

We started comparing notes, explaining about the mystery Proton-Mail from Ray and Marsalek's hope to move the Austrian embassy to Jerusalem. Quadir, meanwhile, briefed us on Akhavan's friendships with Marsalek and the Mastercard contact. Just when I thought I had got to grips with what Wirecard was, a new trapdoor snapped open and a host of bats came flying out.

Quadir's whistleblower had urged her to contact the authorities. The criminal lawyers at the firm her fund used happened to be based in Texas, so in July Quadir had walked into the Dallas branch of the Department of Justice to speak to half a dozen prosecutors and FBI agents specializing in money laundering, digital crimes and payments. It had quickly turned into a brainstorming session about how they could recreate her work and the avenues for prosecution.

The reporting urge came surging back. I'd been concentrating on Wirecard's fake customers. What if I took a look at some of their real ones?

In North Devon, staying with my parents at the end of August, I finally switched off. We held sandcastle competitions on Instow beach

---

* An inquest into the incident, in which two people died, was ongoing.

and told the kids to keep their mouths closed when they splashed in the water, which wasn't clean enough for swimming. The pollution was at least less obvious than the mounds of brown and white foam my sister and I had played with in the same spot when we were their age. A week of Mum's cooking, lazy days and sipping wine with Charlotte as we watched sunsets over the water was a balm.

We got back to St Albans on the first Monday in September. As we were bringing everything in, I checked the post. There was no letter box; it was one of the final jobs which fell victim to the inertia which set in once the house was built. Instead we had a plastic recycling box with a sheet of wood on top. Lifting it up, I saw a big fat envelope marked 'by hand'. Pulling it open, I felt a knot in the pit of my stomach. It was Wirecard's lawsuit. I looked around, half expecting someone to be watching. It had been an abstract curiosity for so long I'd forgotten about it. Looking at my name on the first page next to that of the *FT*, it felt suddenly, nauseatingly, all too real.

For three days I hid from it. I couldn't bring myself to read any further and anyway I had other things to think about. RPC had finally summoned Murphy and me to our interviews.

27

Attack and Retreat

July 2019 – St-Tropez
Wirecard share price €152, market capitalization €19bn

A FTER HIS TRIUMPH WITH *Handelsblatt* and the Nick Gold record-ing, Jan Marsalek flew to St-Tropez. He and Markus Braun were both drawn to the French resort town with its yachts, clubs and boutiques, but their social circles were different. Braun cultivated other senior executives while Marsalek hung out with oligarchs, and that weekend there was a particularly entertaining diversion. Dissatisfied with the French police response to a number of thefts, some of Marsalek's Russian friends decided to take matters into their own hands. They left a Porsche in a driveway with the windows down, music on and boot open to display a couple of Louis Vuitton bags. Satisfied with the honey pot, their security men retired to the bushes to wait. Sure enough, it caught the interest of some passers-by. A sound beating later, they knew well enough to give the area a wide berth in the future.

Marsalek, proudly telling the story to his PR man in Munich on Sunday evening, thought the whole thing was 'brilliant', his favourite term of endorsement. He was fresh back from France, in a tight white designer T-shirt and jeans, the exposed gearwork of a Vacheron Constantin watch spinning on his wrist. Mr Samt was starting to get the measure of his client. Marsalek talked a good game, but he seemed more like the person to let others do the fighting, running in with a punch once his opponent was firmly tied to a chair.

Samt had actually started with two masters at Wirecard, reporting initially to the CFO, Alexander von Knoop. What Samt liked to do with clients was give them a large box of Kinder Surprise as a personality test. If he started to see the plastic toys dotted around the office on return visits, it was a sign of a healthy workplace. He arrived one day in the Aschheim headquarters with 108 eggs each for von Knoop and Marsalek, offering them as a small token to cheer staff; everybody loves the little reminder of childhood. Within a couple of weeks the finance director had given away most of his and thanked Samt for the idea. Marsalek's were barely touched. The box sat on a cupboard unit in his office, between a couple of his Russian *ushanka* military hats.

That Sunday Samt met Marsalek for drinks in the wine bar of the boutique Cortiina Hotel in the centre of Munich. They were planning further strategy to go after the *FT* when Markus Braun called. Samt had seen Marsalek send those to voicemail before, declining as many as thirty times in a row when he didn't want to pick up. This time he did, and Braun sounded like he'd spent the weekend stewing. 'We will need the *FT* later and we cannot afford to make them furious,' he shouted.

Marsalek was (rightly) of the opinion that the *FT* was already furious with Wirecard and unlikely to change. Yet Braun's sensitive ego couldn't seem to bear the idea that the newspaper wouldn't eventually come round and show him the respect he deserved. He continued to complain, ringing Marsalek back to shout at him again. Afterwards Samt offered himself up. Marsalek could always blame the dirty tricks on his PR guy if he needed to.

Massaging egos wasn't Mr Samt's only interest. The following Friday, 2 August, he met Marsalek again, back outside Käfer-Schänke. Thanks to their efforts to discredit the *FT*, Wirecard's share price had recovered to €150. Samt had an immodest proposal: reshaping the European financial system. Wirecard should buy Deutsche Bank, he said. It was Germany's leviathan, with €1.4tn of assets on its balance sheet, yet it had been mismanaged for years, ricocheting from one restructuring to another; the stock market value of its equity was actually less than Wirecard's €18bn. It was ripe for a takeover.

Marsalek thought this was brilliant too. He revealed there had been some exploratory discussions with the top men at Deutsche Bank earlier that year. On the eve of the Munich Security Conference, Markus Braun met Paul Achleitner, the Austrian chairman of Deutsche Bank's supervisory board, and its German CEO Christian Sewing, to deliver a pitch for turning the bank into a technology company. Marsalek had joined a second meeting a week later, but Achleitner and Sewing weren't impressed. 'They refused to talk to us,' Marsalek said.

Samt went to Käfer's newspaper stand to borrow some paper. The cashier opened a printer and pulled out a few sheets. Back at the table he began sketching out the plan in detail, explaining the lines of inquiry he'd already made. Samt had sounded out a senior figure at UBS, and the investment bank was interested in supporting the transaction by picking up pieces of its rival that Wirecard didn't want, to be carved off later.

The big question was politics. Deutsche Bank was systemically important to the whole of Europe, a financial counterweight to the dominant American investment banks. It was also a national champion, essential to Frankfurt's aspirations to be a major financial centre, and an institution whose troubles prompted nightmares in Berlin. That was why the support of UBS was so important when it came to securing political backing for a takeover. As a German-speaking Swiss bank, UBS was seen by some as the only acceptable white knight to ride in if Deutsche ever tottered. Samt said his UBS contact had made discreet enquiries in Berlin. Annegret Kramp-Karrenbauer, then a leading candidate to succeed Angela Merkel, was thought likely to support a UBS-backed Wirecard bid, along with Jörg Kukies, the former Goldman Sachs banker who was now deputy finance minister.[*] The key would be to get cornerstone Deutsche Bank investors such as Qatar and the US fund Cerberus on board, to make it a fait accompli.

---

[*] Kukies said he wasn't approached and wouldn't have blessed a takeover if he was.

Samt and Marsalek began to make personnel decisions. The chairman, Achleitner, would have to be axed immediately – too much of a canny operator. Sewing, the CEO, would be offered the supervisory board to run. It would be an audacious takeover of the decrepit by the new. The PR man jotted down a tagline for the deal: the Carnival whore buys the demented old lady. A luxury blended cognac on show inside Käfer inspired the project code name: Louis XIII.

In a deal of this magnitude, problems with Wirecard's balance sheet would disappear into the depths of Deutsche Bank, never to be seen again. And the merged company would be so big, it wouldn't be allowed to fail. Deutsche Bank did everything which mattered in banking. It had 90,000 employees, €1.4tn worth of assets, and was responsible for more than half a trillion euros in bank deposits. A takeover would be the greatest bank robbery in history. If Wirecard could pull it off, it would insert itself into the beating heart of Europe's financial system. It could do anything.

Marsalek took Samt's idea to Markus Braun and reported back; the CEO liked it, but it would be better to do it from a position of strength. They would wait for Wirecard's share price to reach €160, a €20bn market capitalization and a premium to Deutsche Bank, then they would make their move.

On 21 August Wirecard's supervisory board met in an Austrian hotel for a two-day retreat. The Schloss Fuschl commanded a peninsula at the head of a picturesque lake in the hills beyond Salzburg. Once an aristocratic hunting lodge, and still decked in the trappings of bygone glory, it was a fitting retreat for a group riven by suspicion and intrigue.

After an evening dinner on the terrace they set to work the next morning in an ornate room with high ceilings and windows offering more of the view, but the tables were arranged in a U, the chairs facing inwards. Nominally in charge was Wulf Matthias, a venerable former banker of seventy-four whose white hair was slicked back and best years were behind him. He'd run the board since 2008 and his sleepiness at times was quietly attributed to medication related to problems with his joints. The second longest-serving external director was Stefan Klestil, the venture capitalist son of a former Austrian president, who joined in 2009. He was the industry expert, having previously run a payments company. A friend of the CEO, Klestil was also on the board of Wirecard Bank and had just been elected deputy chairman in a contentious boardroom vote.

The newest man had only joined that summer. As the supervisory board needed to add a heavyweight, given the swirl of controversy around Wirecard, headhunters conducted an international search for candidates. In a coincidence, the winner from that process was a peer of Klestil at the consulting firm Roland Berger: Thomas Eichelmann. A wiry, bullet-headed man, he was by many accounts an 'asshole', although some used the term as a sort of grudging professional admiration for his brief stint as the cost-cutting CFO of Deutsche Börse, the stock exchange administrator. It was his only experience as a public company executive, and since then he'd spent a decade whipping the private investment office of a billionaire into shape. Former colleagues there remembered an effective but voluble man with a high self-regard and little tolerance of failure to meet his exacting standards. Eichelmann was clearly media-savvy, as his personal references included one from a PR man. As soon as he joined, press reports began to frame him as the chairman-in-waiting.

Of the three women present, Vuyiswa M'Cwabeni was the longest-serving and, at forty-one, the youngest. An up-and-coming career executive at SAP, German's other large new economy giant, she'd joined in 2016. The other two had arrived the previous summer, giving them just a brief taste of Wirecard's dysfunction before it was engulfed in scandal. Susana Quintana-Plaza was a Spanish engineer with a glittering career in energy, aerospace and venture capital; she had already announced her intention to leave in 2020 due to the demands of her day job at a renewables business. The final member was perhaps the most experienced boardroom operator. Anastassia Lauterbach was a self-made Russian, a polyglottal academic turned executive with a German doctorate and a string of books to her name. An expert in linguistics, reinsurance and artificial intelligence, she was a McKinsey alum who also served on the boards of Dun & Bradstreet, a corporate data provider, and the airline EasyJet.

Lauterbach clashed with Wulf Matthias almost from the beginning, exchanging tetchy emails about the board's administration. She seemed suspicious of the numbers Markus Braun had plucked from the air, a mere quintupling of revenues over the following five years to €10bn. In a July email she told Matthias that she'd asked around and no one knew the basis for the forecast. 'Teams do not support the numbers and they do not understand what they should be doing to achieve them,' she wrote, but the matter didn't make it on to the official agenda.

What the supervisory board was there to consider was the Third-Party business overseen by Jan Marsalek. Lauterbach chaired the new risk and compliance committee launched that March, which immediately commissioned consultants at her old employer McKinsey to conduct a review of procedures at Wirecard. Their verdict, on an operation which was largely run from Jan Marsalek's Telegram account, was searing. Immediate action was required to remedy the lack of controls, the report said.

At the offsite, McKinsey were coming to explain their findings, then Jan Marsalek himself was to brief the board on the future of the parts of the business he oversaw. It was a moment in which Wirecard's reliance on these third parties could be interrogated, the black box quality of the operation laid bare. However, just after 9 a.m. that morning a news story broke in *Manager Magazin*. A PR advisor interrupted proceedings to let them know. It was written by the editor-in-chief and offered an insider's account of the fight over the deputy chairmanship cast as a money-grubbing affair; the deputy got an extra €60,000 a year, on top of the €120,000 earned by the other directors. The position was available because a man even older than Matthias, Alfons Henseler, had finally retired. As the article painted it, a vicious war of words erupted between the 'brave' Lauterbach and the 'resilient' M'Cwabeni over who had been promised the gig, a 'riot' ultimately only settled by the intervention of Markus Braun in favour of Stefan Klestil.

Trapped together in a country hotel, the lake lapping outside, it was like a scene from Agatha Christie. They looked at each other knowing that someone in the room had broken the covenant of trust. (And the law – supervisory meetings are supposed to be confidential.)

Just when the supervisory board needed to focus on the dark heart of Wirecard, they were tipped into recrimination over leaks. Markus Braun (another suspect with means and motive?) called in to give the pot a stir, sharing his disgust at the unpleasant situation.

The CEO had already tried to blunt McKinsey's presentation with another angry phone call. One of the Wirecard lawyers who had supported the review was driving from Munich to the hotel that morning when he took a call from Markus Braun. The Austrian's stern voice filled the vehicle.

'Turn around. Come home, you should not attend.'

It was an order. Braun insisted that he would be the one to answer any questions.

The lawyer kept going. 'I note your protest, but I have accepted the meeting, and I won't disappoint the supervisory board.'

'Turn around. I instruct you to turn your car around and get back home.'

In the face of this tantrum by Braun the man apologized and hung up.

At the hotel, the McKinsey partners ran through the alarming deficiencies in Wirecard's business. Controls and compliance policies in the Third-Party operations barely existed. There were risks that managers could cut corners to hit internal targets, but that was just one part of it. If anyone was doing the anti-money-laundering checks required by law on the money gushing through the systems of these third parties, it wasn't Wirecard. The board appeared to be paying attention, although the lawyer noticed that Anastassia Lauterbach and Thomas Eichelmann seemed to detest each other, vying for prominence and the last word.

They also sat through Marsalek's brisk review. Instead of stepping back, asking if anything about the structure made sense, the focus was governance. Marsalek was regarded by his colleagues as Wirecard's 'chaotic genius'. Details of Third-Party Acquiring were all inside his head. The group had somehow reached the DAX without anyone seriously considering what would happen if he was hit by a bus. And by the time the offsite arrived, Wirecard's executive board had already decided on the next stage of the project: a different and cheaper set of consultants from PWC were given the mandate to implement the recommendations made by McKinsey. Somehow, when it came to the list of 'workstreams' the consultants had to deliver, the Third-Party business was left out.

In the office of Greenvale Capital above Oxford Street, Oliver Cobb never really gave up. The hacking attacks and Burkhard Ley's strange visit had convinced him and his colleagues that something wasn't right, and when Wirecard entered the DAX 30 they found an excuse to start shorting the stock again. So Cobb had been infuriated that the *FT* stories about Singapore and the Philippines didn't seem to be working. Then, in May 2019, he saw Markus Braun speak at a lunch for investors. Over the clinking of plates and cutlery he heard something which stood out, because the CEO normally avoided specifics.

Braun said that Wirecard had successfully started to lend money to its merchants. An online shopkeeper typically waited thirty days to be paid for credit card transactions, so Wirecard offered to pay them early, for a fee. It claimed to have extended €400m in such Merchant Cash Advances (MCAs), and Braun said most of the lending took place in Brazil and Turkey. Here were facts Cobb could check. Or at least, he would have checked if he and Amelie weren't trying for a baby. As the Zika virus threatening birth defects was spreading in South America, Cobb's boss Bruce Emery went instead and came back with a revelation. Wirecard's business there wasn't lending any money in Brazil, and wasn't allowed to. It was the same in Turkey; such a product was flat-out illegal. So if €400m hadn't been lent to Wirecard's merchants in those countries, where had the money gone?

Cobb's guess was that €400m had been stolen, or recycled back into Wirecard in a much larger version of Edo Kurniawan's round tripping scheme. Wary of countermeasures from the company, Greenvale launched an anonymous short seller campaign, calling itself *MCA Mathematik*. It was a hyper-reasonable version of Zatarra. Instead of the smash-and-grab approach of throwing as much mud as possible, Cobb tried to gently walk analysts up the garden path of logic: if €400m was unaccounted for, maybe that explained why a supposedly profitable and cash-rich company needed $1bn of SoftBank's money.

MCA Mathematik spoke to financial analysts and investors in their own language, offering them a puzzle to solve that prompted them to take up the issue. In August and September Greenvale added to the campaign with a series of anonymous letters to regulators, to Wirecard's supervisory board and to SoftBank. With the *FT* out of the picture due to the internal investigation, Cobb was trying his best to disrupt Wirecard's imminent fundraising.

In that respect, *MCA Mathematik* failed. The supervisory board was told by its lawyer that Ernst & Young had looked into their files and spoken to Wirecard about the €400m of lending: 'The good and most important news is that EY sees no issues that the financial statements could be wrong or that there would be any money missing that was reported (as the short sellers are indicating),' the lawyer wrote by email.

Moody's, the credit rating agency, was happy with Wirecard as well. It awarded an investment-grade credit rating to the company's inaugural €500m bond issue.* With that important label secured, and a clean audit from Ernst & Young, SoftBank handed over its promised €900m as well.

Except it turned out Akshay Naheta wasn't quite as soft in the head as Paul Murphy thought. Naheta and his colleagues spent the summer using the Japanese conglomerate's reputation, connections and resources to pitch Wirecard to various of the companies beholden to SoftBank, as well as takeover targets to Markus Braun. He also showed up in London at the party thrown by the head of the Vision Fund each year just before the final weekend at Wimbledon. At the annual meeting shareholders had waved through the proposed generous terms of the €900m convertible bond announced in April, thankful that SoftBank's backing and its strategic co-operation with Wirecard had helped to levitate the share price.

It was the trade of the decade. Even before any cash changed

---

* Bankers call the formal notice advertising details of a transaction the 'tombstone'. This one listed the banks co-ordinating Wirecard's five-year bond issue as Crédit Agricole, Deutsche Bank and ING, with joint bookrunners ABN AMRO, Citigroup, Credit Suisse and Lloyds Bank.

hands, SoftBank's investment was 'in the money', thanks to the convertible bond's terms and movements in interest rates between April and September. So there was the opportunity for a bit of ingenious financial structuring. As soon as the €900m convertible bond was issued to SoftBank, bankers at Credit Suisse arranged to sell it straight on to their clients eager for investment-grade debt. (A side benefit of Wirecard's €500m bond sale was the credit rating which made the Credit Suisse deal possible.) SoftBank immediately got its €900m back, plus cash profits of more than €60m. It also held on to some of the rights to take ownership of Wirecard stock in the future, assuming the share price remained high enough, without any of the associated financial risk. It was like flipping a house. SoftBank had bought a mansion, carved out the gamekeeper's cottage and some of the grounds, then sold what remained at a profit and laughed all the way to its Swiss bank.

Except the strange thing was that SoftBank didn't do the deal. There had always been some ambiguity about which part of the conglomerate was making the investment; was it for the benefit of the group, or for clients of the Vision Fund? As it would turn out (revealed by Paul Davies at the *Wall Street Journal*) it was neither. The SoftBank group and the Vision Fund both declined to invest. So instead it was offered to SoftBank senior staff, and an Abu Dhabi sovereign wealth fund called Mubadala that was deeply enmeshed in the Vision Fund. To them the easy money was as tempting as a Louis Vuitton bag left by the side of the road, and they snapped it up. SoftBank's involvement was to manage the juicy Wirecard investment on their behalf, earning a share of the profits.

Was it a deception? It's impossible to know how Wirecard shareholders would have reacted if the arrangements were made clear when SoftBank's investment was announced by Wirecard the previous April. (SoftBank itself was silent, as it doesn't announce such investments.) The flip to clients of Credit Suisse was also well reported. Either way, it armed Markus Braun with €1.4bn to spend, while Akshay Naheta and his colleagues had dived into the middle of a scandal and, less than six months later, waddled out with pockets full of gold. So great was the bounty, in fact, that it was only fair to tip the middleman. Christian Angermayer, the handsome psychedelic enthusiast who had brokered the deal, got his €11m from Wirecard. As a thank you, the SoftBank crew threw in another €2m on top.

Marsalek's personal conference room at Wirecard HQ contained a large plasma screen hung at the head of a table seating seven in big, heavy chairs. On 3 October, German Unity Day, one of them was filled with Burkhard Ley, Wirecard's wily former numbers man, whose shock of hair was greying and receding, now the wise counsellor who continued to advise the company as a consultant. Marsalek acted like a doting son around him. He was warm, full of compliments, and seemed intent on soliciting them back. They were there to discuss Wirecard's audacious ambition to take over Deutsche Bank. Mr Samt's Louis XIII plan, sketched on the Käfer-Schänke terrace, had progressed to become Project Panther. Over the summer Marsalek had promised his PR advisor millions of euros in fees were the audacious bid to succeed, and Samt made sure he was there to discuss next steps. Wirecard's valuation had approached but not quite reached the €20bn mark in September, and was hovering above €140. With Wirecard's coffers full of freshly borrowed money, it was time to move preparations to the next stage by commissioning McKinsey. The firm that was deemed too expensive (or effective) to implement proper compliance procedures was the ideal choice for the blue-sky thinking required to sell the deal when the moment was right.

A McKinsey team set to work. They imagined the chaotic alchemy of Wirecard let loose inside a ponderous and scandal-prone bank, then translated it into the bromides of international finance. A deal would 'fully unlock the value in the complementarity of Bank & Tech', the draft pitch deck read. McKinsey predicted an extra €6bn in profits by 2025. The combined market capitalization of the two companies could be €50bn, making them much greater than the sum of their parts. Everything was coming into view, and this imagined new Frankenstein of finance even had a name: 'WireBank'. The heist of the century was only a matter of time.

28

Exocet

September 2019 – London
Wirecard share price €157, market capitalization €19bn

T HE RPC LAWYER CONDUCTING the internal investigation at the *FT* was polite as he explained the process. He would ask questions while his mostly silent colleague next to him took notes on her laptop. They weren't recording. We sat around a table in one of the *FT*'s posher executive meeting rooms on the top floor.

I was on my best behaviour, trying to be open and relaxed, but as I knew I hadn't done anything untoward I found myself more intrigued than afraid. What on earth might they have found? The lawyer produced one of my emails from a binder. Presenting it to me, he asked if I could explain its contents. The email was from a French trader, sent to me that March. He'd mentioned that there was a way to get around BaFin's short selling ban using derivatives 'the old-fashioned way'. I only had a vague sense of what the Greek terms and trader slang he was using meant. I now explained to the RPC lawyer that I tended not to talk to this particular guy on the phone because, while he had great ideas, the combination of his thick accent and financial jargon was incomprehensible.

'And did you take up his offer?'

Nonplussed, I took a beat to realize. 'Did I personally short Wirecard, while a suspect in a German market manipulation investigation and as I was continuing to report on the company? No, I didn't do that.' Did I have to say this out loud? Reporters can't trade stocks. At least not in any company they might write about. Even back in my Citi days my access to the research floor meant I couldn't trade. My last stock transaction was to buy about £30 worth of shares in Millwall Football Club as a youth, a misguided bet on a friend's enthusiasm for their chances of promotion. The lawyer seemed satisfied. There were some more minor questions, but that was basically it. My inbox was clean.

Then he gave me the Nick Gold transcripts to read. I could tell why Wirecard resisted handing them over. At one level the whole set-up screamed dodginess. At the same time, the nightclub owner was obviously bluffing as none of the details were right – there were no invoices involved, for instance. A second conversation was shorter, a follow-up attempt by the private detective to get Gold's business partner Jonathan Dennis to blab some telling fact that had failed. It was only after we'd spent an hour going through the text line by line that the lawyer let on that, yes, there really wasn't very much to it.

Murphy's interview took longer to reach the same destination. In the end, our best guess was that Wirecard got lucky. Gold did have a sense of how we worked because Murphy had been developing him as a source that year. To begin with he'd tried to get Gold to broker an interview with Alexander Nix, the Cambridge Analytica CEO whom Gold claimed to know. Then Gold had been a source about lax money laundering controls at Flutter, owner of the Betfair exchange which allowed gamblers to lay bets with each other. In theory, it would be a neat way to move money from A to B by taking either side of obscure wagers. Using just a Gmail address, the *FT* set up an account with a gambling agency in Curaçao, the Dutch Caribbean island, as a back door into Betfair, and started trying to lose money on purpose.* The first attempt didn't go well; the 250–1 long shot Miss Recycled became the surprise winner in the 4.15 one-mile handicap at Brighton, earning the *FT* account £2,000 that, sadly, Murphy wasn't able to claim. Murphy had told Gold about the

---

* Flutter told the *FT* it conducted enhanced due diligence on all its partners, who were subject to ongoing review through the course of the relationship.

various things that can delay publication, to be as vague as possible about whether something would be published following his input. The *FT* piece about Flutter had little impact when it came out, and a day later a bid rumour (which never came to pass) pushed Flutter's share price up 20 per cent, handing Gold huge losses. In the week before 17 July Gold had called Murphy about something. He'd said he couldn't talk, he was too busy with Wirecard. It was an evergreen excuse and a throwaway comment, but it was enough to set Gold chattering. The fact Gold got the timing of the *FT* piece right was sheer blind luck.

Finally we were in the clear; we just had to wait for the official verdict to be hand-delivered to the editor's office, along with the bill. The invoice for demonstrating the *FT*'s probity came to more than 200 grand, which he cut back to £175k. With the road opening up, the only obstacle left was the German civil legal system.

Once I'd plucked up the courage to look, it turned out Wirecard's fearsome legal attack dogs were time wasters. The company was suing us using an untested law based on a European directive designed to protect trade secrets. What trade secrets had we spilled? Did forging contracts count as a special sauce these days? The whole thing was spurious, as there was a specific exemption for investigative journalism in the law, but we still had to defend the suit. The insurance kicked in (the excess adding another £100,000 to the *FT*'s mounting Wirecard tab) and I soon had a set of litigators from the German firm CMS to go with my criminal representation. They were relaxed about Wirecard's renowned lawyer Franz Enderle and his firm, which they regarded as a commercial specialist not known for its media work. One of the first surprises for us in London was the lack of forced disclosure. In a UK or a US suit, mandatory disclosure of relevant documents is when all the skeletons fall out of cupboards. Preparing for it and combing through the material which the other side is obliged to offer up is costly and time-consuming.

Germany's system was cheaper and faster. Our case would be fought essentially on the briefs, with each side getting two punches. We would respond to the suit; Wirecard would have a chance to amend its arguments; then we would have a final counter. A panel of three judges was then likely to decide the case in a trial based largely on the documents; if you didn't have them to expose that the other side was lying, well, bad luck for you. In this case I did, because Wirecard had given them to the Munich prosecutor; a draft final report from Rajah & Tann in Singapore was right there in the criminal file, directly contradicting what the company claimed in its civil suit. In a conference call with CMS, Nigel Hanson and I ran through the response. At certain points they said we should indicate people willing to testify, in case a judge did ask to hear from them. Would Stefania Palma be willing to travel from Singapore to Munich if required?

'Er, ideally not. Would that be completely necessary?' Hanson asked.

As well as the cost and inconvenience, there was the small matter of the open criminal investigation hanging over our heads.

The German lawyer said it wasn't essential. 'In that case we could perhaps identify someone such as yourself, Nigel. You could talk to Stefania and if required appear for her.'

He arched an eyebrow. 'Really? Because in the UK courts we would call that hearsay evidence.'

'Oh no, that would be quite all right,' the lawyer said.

It was an education for both of us. After the call ended and Hanson was gathering up the papers he'd covered with his usual meticulous notes, he shook his head, still digesting what he'd heard. 'The German system. It's just not robust.'

Shepherd Market is a couple of Mayfair back streets filled with bars and restaurants. It was also neutral territory, a place where various gangsters from around the capital could relax without fear of a fight with their rivals. Paul Murphy was burning a bit of shoe leather in a tiny wine bar and gallery with one of the more successful bandits, who'd once made a small fortune from the float of an Indonesian coal mine that was later found to have dug a black hole in its balance sheet. He was the sort of florid character who liked supermodels to drop by the table to chat while he was entertaining. This time, as he and Murphy sipped gin and tonics, they were joined by a source

Murphy had nicknamed the Coathanger King, an ageing English millionaire who'd sold his business years earlier, and another man who introduced himself as 'Bill', a new Wirecard source. Bill was an IT guy, he said, who'd worked on the company's systems. He started dropping all sorts of juicy hints, of the real story, of a dead body in Costa Rica, but his tale came with a catch. He was ready to fill Murphy in, but he'd like a heads up if there was going to be a story. It didn't work like that, Murphy explained.

Not long afterwards the Coathanger King tried again. He met Murphy for lunch at Franco's, a stuffy Italian on Jermyn Street with a range of Barolos to suit deep pockets. This time the bandit was explicit. Bill wanted to give Murphy the goods, he said. But if he was going to risk betraying Wirecard, he needed a payday. Bill wanted four or five days' notice of any article. Murphy glanced around him. The tables were full of pinstripes, old money and expense accounts. The King had made a packet years ago, had he fallen on hard times? Wirecard had made Murphy intensely paranoid; the whole thing felt like a set-up. In decades of conversations as a financial journalist handling sensitive information, no one had ever invited him to do anything corrupt. For the benefit of any microphones he said it again: he didn't do that and he wasn't going to. The King persisted, but eventually he said he understood. Still, the following day he tried again by phone. Bill would soon be back in the country and ready to talk. 'All he needs is a four or five days' heads up on when you are going to publish.'

We briefly considered trying to turn the tables with a sting of our own, but given our previous record, trying to be cute again seemed likely to backfire. Another story about tip-offs and market manipulation wasn't going to help matters. We had to change the subject. My Wirecard accounting fraud story was coming along, but we were also pushing to write that Marsalek had been waving around top-secret documents about the Russian poison Novichok. It would catch the company off guard, not to mention grab the attention of every intelligence agency out there. Lionel Barber didn't see it that way. The editor thought the nerve gas line was so left-field that people simply wouldn't believe it. It would read like a desperate retribution for the

Nick Gold affair. He wanted a straightforward, unimpeachable case that Wirecard was a fraud.

I was getting there. At the start of October 2019 I flew to Dublin to meet a new whistleblower, 'Dale', who filled me in about life at Wirecard's Irish outpost. Like the rest of the company, it was perpetually short of cash. Wirecard UK & Ireland was still based in the old G2Pay office in Ulysses House, and its day-to-day business was tiny. It administered voucher programmes for companies like Vodafone. The rest of its revenues were commissions from Al Alam in Dubai, which I thought were all fake, so after my meeting with Dale I went to visit. Wirecard was on the first floor, its reception empty. I rang the bell and, when someone eventually appeared, I said I was there to see the finance director, Alan White. The guy who answered was casually dressed and didn't ask who I was, he just showed me in and left me standing outside the glass door to Alan's office. I could see he was on the phone; he gave me a wave and carried on talking. The radio was on, playing Florence and the Machine's 'Dog Days Are Over', and I had plenty of time to take in the layout. It was mostly open-space, about fifteen metres long and untidy. There were two offices at the end, Alan's and another of the same size. On the walls were accumulated posters and calendars of old projects. Only two desks were occupied, by long-standing employees judging by the amount of dusty knick-knacks and junk on them. A tinny Crowded House 'Don't Dream It's Over' was next on the playlist, which gave way to Eagle-Eye Cherry's 'Save Tonight'. Loitering by an empty desk and a shelving unit filled with binders, I resisted the temptation to pick up one marked 'UAE invoices 2018' and flick through. I peered back into Alan's office; he was still chatting away. It was becoming awkward, so the man showed me to the boardroom behind the reception area. With time to kill, I let Murphy know I was inside, and he updated me on progress with my Wirecard story; the latest edit of the copy was with the German lawyers for a once-over.

After five minutes, Alan came in. 'Hello?' He was tall, balding, in a pale-green jumper. He had an office build: narrow shoulders, pot belly. There was an impatient, possibly arrogant air about him. I introduced myself and stuck out a hand. He looked startled, took a step back and crossed his arms. 'I'm not going to talk to you.'

'I thought you might be interested to hear . . .'

'I have a fair idea of what you want to talk about and I'm not going to get into it with you.' I tried again but he was resolute. 'If you have any dealings we put 'em in writing.'

'Al Alam?' I ventured.

'This is the end of the conversation. I am absolutely not interested.'

He opened the door into the reception, walked me out to the stairs and I left. That was fun, I thought.

This time Murphy's recommendation was the Horseshoe Bar in the landmark Shelbourne Hotel as a place where senior police, politicians and hacks might mingle. It was too early to tell if he was right because it was closed, so I had a glass with the wrinkly tourists in the main bar to celebrate this latest piece of evidence to throw on the mounting pile. Dublin was supposed to be Wirecard's second-largest outpost, judged by its profits on paper. For 2018, internal Wirecard budgets had predicted sales of €230m and Ebitda of €108m. (From those various budgets, sent out to each country by Edo Kurniawan in Singapore, I'd pieced together a spreadsheet I called The Enchilada: a financial map of the whole company. There was also a file which gave a breakdown of Wirecard's business by product, another big clue. It was password-protected, but Kurniawan was sent the key 'WDPayment$' in a separate email.)

The Guinness tasted just the same as every other one I'd had, and it was good. I was closing in, and I wondered what Marsalek and Braun had done with their time to prepare, if they had any inkling of what was coming or if my visit would spark a new round of countermeasures.

Indeed, we faced the question of how to approach the company again. I'd cornered Wirecard into claiming that the key spreadsheet with the non-existent customers was 'inauthentic', but that response from the company, through Herbert Smith, was two months old. To publish now, and to remain professional, would mean going back to Wirecard with fresh questions about Al Alam in Dubai and its fake customers. That would give Marsalek another opportunity to come up with some outlandish explanation. Murphy's idea was to distract Wirecard from the spreadsheet and throw them off balance: before asking again about the fake customers, we threw in a selection of eye-catching queries about Jan Marsalek's extracurricular interests. Why was he working with a CIA operative and the Austrian Far Right to move the location of the embassy in Israel to Jerusalem? Why had his interest in Libyan cement plants not been disclosed to shareholders?

The questions were sent to Wirecard on the evening of Thursday, 10 October, without any deadline for comment. First thing on Monday morning I chased for the responses 'without delay'. They arrived that evening and we were ready. Lionel Barber's instructions had been clear. 'I want us to draw blood. I want an Exocet missile. I want them dead.' On Tuesday, 15 October we took aim and fired.

29

Chasing the Joker

15 October 2019 – Aschheim
Wirecard share price €108, market capitalization €13bn

'SUSPECT ACCOUNTING PRACTICES REVEALED' blared the *FT* headline on 15 October. It was a warm and sunny Tuesday in Aschheim, and Markus Braun took refuge in denial as the Wirecard share price crashed. The CEO personally called analysts to brush off the allegations as more of the same, even as most of those around him realized they weren't; the allegations of fake customers and invented profits were too serious. Alongside the news story, the *FT* had published the spreadsheet showing all the names of these imaginary clients, plus their fictitious revenue and profit figures. What's more, it had published a selection of internal emails and chat transcripts showing Wirecard's finance team discussing the spreadsheet which Braun was now trying to tell the outside world wasn't real. The evidence was overwhelming and demanded an explanation. The obvious answer was to hire an independent set of accountants to definitively review everything, the same process which had brought Ernst & Young into Wirecard a decade earlier. If the company didn't offer to investigate itself, then it was surely inviting the blue lights and uniforms to intervene.

To begin with, Jan Marsalek told people a special audit wasn't necessary, the whole thing would blow over like it always did, and the finance team was already exhausted by the strain from the year of controversy. Their intransigence couldn't last. Anastassia Lauterbach on the supervisory board had raised the possibility of a special audit as soon as the regular one finished that year. Thomas Eichelmann, the new arrival and head of the board's audit committee, leaned in, so did the SoftBank executives who had a stake in the company's future. Outside the company a drum beat of protest from shareholders and analysts was building. By Friday the 18th, Markus Braun even professed to be relaxed about the prospect. The only question was which accounting firm to choose.

Wirecard's chairman Wulf Matthias was out of the loop. That day *MCA Mathematik* published the letters it had sent to the board in August and September, and joined the voices calling for a forensic audit. The *FT*'s Frankfurt correspondent, Olaf Storbeck, reached Wulf Matthias for comment and he was dismissive: 'It is just an impertinence at the moment. We have endless anecdotes, three per day. I have not looked at them in further detail as I have other things to do. It is just another attempt to write things in one direction.' The chairman said there was no need for a special audit, as 'EY is evaluating the matter sufficiently.' Within hours he was contradicted. *Manager Magazin* got the news; a special audit was coming. There was only ever one serious candidate, Braun's *alma mater* KPMG. That weekend it got the gig to look afresh at everything: the allegations from the *FT*, from MCA, and any other lingering areas of concern. The firm would report to the supervisory board, and it was to consider arrangements with all three of the suspect partners: Al Alam in Dubai, Henry O'Sullivan's Senjo in Singapore and Christopher Bauer's PayEasy in Manila. The announcement purchased time – almost six months of breathing space – before KPMG's report would be published. The question was what to do with it.

The fifth of November was special for Markus Braun; his fiftieth birthday. He was up early, welcoming Germany's deputy finance minister, Jörg Kukies, to the Wirecard HQ for an 8.30 meeting. Kukies, a former co-chief executive of Goldman Sachs, was no slouch, and Braun stayed in his comfort zone up in the blue sky of German international competitiveness. Start-ups needed more venture capital finance to succeed, was his considered view. He bent Kukies's ear about taking Crypto mainstream; Wirecard's prepaid card service could be used to transact Bitcoin, if the regulations were supportive. Then it was on to a curious bugbear. Due to Europe's lack of other technology companies, its financial institutions had to rely on the American giants if they wished to store their data in the cloud.

Shortly after they spoke that day, Braun announced a transaction Wirecard had prepared for months, its entry into China with the €109m purchase of a Beijing payments company, Allscore. To ease the way it had hired the former defence and economics minister Karl-Theodore zu Guttenberg and the former intelligence service commissioner Klaus-Dieter Fritsche as consultants to lobby for support earlier in the year, with apparent success: on a trip to the country that September Chancellor Angela Merkel had raised the Wirecard deal with Chinese officials.*

The day after his birthday, Braun spoke to analysts on a conference call to discuss the third-quarter results. He was in black turtleneck mode, addressing them from one of the all-white meeting rooms in Aschheim. The first question was about the special audit, and Braun giggled at his own metaphor for the cycle of accounting allegations and company denials. 'There was this film with Bill Murray called *Groundhog Day*. So the KPMG approach is bringing this really to an end.'

The special audit, meanwhile, was off to a slow start. A group of forty forensic accountants from KPMG had begun their work, publicly promised access to all areas, whatever documents they needed. Regular meetings began in the Wirecard legal department which occupied the ground floor of building 28 on the Aschheim campus. There were normally three or four representatives each from Ernst & Young and KPMG. On the Wirecard side regular attendees were Jan Marsalek and Stephan von Erffa, the company's aristocratic deputy

---

* Merkel's travels in 2020 also took her to New Delhi, where she visited a metro station equipped with solar panels funded by a German development bank to publicize a Green transport initiative. While there she posed for the world's press at a stand for electric rickshaws operated by the company SmartE that, in a remarkable coincidence, was backed by O'Sullivan's Mauritius fund 1A.

CFO, who had been a lynchpin of the finance team for more than a decade and was developing a reputation for plum-faced shouting as his approach to managing stress.

An older woman from the finance team, Dagmar Schneider, seemed to be co-ordinating everything. She had worked closely with Marsalek for a year, and was in regular Telegram chat contact. For instance, after the *FT* had published pictures of Christopher Bauer's office in Manila, where the payments operation PayEasy shared space with his bus company, Marsalek told her the partner was irritated, and that he'd been surprised to get a call from the son of President Rodrigo Duterte about it, who Marsalek said regarded it as Wirecard's problem to fix.

Schneider replied: 'I have no idea how we should react. As you say – nothing is clear, everything just insinuated.'

'Yes, that's the problem. I have been working on this for hours, and somehow this is really tricky.'

What version of the truth Marsalek was feeding Schneider is impossible to say. She knew enough about him to broach one menacing idea: 'I opt for YOUR Russians. They should generate some silence for us.'

The meetings with Ernst & Young and KPMG were joined by a couple of legal staff as well. One of the surprises was the confidence held by EY. Martin Dahmen and his EY colleagues in particular talked about their understanding of the Third-Party arrangements. They were used to dealing with the mindset of a growing start-up; they knew how a fast-paced environment worked, how IT worked. Wirecard's processes were not ideal, but they were open to working with them. The lawyer who had helped McKinsey's review of compliance and struggled to get his own grasp of Marsalek's black box empire marvelled at EY's apparent certainty.

KPMG, by comparison, were sticklers. The two veteran partners running it, Sven-Olaf Leitz and Alexander Geschonneck, came from a very traditional bank audit point of view. They expected policies and procedures, with everything documented. If someone had ordered a box of pencils, they wanted to see the procurement order. They were in for disappointment. Wirecard's freewheeling culture and resistance to record-keeping was set from the top. KPMG kept requesting meetings which didn't happen. In late November, Oliver Bellenhaus finally flew from Dubai for the day, grumpily tolerating the inquisition and supplying bare-bones answers. He left the accountants with more questions than they'd started with, and refused to come back. Dagmar Schneider informed the group that Bellenhaus was burnt out and needed a vacation; they shouldn't expect to see him that side of Christmas.

Jan Marsalek remained unruffled as he slow-walked the special audit which took up most of his time. His only complaint was about his back, which still troubled him. He'd even experimented with an inversion board at home, strapping his ankles in and flipping upside down without heed to the instructions for calibrating the balance. He found himself stuck, alone, the blood rushing to his head and in danger of passing out, his phone just out of reach. Bright red, swinging at full stretch, he got a fingertip to it and called for help. He still recommended it to friends after that, just with a warning to be careful.

At work, he and Andrea Görres, Wirecard's general counsel, camped out in Marsalek's penthouse conference room for several hours a day to deal with issues and requests raised by KPMG. Arriving one Monday evening in December, however, Mr Samt found Marsalek alone in his corner office. Inside were Marsalek's Russian hats and the box of Kinder Eggs (still three-quarters full). There was also a set of wooden *matryoshka* nesting dolls; Vladimir Putin was the largest, with the former Russian leaders inside all the way down to a tiny Lenin. In the drawers Marsalek kept a selection of eggshell-blue Tiffany bags, pre-purchased in bulk for his long-suffering partner Viola, whose plans were at the whim of his hectic schedule. 'Is this an €8,000 apology or a €12,000 one,' he once mused while selecting the appropriate trinket. On the floor next to Marsalek's desk was a spherical PC, a designer computer which Marsalek never appeared to use. He always had his personal MacBook with him, secured with a safety-conscious passcode: three German letters, three numbers and an exclamation mark. The desk was clear except for a red 'Make America Great Again' cap, to go with the life-size cardboard cut-out of Donald Trump next to it.

As usual Marsalek was running behind that day, so Samt had taken a detour to a nearby mall to kill time. He loaded up on gourmet chocolates and biscuits, then wandered into a store stocked with Lego. It meant he arrived with a gift, a €39 Batmobile kit called 'Chasing the Joker'. Laughing, Marsalek tore it open and began to build. Samt sat down; for €850 per hour he would happily play Lego. They talked while they assembled the pieces. Marsalek took a call from Viola; he was supposed to be having dinner that evening with her and his father. He said he was still busy, he would be there later. Marsalek continued to put together his new toy. As time wore on Viola called a few more times. The table was reserved and they should go ahead without him, Marsalek said. He would join when he could. 'Tell my father there is food served in Munich after 9 p.m.' It was evident he didn't want to go. When Samt said goodbye, Marsalek asked him to leave the cookies behind. On his next visit the Batmobile was displayed on the desk next to the Maga cap. The Joker was nowhere to be seen.

30

Tradecraft

November 2019 – Mayfair, London – Wirecard
share price €121, market capitalization €15bn

TUCKED AWAY INSIDE CLARIDGE'S Hotel was the Fumoir, a cocktail bar of heavy wood, velvet banquettes and gilded mirrors. Its lack of windows and discreet corners made it ideal for assignations, backroom dealings and double agents. Paul Murphy arrived to find Nick Gold waiting for him, with a former copper called Jon whose morals and loyalty were negotiable.

At the time, Jon's motivations were brushed over. He came from the overlapping circles of bodybuilders and martial artists, ex-Services types trading on a spooky mystique, and grunts with negotiable morals and a taste for subterfuge that supplied London's bouncers, bodyguards and private detectives. Murphy assumed that after Marsalek's sting Gold had put the word out and was paying Jon to sing. (In Gold's version of events it was a matter of charisma. Jon had seen him holding court in the Chiltern Firehouse, dancing with the waiters, jumping over the bar to pour drinks, schmoozing one and all, and it had prompted an attack of conscience. Jon was Jewish too, and couldn't live with his part in trying to destroy such a generous-hearted guy.)

Murphy was paranoid about dirty tricks and wary, as Jon's stories were hard to believe. He spied on journalists all the time, it was incredibly common, he said. Challenged for proof, Jon thought. '*FT* people, hmm. Do you know a guy called Kadhim Shubber? Yeah, we have loads of stuff on him.' Murphy knew him well. Kadhim was a sharp young Iraqi hack raised in Derry, Northern Ireland. At that point he was in the US, but he'd previously written for *FT* Alphaville in London, earning a reputation as the 'Unicorn Slayer' for his exposés of overhyped British tech companies. 'Actually, I have a copy of his mother's passport.' Jon looked at his phone for a second, then sent over a picture of the passport flat on a table. He seemed to relish Murphy's shock.

There was more. Jon described sprawling snooping operations. It wasn't just Paul Murphy and me who had been targeted. More than thirty private detectives were running around London with hidden cameras trying to find evidence of short sellers colluding. Those involved were told that the police were aware of their activities, and that it was the largest private surveillance operation ever conducted in the country (for obvious reasons an impossible-to-verify fact). They were sticking to non-electronic methods, aiming for material which could stand up in court. Overseeing the project was a Manchester private detective, Greg Raynor. It was his firm, APG Protection, which had secretly recorded Nick Gold. Jon said a former MI5 agent, Hayley Elvins, was organizing the grunts on the ground. The cost was staggering, around £18,000 a day for the multi-week operation.

Were Wirecard shareholders funding this?

Jon said the person at the centre of it all was an extremely paranoid man who went by the name 'Dr Rami' and claimed to be a large Wirecard shareholder. He lived in an apartment in the Raffles Hotel in Istanbul, and when he came to London he always stayed at the Dorchester in Mayfair, barely leaving the premises. It was where he'd met representatives of the UK market regulator, the Financial Conduct Authority, in a two-and-a-half-hour meeting where he presumably urged them to investigate the corrupt *FT*. Dr Rami spent most of his time in the Dorchester main bar or its Cantonese restaurant, China Tang. When Dr Rami's doll-like girlfriend wanted to go shopping he had her escorted. The close protection team even accompanied him in the lift up to his room each night, and he didn't trust the hotel's safe. Instead he gave his passport to Jon for safekeeping. His full name was Rami El Obeidi. After Muammar Gaddafi was killed in 2011, Dr Rami became the head of foreign intelligence for the transitional government which briefly took over in the chaos. He was a Libyan spymaster.

Murphy left this briefing staggered by what we were up against and driven to expose the people who had set him up. We'd been picking up hints of Marsalek's intelligence connections, his Libyan business interests for a while, but this was something new.

Back at the office, Murphy laid out what he'd heard, including a contingency plan that Jon said he considered.

'One option, not yet acted on, is to plant drugs in your car and call the cops.'

'Huh, that would be interesting.'

Was it reassuring that they hadn't? My world was so far removed from normal I wasn't sure any more. So this is what it's like to have enemies. I imagined the knock. Hello officer, yes that is my car. Look, this might take a while, you better come in, I've got the number for the editor of the *Financial Times* here . . . Much later, when we learned more about Jon, Murphy and I began to wonder whether everything he told us was reliable, but at the time, the journalist part of my brain relished each twist: just wait till everyone gets a load of this. We were on to them, that was the relief, the consolation. It was only at home, talking to Charlotte, which made real what I'd brought to our door; it could blow up our lives.

'I feel sick to my stomach. You know how the world works, it's the people with the most money who win,' she said.

While I focused on Wirecard's business, Murphy was on a mission. He set about trying to get more evidence on the spies, contacting Hayley Elvins and trying to flip her. The gloves were off. The choice he offered was the one which motivates many a source: co-operate and get anonymity, potentially a more sympathetic hearing. Refuse and you'll be exposed, with everything that means for your reputation. What Murphy should perhaps have avoided doing was sending text messages at 11 p.m. on a Friday night which made that choice quite so explicit. 'I can obv see the damage to your firm we are about to do,' he wrote in one. Invoking the Security Service contacts of the editor and a senior *FT* columnist in another was also a little unwise:

'Lionel Barber and Philip Stephens are close with the top people at both 5 and 6. Work with me and I promise we won't fuck you over.'

A complaint landed from her law firm (helpfully confirming that she was a former counter-terrorism specialist).* After everything we'd just been through with the internal inquiry, the editor was furious. We were in the middle of a very public battle and we couldn't afford to put a foot wrong. (Never mind bragging about someone else's sensitive sources.) Murphy was hauled in for a bollocking and he looked worried. He had a suit and tie on, for starters. 'I think Lionel might actually fire me this time,' he said. That was never going to happen, and while Murphy offered his resignation, he also stood his ground as the temperature rose. 'Where do you think these stories come from? They don't just float in through the window.'

What did waft in next was a pile of evidence from the three-week spying operation called 'Palldium phase 2'. We skimmed through timed and dated surveillance pics of various targets from the last weeks of October. The grunts had followed Nick Gold, and had the Coathanger King at the door of Gold's office. There were photos of Zatarra's Matt Earl in a coffee shop, and his playboy friend Brett Palos on the street. Fraser Perring was caught close up, standing on a train platform in a body warmer and flat cap, no sign of a cane or cast. 'Hang on a second,' I said, going back through the pile. 'Are we sure that's Matt?' I checked and the pictures of someone buying coffee couldn't be him; he was on holiday on the other side of the world. Then Murphy showed one to Crispin Odey, a British hedge fund manager who had a long-standing public short position in Wirecard. His response: 'I'll admit that chap does look a bit like me. But I don't have a red phone and never in my life have I worn a pair of yellow trainers.'

I started taking absurd precautions, half-remembered tradecraft from spy novels. On the way to meet sources on the Tube I'd wait until the warning beeps at my stop, only stepping out just before the doors

---

* Elvins, Raynor and APG all denied any involvement in operations to surveille or discredit journalists and said they had done nothing illegal. It was unclear whom Jon discussed the drug-planting gambit with or if it was ever taken seriously: Raynor said he knew nothing about it and would have rejected it out of hand if he had.

closed. There I'd be, standing on an almost empty platform, spinning around like a madman to see if anyone else had rushed off. In conversations it had become automatic to add lawyerly qualifications for the benefit of any recording devices. On another trip to Ireland I stayed with friends on the coast outside Dublin. It was a joy to see them, and the out-of-the-way location gave me confidence I hadn't been followed when I met a new whistleblower the next morning, Simon Smaul the former G2Pay salesman, at the Mespil Hotel, away from the main life of the city. We spent hours in its café as rain drummed on the windows, eating club sandwiches in Jan Marsalek's honour as Smaul ran me through his history with G2Pay, Wirecard and Sunsont. He was nervous, and it was clear he had things to get off his chest, that he'd been conflicted by his knowledge as an insider. Watching the company's rise, he'd known enough to be suspicious of its incredible financial performance, but he'd been too wary of the people involved and too far removed to do anything beyond post helpful comments on *FT* Alphaville.

Smaul's insight into the early days boosted my conviction that Wirecard's accounting fraud had started in at least 2010, and that its Third-Party Acquiring business made no sense at all. What the company claimed to be doing with its three partners – Al Alam, Senjo and PayEasy – was processing payments for multiple currencies in multiple time zones. Just reconciling one twenty-four-hour batch of payments would be heroically complicated. Then throw in the claims for refunds which characterize high-risk payments processing; for the huge volumes Wirecard was supposedly sending through these partners, they would need hundreds of staff just to deal with the admin, and there was no sign of them. Smaul also helped with a fundamental question: where was all the money?

I knew there was no cash to spare at all in Wirecard's business. It was something I'd heard from whistleblowers all over the globe and could see in Edo Kurniawan's emails. Money was always tight. Yet bank balances are supposed to be straightforward for auditors to verify, and Wirecard's balance sheet was overflowing with cash. The cover story for the Third-Party arrangements seemed to have been pieced together from business experiments which Marsalek had tried and failed, in the same way the customer names were those Wirecard had lost or failed to win in the first place. Some of the documents the *FT* had published referred to large sums in something called 'trustee accounts'. There was no explanation, but Smaul's tale of the trustee who had run off in Israel pointed to a possible answer. Maybe Wirecard claimed its cash was held in trust somewhere.

In London I found a weird document in the trove. On April Fools' Day 2017, Edo Kurniawan sent Wirecard's deputy CFO a draft accounting opinion written inside an Excel spreadsheet. It suggested there was an argument with Ernst & Young over what constituted cash on the balance sheet, as the timing was just before the firm signed off the 2016 annual figures. The opinion, which showed traces of the Indonesian's grammar, said, 'management believe that trust accounts held in third-party acquiring business is cash equivalent, part of operating cash flow and not restricted.' To put it another way, Wirecard was leaning on the bonnet of a Bentley. When the auditors asked to see the keys it pointed to a friend across the street who held them up and gave them a jangle. 'Don't worry, we can take it for a drive whenever we like.'

The timing made sense. From 2010 to 2014 it looked like Wirecard invented sales using takeovers in Asia, then hid the hole in its balance sheet using the spinning wheel of payment processing; that was the stack of unpaid invoices left behind by the adjusted versions of its financial statements. When I showed up asking questions, the fraud had to change; there was one more big fraudulent transaction in India in 2015. Maybe that was a pot of escape money in case it all went south. By the end of 2016 the Third-Party Acquiring scam was in place. If Wirecard had found a way to fake cash balances, then it must have been plain sailing after that; each year they added another zero. That would explain why there were only three partners producing so much sales and profit; Marsalek didn't need any more.

When I asked Wirecard about the trustee accounts at the start of December, the company surprised us all by coming back with an offer. Suddenly, after a year of hand-to-hand combat, Markus Braun wanted to give the *FT* an interview. Except it came with terms. He wouldn't talk to me. The *FT*'s Frankfurt correspondent, Olaf Storbeck, was invited for a two-hour meeting with Braun in his Aschheim office. Lionel Barber or Roula Khalaf, his deputy, who was about to take over in the New Year, would be welcome to join in by phone. It would be on the record, but for reasons of 'compliance' discussion of the Third-Party business had to be off the record.

Letting the company choose which journalist it dealt with was out of the question, but could I even go to Germany? Was it safe, would I be arrested? Unlikely, said my criminal lawyer, the investigation had gone in another direction. As for the personal risk, I was tempted; it could be my only chance to look Markus Braun in the eye. However, if we listened to him we would have an obligation to print at least some of what he said, which would serve his purpose of normalizing the company. Murphy and I came back to the question of who gets a journalistic ear. Wirecard had forfeited that right through its smears, lawsuit and army of spies. We argued it all had to be on the record, including the Third-Party business, or not at all. The *FT* declined.

When Murphy's spy story was published he was in Mozambique, so I went down to the *FT* post room to collect Dr Rami's thank you: he asked the concierge of the Dorchester to drop round a £500 spa voucher and £500 of roses '(if possible slightly thorny)'. He got two dozen large, plump flowers for the money, with his email stapled indiscreetly to the side of the bag. His message to Paul read: 'I am grateful for the recent press coverage you have given me. I am uncertain as to why I deserve that much of an honour but I appreciate the attention.' Dr Rami had asked for the text in a medium size and 'elegant font'. I was chuckling away when the thought suddenly occurred: was this a trick? The flowers still stood in the hatch to the post room. 'Did you check them out?' I asked the guy inside.

'What do you mean? No, we didn't run them through the X-ray.' It was a bunch of flowers, why would he do that? Without really thinking about what I was saying, I offhandedly mentioned they were from a Libyan spy who'd been keeping us under surveillance. Wide-eyed, he sent the post room into full suspicious package mode. A metal grille whirred down to seal the hatch. Five minutes later it trundled back up and he handed me the tousled bouquet. 'Yeah, it's just a bunch of flowers.' I gave them to the church next door, the St Nicholas Cole Abbey. There was a brief flurry of excitement that the gift card might go into the Christmas charity raffle as a prize. However, the compliance team got hold of it and it was never seen again.

The week ended on a high when the magazine *Wirtschaftswoche* published an in-depth investigation into Al Alam. The article said Al Alam seemed to be run by Oliver Bellenhaus and three staff. I was delighted to see that a couple of German hacks had actually taken the trouble to fly there and follow up rather than take Wirecard's word for it. (We were so pleased, in fact, that Murphy handed the lead reporter, Melanie Bergermann, a copy of the document trove on a USB stick to inform her future reporting.)

It had taken a year, but it felt like we were finally cutting through. On the Friday before Christmas, however, there was a reminder that Wirecard's tactics were spreading. The American short seller Carson Block launched an attack on a FTSE 100 hospital group called NMC Health. Block had unwittingly scooped the *FT*'s Cynthia O'Murchu and Robert Smith, who rushed out an *FT* story about hidden off-balance-sheet debt. Just like Wirecard, NMC was audited by Ernst & Young and used FTI Consulting for its public relations. An NMC Health official statement called the story 'the latest in a long line of malicious attempts by certain parties to influence commentary around the company . . . via methods which are at times nefarious, unethical and illegal'.

We'd already caught FTI trying to get the *Mail on Sunday* to reprint the *Manila Standard* allegations, but this was out in public. The impunity of it rankled. Three FTI staff were named on the press release calling our colleagues crooks: Brett Pollard, Victoria Foster Mitchell and Shane Dolan. Murphy had also heard that FTI was briefing journalists at other organizations that he was to be fired as soon as Wirecard's special audit was finished. He wanted Lionel Barber to go nuclear, to issue a press release announcing that FTI had lost all privileges. 'Their entire business rests on access to journalists. They can't lie about us one day then turn around and ask us to trust them the next. Cut them off and see how long their clients stick with them.' Lionel Barber, about to begin the final month of his long tenure, didn't go that far. Instead, after a festive lunch, he made the call in front of the main news desk to give them some sport. He put on a theatrical swearing routine as he harangued the head of FTI for taking dirty money and said that this was their very last chance. 'Otherwise we'll have nothing to do with you people.'

31

Closing the Border

2019 – Vienna
Wirecard share price €144, market capitalization €18bn

IN MAY 2019, A SCOOP caused the collapse of the Austrian coalition government. *Der Spiegel* and *Süddeutsche Zeitung* published a video taken at a luxury villa in Ibiza, in which a woman posing as the niece of a Russian oligarch told the head of the far-right Freedom Party that she might purchase Austria's most widely read tabloid. He then suggested, so long as it was legal, he could offer lucrative government contracts in return for media favours. All the fuss, and the early election which resulted, led the *FT*'s new Switzerland and Austria correspondent, Sam Jones, to spend far more time in Vienna than he'd anticipated.

While Murphy and I had been battling Wirecard that year, Jones was preparing to move from the investigations team to his new beat in Geneva, showing us for entertainment the selection of basements and cupboards that were in reach of his meagre housing allowance. Before Jones left, Paul Murphy had asked him to look into Jan Marsalek's dealings in Vienna. We wanted an on-the-ground perspective, and it was a classic Murphy gumshoe request, to dig into the networks in Marsalek's home town. He promised air cover to keep the news desk off Jones's back if he needed it. Sure, Jones said, not fancying his chances of landing in Austria for a week and picking up the threads of an international conspiracy.

On the ground, he found there were plenty of corrupt shenanigans going on, and the approach Jones took to getting stories was to start by finding interesting people. One of those was a political figure, Stephanie Krisper, who had insight into some of the more fascinating Austrian affairs. Jones met her several times, and was invited to her office on Ringstrasse, the grand boulevard of architectural confections in the city centre. The office was an immense fin-de-siècle space in the neo-baroque style, with a small collection of modern bureaucratic furniture in the middle dwarfed by its surroundings. The politician was there with a couple of officials in tow, piles of paper and pages scattered all about. Jones chatted for a while. Only at the end he ventured: 'You don't happen to know, or, er, have come across this guy called Jan Marsalek do you?'

For a moment Krisper's guard dropped. A light clearly went on and her eyes flicked to the others in the room; an inconvenient audience. 'Yes, yes, I have heard of that name and I'll come back to you. Why are you interested in him?' Jones explained that his colleagues were investigating this fellow and he seemed to have all of these suspicious political connections. Inside, he was thinking: oh my God Murphy was right. 'I'll have to see,' she said, and Jones was ushered out.

The next time they met was a Saturday afternoon in the autumn of 2019, on the Danube; a moored floating restaurant. Krisper ordered coffee, while Jones drank beer. There was someone who knew Marsalek, a humanitarian who was very concerned about their personal safety. She said she trusted Jones, that she would encourage this friend to speak. If he was willing, he would be in touch. Jones, his reporting radar pinging like crazy, urged the politician to let him know.

The call came the next morning. Jones was at the Hilton Plaza, a five-star mock-Viennese modernist treat that he could finagle through *FT* expenses. He was packing, due on the night train back to Zurich, when the phone rang. The humanitarian was on a similarly tight schedule to get to the airport. There was a half-hour window at 5.30 p.m. Jones paced back and forth in the room, buoyant at the prospect of this mystery encounter.

He arrived early. Café Prückel was an iconic part of Vienna's coffee house scene, its interior preserved untouched since the 1950s. Jones didn't see anyone who looked likely, so he picked a quiet spot, placed a two-day-old copy of the *FT* on the table to indicate his presence, and ordered a beer. Five minutes later the politician arrived with her friend, a heavy-set man in a long overcoat, and set the ground rules. The conversation was for Jones's background knowledge only, there could be no identification of the source whatsoever due to the dangers. Jones agreed, then marvelled at the story which unfolded. Kilian Kleinschmidt lived in North Africa and was tanned, with receding blond hair and a grey stubble beard. German, at the age of eighteen he left for the Pyrenees, where he made goat's cheese and helped found a co-operative. In the late 1980s he set off on his motorcycle looking for adventure. Riding across the Sahara, he made friends at a bar and joined them building a school; the beginning of his humanitarian career. He joined the UN and worked at the sharp end. He was head of the UN High Commission for Refugees in Mogadishu, Somalia when a US Black Hawk helicopter famously went down. He spent time with the Tamil Tigers in Sri Lanka, and in 1997 got 40,000 people out of the Congo in an airlift. There were five years in Pakistan, and a hostage situation, just one of the tough, complex assignments he took on. He ran a refugee camp in Jordan for 100,000 Syrian refugees. Kleinschmidt had faced torture and suicide attacks. He did not scare easily, but whatever Marsalek was involved with had him spooked. He'd tried to raise it with an Austrian ambassador in Africa, and the diplomat had looked at him with concern. 'How do you know I'm not one of them?' He was relieved to finally have someone who was interested. Jones only had a tiny pocket notebook, and as he furiously scribbled he realized they had just fifteen minutes left. Was this the only chance he'd get?

Where Kleinschmidt and Marsalek crossed paths was the defining political issue of the time: migration. In 2015 there were a million people on the move and parts of Europe were overwhelmed. Kleinschmidt had left the UN, set up on his own as a consultant, and was advising the Austrian Interior Ministry on policy. After the first rush, the big question became how to prevent these flows of people at source. In 2016 Kleinschmidt was invited to a meeting with an

Austrian billionaire known as a bridge between the East and the West; before the wall fell he did business with the Stasi, the East German secret police, who called him 'The Count', and for a while owned a casino with the Palestinian leader Yasser Arafat. Also there was the head of one of Europe's largest construction groups. They wanted to do something on migration in Egypt, so Kleinschmidt wrote a paper on stabilization, advocating solutions such as refugee cities and special economic zones. What the money men appear to have wanted was his good name as an expert behind the idea of controlling migrant flows, because immigration won elections.

In May 2017 Sebastian Kurz, the future Austrian chancellor who was then foreign minister, travelled to Libya to use Tripoli as a backdrop for some of his right-wing talking points: 'migrants who are saved in the Mediterranean should not be guaranteed a ticket to Central Europe', etc. Kleinschmidt said that shortly afterwards he was approached by Wolfgang Gattringer, a former official at the Austrian Ministry of the Interior, who invited him to meet a good client of his to discuss a project in Libya. In June, Kleinschmidt met this client for lunch on the terrace of Käfer-Schänke in Munich: Jan Marsalek.

Trying to compete with Kleinschmidt's tales of derring-do in the world's hotspots, Marsalek talked about his own trip to Syria as a guest of the Russian military, just after Isis had been forced out of Palmyra. (The trip put Marsalek on the radar of at least one intelligence agency in the region. He omitted to tell Kleinschmidt the part told to Marsalek's friends by the fixer who took him to Syria, that Marsalek arrived with the finest body armour and helmet money can buy. As the soldiers admired the mix of kevlar and carbon fibre, one of them gave him bad news: 'Jan, if you wear this every sniper in the area is going to think you are the number-one VIP, and they will shoot you dead.' He left it all in the hotel.)

Marsalek said he was gripped by the possibilities of reconstruction, and as he had personal business interests in Libya he asked Kleinschmidt to come up with strategies for stabilization in the country. It would combine economic and social elements, but it was clear that Marsalek's main interest was the highly political issue of migration. 'We must stop them at the Libya border,' he said.

Kleinschmidt, who knew nothing about Marsalek or Wirecard, thought he was dealing with a typical Austrian smartass; a well-dressed, rich narcissist. However, there was something he could work with there, and he liked the idea of public- and private-sector interests combining. His pitch was that Libya was once home to 2 or 3 million guest workers; stabilization would make it a destination for migrants, rather than a source. Marsalek, with signature ambition, wanted a plan to present to the international community. He committed €200,000 to a study, along with the help of connections in Libya he had through his investments in cement plants there. Gattringer said he could advise on how to secure further funds from the Austrian government. Kleinschmidt declared it enough to get started and to develop a project to present to donors. As Marsalek and Gattringer seemed to know each other well and had things to discuss, Kleinschmidt left them to it.

Later, in Vienna, Kleinschmidt asked about a contract. Gattringer told him that Marsalek always paid his bills, but he was a handshake guy. As Kleinschmidt set to work, a serving member at the Austrian Ministry of Defence popped up, Brigadier Gustenau, another acquaintance of Marsalek's. He said the ministry would consider commiting €20,000 to the study, and that he would evaluate the project.

Sam Jones, mind racing, had filled his tiny notebook. Both he and the humanitarian had to go, and they resolved to stay in touch. On the night train he couldn't sleep, and tried to get down every detail of what he'd just heard. Jones secured documents, evidence and arranged to meet Kleinschmidt again in the New Year for dinner in Berlin. It was a miserable day; freezing and wet. Jones chose a restaurant in the upscale area of Schöneberg based on the high quality of its food cited in reviews, unaware that its interior was staged for romance. They arrived, dripping, out of the rain to be shown to an intimate table for two with others close by. In hushed tones, by candlelight, they whispered of Russian spies.

Wolfgang Gattringer, who had made the initial introduction, advanced enough money to keep the project going. Work reached a point when a trip to Libya was required. The question was who would arrange visas and assure security, which is when the Russian 'colonel' came in.

Kleinschmidt was told that the person co-ordinating Marsalek's security interests in Libya was Andrey Chuprygin. An expert in the shifting politics and tribal dynamics of Libya who taught at Moscow's Higher School of Economics, Chuprygin had a long career in the military. He was also, in the assessment of British intelligence, a former officer in the feared GRU, Russia's Military Intelligence Directorate.

Here was the reason for Kleinschmidt's concern. The GRU was the bogeyman of the modern world, a murderous cloak-and-dagger agent of chaos. It was GRU agents who had poisoned Sergei Skripal with Novichok in Salisbury; GRU's little green men who invaded Ukraine; it was the GRU which stood accused of meddling in the 2016 US presidential election to tip the scales in favour of Donald Trump. And, according to Western intelligence agencies, it was the GRU advancing Russia's interests in Libya by co-ordinating the clandestine use of mercenaries. For instance, a tactic used with success by Russia in Syria and Ukraine was the deployment of soldiers from the Wagner Group, whose precise ownership and control remains unknown. The dissolute lines offered deniability; indeed, the Russian government always denied any relationship with the company. Soldiers of the Wagner Group had also been operating in Libya since at least 2017, officially hired on 8 May that year to assist with mine clearance operations at the cement plants which Marsalek told multiple people he had backed. (The Libyan Cement Company denied any connection to Marsalek.)

Kilian Kleinschmidt said a January 2018 meeting was arranged to discuss a Libya trip with the Russian, Andrey Chuprygin, but this was cancelled due to Marsalek's continued failure to pay up. (Chuprygin denied ever being a spy and said his consulting for Marsalek was limited only to Libya's security situation, his academic speciality.) Instead, everyone was invited to Marsalek's villa to clarify his commitment to the project.

The humanitarian, Kleinschmidt, attended with an Irish colleague and the two Austrians, Brigadier Gustenau and Wolfgang Gattringer. They were shown through the austere rooms of the villa, with its fussy art, by Marsalek's personal assistant, Sabine, her heels clicking on the hard floor. While they were still passing out coffee and cookies, making themselves comfortable, Marsalek was engaged in a side-conversation about some super-cool new equipment, and the fantastic footage from body cameras worn by troops in the field. Laughing, he said it could never be shown in public, and proceeded to view some of it. Mercy was not a guiding principle of the gunmen.

Kleinschmidt pretended not to notice. The meeting proper began and Marsalek said that the project had not been thinking big enough. Its plan to start in stages, build civil society, was all kids' stuff, too humanitarian. He wanted highways, factories, but most important of all he wanted to control the border. To do that he desired an army, a 15,000-strong border force composed of former militias. The point of the project should be to train and equip this force, Marsalek said. He was excited by Humvees, night vision goggles and other toys of military men. It became very clear that Kleinschmidt's research was a fig leaf for a hard solution to the migrant problem.

Was Marsalek trying to advance Russian interests, or to use Russia to advance his own? Did this explain his regular trips to Moscow? It's possible he was a fabulist, improvising another hare-brained scheme. Under the government of Vladimir Putin, foreign policy is not necessarily a top-down process. There is a speculative quality to the efforts of oligarchs vying for favour and influence. The apparent aims of Marsalek, the Austrian Far Right and Russia broadly aligned: immigration was a political weapon which destabilized the existing order. Libya also held multiple attractions for Russia. It was in the NATO sphere of influence, and any role in eventual peace would maintain Russia at the top table of world diplomacy. Military influence also put Russia's hand on the tap; a point of control for the boats packed with desperate people heading for Europe's southern shores.

Kleinschmidt read the room. Repurposing militias is actually a proven tactic of demobilization schemes in former combat zones. It was not, however, within the expertise of his humanitarian team. His objective became to secure some of the promised €200,000 from

Marsalek before the relationship collapsed. A couple of weeks later €50,000 arrived.

At the end of January Sam Jones flew into London for a gathering of European country correspondents, a few days before Lionel Barber's big farewell. I saw him at the bus stop coming out of Barber's office. The editor, naturally, was taken aback by what he'd just heard. Intrigued, I joined Jones in Roula Khalaf's office as he briefed the new editor. (To begin with I thought we were talking in hushed tones for security, but then realized she had laryngitis and I was just copying her.) Aside from the hair-raising details, Jones was keen to manage expectations as the account was so out of this world we were almost certainly never going to be able to print it. The main message, however, was that we had to be even more careful than before. There was nothing digital on this one, it was in-person conversations only. We had to consider the possibility that Jan Marsalek wasn't just a criminal fraudster. He appeared to be linked to at least two different intelligence agencies and connected to some of the nastiest people in the world. Maybe Wirecard really was protected, after all.

32

Police Escort

22 January 2020 – Aschheim
Wirecard share price €129, market capitalization €16bn

K PMG WANTED TO KNOW where the cash was. When its team of forensic accounting specialists first arrived at Wirecard they were told that more than €1bn of Wirecard cash was in Singapore, in bank accounts overseen by a trustee. The man holding this great responsibility was Shan, the oval-faced paperwork expert and bar owner used for years by Henry O'Sullivan. However, his company, Citadelle Corporate Services, was not co-operating. It wasn't answering calls or emails and, a couple of months into the special audit, that was becoming a sticking point. Given that Wirecard had history of a trustee disappearing with its money, and well over a billion euros was at stake, the situation might perhaps have caused some alarm.

In public the message was that all was well. On 22 January 2020, *Manager Magazin* carried an interview with the new chairman of Wirecard's supervisory board. Wulf Matthias had resigned due to health reasons, and Thomas Eichelmann was now in charge. He backed Markus Braun, took credit for leading the special audit and, when asked the status of it, said: 'You can draw your conclusions from the fact that we have not yet submitted an ad hoc disclosure.' Investors read it as nothing to see here, please move along; within a couple of days the share price was back above €140, as if the *FT*'s Exocet from October was never fired.

A week later, at one of the regular meetings in the legal department with the various auditors and Wirecard staff, KPMG raised the lack of communication from the trustee once again. One of the forensic investigators said that if it wasn't possible to get bank confirmations from Citadelle, they wanted to know the best way to approach the relevant partners about the accounts. After all, the point of the trustee structure was to give Wirecard's partners – Al Alam, Senjo or PayEasy – access to the money if they needed it for their operations.

Jan Marsalek, as if remembering that he'd forgotten to pass on a phone message about the catering, made an announcement. The trustee had changed, months earlier. Wirecard had become a negative issue for Citadelle's business and Shan informed Marsalek that he would like to terminate the relationship. The money, a mere €1.9bn, had been transferred elsewhere. Asked where, he said: 'Give me a little time to figure, I forget the name.' As for the location of the banks, he wasn't sure either, possibly the UAE or Russia. 'I need to check, but the new trustee will be able to confirm and provide this information,' Marsalek said. He should have mentioned it – it was a total oversight on his part. Most of the people around the table were in too much shock to say anything. Did that just happen? Did Marsalek momentarily misplace over a billion euros? It took about ten minutes to sink in.

A few days later Marsalek followed up. The cash was in Manila.

Mark Tolentino, the man in charge of Wirecard's money in the Philippines, was late. At 10 a.m. sharp on 4 March 2020, the group from Germany had arrived at the lawyer's penthouse office. It had a small front desk, and on the wall behind it were pictures of the man and his professional certificates. They'd been shown into a meeting room with space for about eight people, tiles on the floor and an air conditioner unit humming. From Ernst & Young there was Martin Dahmen, the lead partner, and a local delegate from the firm. The KPMG delegation looked at their watches and chatted quietly. There was a lawyer from Clifford Chance representing the supervisory board who had travelled from Singapore. Jan Marsalek was there, with Dagmar Schneider and a Wirecard lawyer. A woman called Maria, who introduced herself as a paralegal for Tolentino, joined them.

After thirty minutes the group, most of whom charged their time at not insignificant rates and had flown from the other side of the world to be there, began to get restless. Marsalek played with his phone. After fifty minutes Tolentino walked in without apology or explanation. 'Hi everyone, let's get started.' The lawyer was in his late thirties, with a broad nose and thin black wire-frame glasses. Starting meant an introduction by Maria, a laudatory speech extolling her boss. Mr Tolentino was one of the finest and most generous legal minds in the country. He gave advice to the poor and the needy, and his influence was wide and renowned. His reach on social media was large, he appeared as an expert on TV shows and had his own You-Tube channel with more than 100,000 subscribers, which he filmed from the studio right there in his office. (Unusually for a lawyer representing a German financial institution, his speciality in these videos was matters of family law and divorce.) Mr Tolentino also wields political influence, Maria said. He was the son of a politician, and belonged to the same university fraternity, Lex Talionis, as the president, Rodrigo Duterte. It was the university which everyone in the Philippines knew produced important people, and Mr Tolentino won numerous awards while there. After what felt like half an hour of this rendition of the lawyer's prestige, he said he would take questions.

There was a relatively brief period during which he answered queries from Ernst & Young and KPMG about his role as trustee of the Wirecard accounts. Their various boxes appeared to be ticked satisfactorily. Then three of Tolentino's important friends entered the now crowded room. Tolentino introduced them, dwelling on the influence of one, a judge in the highest court in the land who also sat on the election committee for new judges. He was, Tolentino said, one of the most respected and powerful magistrates in the country.

Then it was on to the banks. The group descended the lift to half a dozen waiting cars. When KPMG and the Wirecard lawyer had arrived in Manila, they were met at the airport by a 'friend of Mark' who accompanied them to their hotels with the help of a police escort which whisked them through the streets. This time there were two police motorcycle outriders who took up positions at the front and rear of the small convoy. 'I don't like to wait in traffic,' Tolentino said. His office was in Makati, not far from the financial district and the headquarters of the two banks in which Wirecard held €1.9bn: the Bank of the Philippine Islands, BPI, and Banco de Oro, BDO.

After more than an hour on the road, the cars pulled up to a small bank branch on a street which, were it to be featured in a guidebook, would be characterized as possessing local flavour. There was a pet shop, food courts, a garage specializing in car tyres, and a lot of bicycles. There was also a small branch of BPI. A security guard opened the door and the group pressed in, outnumbering the staff. One jumped up and warmly welcomed Mr Tolentino, who said that this was the responsible branch because he lived close by, as if administering Wirecard's global affairs was something best done while collecting the morning newspapers. All were still standing, practically filling the branch in front of the main counter. There were a couple of other desks with cupboards behind them, and no customers. One of the auditors asked about the money: was the bank aware that Wirecard was the beneficiary of €800m held in the trustee accounts, and could it confirm that the amounts were accurate? There was a pause. The cashier looked at Tolentino, who nodded. 'Ah yes, yes, Wirecard.' His English was not terrific. He produced an envelope and handed it to Tolentino, who solemnly handed it to Martin Dahmen of Ernst & Young. The whole stop lasted less than ten minutes, then it was onwards to BDO.

At a shopping mall half an hour distant, the BDO outpost was much bigger and at least looked like a proper branch. An articulate female manager greeted everyone, handed over the bank confirmations and said how important Tolentino's business was to the bank. Yes, she was aware Wirecard was the beneficiary, it is noted in the bank file, she said.

Jan Marsalek, who had barely engaged with those around him all day, drifted off into an electronics store next door to the bank. He reappeared with a shopping bag, a new mobile phone. When the

Wirecard lawyer asked, he said, 'Oh this? I get a new one every few weeks or so.' Tolentino made a swift exit, and when the Germans returned to their cars the police escort was gone, leaving them to inch through the traffic back to their respective hotels. The Wirecard team were at Raffles, where Marsalek took a two-room suite. The lawyer wasn't sure whether to laugh or cry; the progress of the special audit had been such a mess, with such difficulty obtaining basic paperwork, he was relieved they had at least seen something. There was evidence of people doing things as described. Money was in bank accounts. None of it was normal, but then nothing about these special partners was normal; it was Marsalek's magic moneymaking chaos.

The Manila partner was PayEasy, and KPMG's interview with Christopher Bauer took place in the business centre of a Sofitel. It was early, and the accountants were sipping coffee in the lounge with the Wirecard trio when Bauer strode in with a friend from his motorcycle club, the Iron Cross Sons. The German payments executive looked like an Asian sex tourist. He was over six feet tall, missing teeth, with a belly hanging over black jeans and a matching sweatshirt which showed his dandruff. 'Do I look like a monkey to you? Who do you think you are?' he shouted at KPMG, who'd had the temerity to send an updated agenda with new questions in the middle of the night. He was upset with Wirecard as well. 'These stupid idiots are causing me trouble, they've ruined my business,' he raved, annoyed at all the effort required.

It took some time before he was calmed and seated. Bauer's presentation on PayEasy stretched to two slides. He seemed more concerned to discuss the kitchen at the hotel, which he said could knock up every kind of German speciality, like *Schweinshaxe und Knödel*; pork knuckle and dumplings. It seemed designed to underline that he was a regular guest who got special treatment. Returning to the subject at hand, Bauer said he'd worked with Wirecard for a long time, and PayEasy was owned by him, his wife and two of their relatives. A project was under way to provide Wirecard and its auditors with better access to the underlying payments processing data, and much of the business was in the process of moving over to the

Wirecard ecosystem anyway. There was at least an authenticity to his grumpy complaints.

One issue which came up repeatedly throughout the special audit was a question of the agreements signed by the underlying merchants; the clients whose payments were being processed by PayEasy on behalf of Wirecard. The whole review was prompted by the *FT* reporting that some Al Alam clients simply didn't exist, and that those claimed by PayEasy on its website didn't use it. So signatures on a page would have been helpful. When KPMG asked Bauer for an example merchant contract, Marsalek jumped in. 'Ja, ja, I have it. I'll send it to you later.' The Wirecard lawyer, who had requested the same document for months, felt like jumping out of the window. (Marsalek, as ever, failed to deliver.)

An inspection of the PayEasy office at the Mall of Asia followed the Sofitel confrontation. It was a year since Stefania Palma showed up without warning, and there were now about fifteen PayEasy employees sat at computers, all hard at work. They appeared to have transactions up on their screens and were dealing with the humdrum administration of payments processing; another tick in the box.

By early March 2020, the spread of Covid was beginning to make travel difficult. It was a new excuse to add to the prevarications of Oliver Bellenhaus, but a date with Al Alam in Dubai was set. On the 13th, Bellenhaus and Marsalek roared up to the pair of replica Chrysler Buildings in a sporty BMW M5 with a metallic paint job that glittered blue and gold in the Dubai sun. Marsalek was staying at the Bulgari luxury hotel some distance away. Inside, the Al Alam sign was still on the door of an office no longer in use. A pile of keyboards and old computers gathered dust on a vacant desk. The delegation turned right into a meeting room where extra chairs were squeezed in to fit a dozen people round a table for eight.

Al Alam took a professional approach, supported by two Chinese lawyers from the Hong Kong branch of Withers. There was a relatively young Hungarian called David Yasmineh, who was chatty in a social way but quiet when it came to the business. (It was his name recorded as the owner of Al Alam when it was registered in April

2013, according to a person who had reviewed the filing, three years before the company's first press release announced the launch of its UAE operations in 2016.) In charge was a ginger Brit, Brian Stone, whose card said he was head of group strategy and whose skin suggested he struggled with the climate. He was straight to business, making no effort to entertain or ingratiate. He appeared to know what he was doing and was critical of Wirecard in the manner of a frustrated commercial partner. Due to all the fuss in the newspapers, Al Alam had been forced to relocate and rebrand as Symtric, with a new business licence. It was linked to a range of exciting partners, and he talked about the various functions, its accounting and where its people were based. Contrary to newspaper reports about its tiny and now unused office, Al Alam had staff in the UAE, Eastern Europe and Hong Kong. It was large enough to do its job well, but small enough to be fleet-footed and efficient. Stone also complained that the level of commission paid to Wirecard was inappropriate, given the impact on Al Alam's reputation. Ernst & Young's Martin Dahmen led the inquisition and the meeting lasted around two hours. Having waited four months for this moment, the visitors from KPMG had no further questions.

March 15 was Jan Marsalek's fortieth birthday. There were signs of a small celebration in Aschheim; the Donald Trump cut-out wore a party hat and a 40km/hour road sign covered his face. Fears about the spread of the new pandemic were rising. Germany had recorded its first deaths in March, and as the month progressed schools and borders began to be closed. Marsalek spent most of his time working at his alternative base of operations, the villa on Prinzregentenstrasse known as P61. There he'd already shown hypochondriac tendencies, constantly popping pills, uppers and downers, prescribed by private doctors. He spared no expense to equip the villa for the coming storm, with two rooms given over to hospital beds and medical equipment, including a ventilator and electrocardiogram sourced by his friend Colin. Arrangements were made with medical staff to attend, if needed. One of Marsalek's gophers was dispatched to Moscow, collecting a suitcase full of pills from the airport and flying straight back. The villa's medicine cabinet included Tamiflu, and a full box of the HIV treatment Lopinavir which some thought at the time might be effective against Covid-19. A cupboard was filled with emergency dressings, bandages, masks, gloves and bottles of gin-based hand sanitizers from a Hamburg distillery that made anyone who used them smell like an alcoholic. For his personal use Marsalek had a full-face gas mask with Corpro F1100 filters.

Dr Rami was a regular presence by this time. Colin first met him at the 2018 Oktoberfest on Marsalek's table in the Käfer tent, which began the day weighed down by beer and ended it laden with three-litre jeroboams of Dom Perignon. Colin happened to be sitting next to Dr Rami in Istanbul when he decided to send the roses to Paul Murphy. ('Ja, brilliant, do it,' Marsalek had said.) Colin found Dr Rami frustrating to deal with, however. On a visit to discuss a business idea he kept Colin waiting two hours in Raffles, spoke to him for thirty minutes, then suggested they continue four hours later over dinner. The Libyan had appeared at around the time that the rental agreement for the villa was switched from the name of Goomo, the Indian travel business, to the investment company managed by Colin. He wasn't sure what happened to the relationship with O'Sullivan, but communication seemed to have stopped entirely a few months later after the *FT* articles about Singapore appeared. Money for Marsalek's schemes and investments began to arrive through Turkey. A constant stream of cash was required, both to fund his alternative base of operations, as well as investments like that in Getnow, a Berlin-based grocery delivery service which required regular injections of capital.

Another regular visitor to P61 was the tattooed porn baron Ray Akhavan. He and Marsalek typically spent hours locked away together in a conference room, then went out for dinner; a favourite was Matsuhisa at the Mandarin Oriental, for Peruvian sushi washed down with the finest sake. Without realizing it, the *FT* was giving Akhavan headaches as well. The porn baron used a paperwork factory in the UK called Animo Associates to administer a web of companies. (It was an up-to-date version of Simon Dowson's operation in Consett, County Durham, and was run by a man who

Dowson said told him to start working with Wirecard in the first place, Mark Quirk.)

A frontwoman for one of those companies was upset. 'I received a worrying phone call today from a journalist for the *Financial Times*,' she wrote in an email to the firm. She thought the journalist was a 'Peter Murphy', who wanted to know how she came to be a director of the company. He warned her it was used by Wirecard to channel payments for porn, and that the company was accused of fraud and various scams. 'Below are some links I have found. It has been going on for years, whistleblowers are involved, Ernest &Young [sic], KPMG. I have a gut feeling it is going to blow up & I want no part of it. Whilst I am fully aware of the indemnity of the directorship I do not wish to have my name associated with this ongoing investigation which could be daming [sic] to my position and integrity within St John Ambulance which is my first priority. With this in mind I wish to tender my resignation.'

Marsalek, hands full with the special audit, had no idea how the *FT* had even identified the woman's company and its use for porn. 'They really want to turn off our lights, don't they?' said Dagmar Schneider when he briefed her. He remained relentlessly positive and was, to the outside observer, calm and relaxed when at Wirecard. But at the end of March the mask briefly slipped.

With the Covid lockdown in force, Colin invited Marsalek over for a barbecue. He arrived late with three friends: his personal-life assistant and travel companion, Sabine; a Russian diplomat; and Martin Weiss, an Austrian former spook who became a Marsalek henchman. The atmosphere was Dionysian. The visitors had sunk plenty of vodka before they arrived, and were animatedly discussing politics. More vodka and champagne was opened, and for entertainment glasses began to be thrown, then knives. A competition developed to land one in the wood of a kitchen window frame. Colin didn't try to halt the destruction. 'It's OK, there's nothing you can destroy that can't be replaced or repaired.' The diplomat boasted about his protection squad, men with Kalashnikovs waiting in a van outside, which required the shadow of German police.

After a couple of hours they moved outside to eat, as it was a warm spring evening, and opened a second bottle of vodka. Marsalek collapsed on to the ground quietly sobbing. 'I don't know what will happen. Oh my God, oh my God, oh my God.' While Sabine tried to comfort him, the other men left them to it.

'Too much pressure, I know about that,' said the diplomat, whom Colin knew socially from his regular visits across the road to P61. Then something occurred to the Russian. He pointed at Weiss with an unsteady finger. 'Martin, you are the reason I am not ambassador to Germany.'

'Whoa, whoa, whoa, what are you talking about?' Weiss looked confused.

'Ten years ago I was in Austria, and you invited me to the Ministry of Internal Affairs, and told me I should stop spying. I'm not a spy,' he said with a degree of indignation.

'Ahh, now I remember. You were a spy!' Weiss knew about the whole network, he said. He invited the Russian three times and requested that he stop. 'But you didn't, so we kicked you out of Austria.' Colin looked on with amusement as the two men, reunited for the first time in a decade, continued the vodka-fuelled argument.

Weiss had seen his own career derailed. Until 2017 he was a head of operations for Austria's domestic intelligence service, the BVT (or, to give it its full name, the Federal Office for the Protection of the Constitution and the Fight against Terrorism). After that he went to work for Marsalek, doing tasks such as asking a BVT staff member to look at twenty-five names provided by the Wirecard executive to check if they were spies.

After about forty-five minutes lying on the ground, Marsalek recovered himself and stood up. 'I need another vodka,' he declared.

33

Desperate Punches

27 January 2020 – New York
Wirecard share price €133, market capitalization €16bn

FAHMI QUADIR WAS DREADING going to work. The analyst at her small hedge fund had got to the Safkhet Capital office early and found the lights on, which was strange, and the internet not working, which was less out of the ordinary. Quadir braced herself for a day of IT issues as she left her apartment building on the Upper West Side for the morning walk with her poodle, Maera (named after the dog of the man who learned the secret of wine from Dionysus which, following a Greek tragedy of hungover brutality, became the constellation Canis Major). It was about 8.30 in the morning, and there were people on the street heading to work, children outside the expensive private school opposite. She paused, shivering in the cold, as Maera fussed at the pavement, when out of nowhere Quadir was punched on the side of the head. Knocked to the ground, dazed, trying to hold on to consciousness for the sake of the lead in her hand, she glimpsed a man all in black running away. A black backpack, shoes, gloves and ski mask. The police arrived within minutes. As she recovered in her apartment, the officers asked her if she had any enemies. They must have thought she was concussed as this woman in Ugg boots and a sweater dress with a teddy bear on it talked about an international payments processing conspiracy. They took it seriously enough for a detective to arrive that afternoon. He was annoyed to find the building CCTV hadn't caught the attack. In fact it would turn out that, in a street full of cameras, not one was covering that particular spot of pavement. The FBI arrived as well, because Quadir was their source: it was exactly a week since they had interviewed her in her lawyer's office at the Rockefeller Center. That New York had taken over the Dallas investigation, and they'd taken the trouble to see her on a public holiday, Martin Luther King Day, suggested things were moving. An agent tried to comfort Quadir with stories of his first assault, as if she had joined the concussion survivors' club. But they were both suspicious; the attack smelled like a warning.

Over in London, the Coathanger King and his alleged Wirecard insider, Bill, were back in touch, offering tantalizing details about how the company's systems were set up to withstand online probes by the US authorities. Murphy had become convinced that the King, supposedly a close friend of Nick Gold, was actually in the pay of Wirecard, and this 'Bill' character was probably a corporate security operative looking to set Murphy up. Might the three of them meet for drinks and a chat at Claridge's? Certainly!

On the appointed evening, Bill arrived with a well-thumbed A5 bound notebook. It was said to contain the full secrets of Wirecard's shady past. But to get a peek inside Murphy would have to agree to give prior notice of when the *FT* would run a story on the matter. Bill still needed a payday. Sensing he was being recorded, Murphy naturally declined the offer; he had his own surveillance effort under way, with Cynthia O'Murchu nearby with a camera lens concealed in a button on her coat. But efforts to identify this mysterious Bill came to nothing: the button was wonky and all she caught was Bill's shoes.

After Bill, the King and Cynthia had departed, Murphy lingered at the bar to jot down what was said in a notebook. A couple of young women in party dresses came to stand next to him and, to Murphy's surprise, were keen to strike up a conversation. He quickly mentioned he was a lowly hack, to save their valuable time, and was obviously trying to work. Yet they persisted, and Murphy became suspicious, his paranoia flaring again. In all the time he'd spent in Mayfair hotels, not once had he attracted the interest of working girls. Now a duo? When would the dirty tricks end?

Wickford was not on the Oyster card system. The office of Animo Associates was so deep into Essex I got a fine from the train conductor for not buying a ticket from Liverpool Street. It was 5 March, drizzling, and Animo was a short walk from the station in a small building two flights above a branch of Barclays Bank. I took a deep breath and walked in. 'Afternoon. I'm here to see the person who deals with the porn companies please.'

The room was long and narrow, with desks arrayed down both sides. There was a mural advertising the firm's corporate services in company orange, along with its tagline: Experience – Foresight – Discretion. Heads swivelled all the way down and there was a small amount of giggling. The person nearest the door said, 'Er, Steve maybe,' and looked at a man of South Asian descent in the corner who seemed to be in charge. I said I was from the *FT*, and the greeter quickly showed me into a meeting room and offered me water, then stuck his head back in to check my name.

Two minutes later the boss walked in and started talking quickly.

'I'm afraid there's nobody here to speak to you. You'll have to make an appointment.'

His volume was rising rapidly. 'You don't have the right to walk in here and start asking questions, are you from the police?'

'No, I'm a journalist. So who is it here who deals with all of your porn companies?'

'I can't answer your questions.'

I put my bag on the table and opened it.

'OK, well who should I give these letters to? I've got 130-ish of them here for clients of yours.' They were in A4 envelopes, a few inches' worth. At this his tone changed.

'OK we can take these.'

The letters resulted from my lack of faith in Wirecard's special audit. I couldn't believe it when Wirecard's chairman, Thomas Eichelmann, had said everything was fine in January. KPMG had found nothing? Neither Murphy nor I felt like we could relax or let it go until every facet of this company was exposed to the light. I'd gone back to the customers revealed in its files, and what stood out were the suspiciously high profit margins on some of the business. Why would a legitimate merchant pay upwards of 15 per cent to process its payments?

Working down in the bunker, where colleagues wouldn't stumble upon my screen in shock, I found about 4,000 websites in different networks of porn and dating companies, mostly registered to companies in the UK and Cyprus. The Wickford network was sixty-eight companies controlling about 1,200 porn and customer service sites. They were ostensibly independent but obviously linked. Each had a generic sort of name, *Latin Juicy Squirting* or *Eat My Kinky Milf*, for example. Everything else was almost identical, from their outdated technology (the virus-prone flash player), design, and use of anonymous customer service pages for credit card billing. At the bottom of each porn site and corresponding customer service page was the name and address of a nondescript UK company. Every porn site had its own phone number, with an individual voice message that then led to the same few call centres in Miami.

The staff were trained not to give out any details of the operation, beyond untraceable company names (I gave up after a few dozen calls when I kept hitting the same operators), and they were primed to give refunds and cancel subscriptions, presumably to avoid chargebacks.

Murphy and I risked our cards on a few porn sites. For some sites our banks blocked the payment automatically, others overcharged us. It looked deeply suspicious. Who on earth would pay $39.95 a month for access to the shonky sites in the days of free online porn? I finished summarizing this investigation into the sixty-eight companies for the Animo Associates man. 'What you have there are letters asking for comment from all the directors and former directors, and all the owners listed since 2017.'

He'd calmly taken notes and asked questions, appearing to be familiar with the concepts. He suggested I speak to the head of Animo, Mark Quirk (who declined to comment when I did). Not one of the 130 letters sparked a response.

*

While I'd been digging, the world changed. A cough became something that turned heads. Alcoholic gel dripped near every doorway. The news was all numbers, rising fast; for cases and then, with terrifying inevitability, deaths. By the time everyone in the UK was told to stay at home on 23 March, Charlotte and I had already been there for a week. The newspaper was frantically trying to work out how to operate remotely and investigations were suddenly beside the point. There was only one story and everyone was on it. I pitched in with editing markets stories to help with the flood of copy.

Wirecard had meanwhile delayed its financial results and the conclusion of the special audit by a month. The company's statement beggared belief: after five months KPMG had 'not produced any substantial findings in these areas of investigation that would result in a need for correction of the financial statements'.

I knew what I would do if I were Markus Braun: blame Covid, fudge the audit when no one is paying attention and use the pandemic to reset the business. Wriggle, wriggle, wriggle, and off the hook he flies.

On 27 March 2020, Ray Akhavan was arrested in California. He was accused of conspiring to trick US banks into processing around $160m in marijuana-related purchases for the online weed marketplace Eaze, using shell companies and false merchant codes. A German accomplice was arrested as well, and a Wirecard salesman showed up to pay his bail money. Reflecting on the proactive approach of the US authorities, Fahmi Quadir was reminded of something her whistleblower had said to her. The fates of Akhavan and Marsalek were intertwined: if one fell, the other would soon follow.

34

Show Me the Money

April 2020 – Munich and Austria
Wirecard share price €120, market capitalization €15bn

SUNDAY EVENING, ALMOST SIX months to the day since the special audit was announced, couriers masked against the spread of Covid knocked on doors at different addresses in Germany and Austria bearing heavy packages. Inside were individually watermarked copies of KPMG's draft report prepared for Wirecard's supervisory board. The document was top-secret, relentless and damning; a shock for the three men and three women, who had all visited the flourishing Aschheim campus. Wirecard had long ago taken over the five blocks of its U-shaped formation at the Einstein business park, and before the pandemic hit was expanding deeper into the neighbouring buildings. Staff could view scale models of the expensive outfit planned, and on some days whole schools of new employees crowded the pavements and corridors as they were oriented to their surroundings. Yet within a matter of weeks KPMG had realized the truth of Wirecard's business: its core European payment processing operations made no profit at all. Since 2016 practically all of Wirecard's much vaunted Ebitda, the astounding performance which had vaulted it past its rivals, came from commissions supposedly paid by the three partners in Dubai, Singapore and Manila.

Of that trio – Al Alam, Senjo and PayEasy – KPMG verified next to nothing. Its team of forty experts saw no transaction data, in some

SHOW ME THE MONEY

cases no contracts at all. Pretty much the only money flows it could trace were those going out; there were €250m of unsecured loans to PayEasy and Al Alam; another €115m for a business spun out of Senjo and run by a former Wirecard employee. What KPMG had no evidence to support were €1bn of commission payments Wirecard claimed these partners had paid into the special bank accounts managed by the Manila trustee.

What would stun some who read it, however, were the small details. Minutes were not kept of Wirecard's executive board meetings. This was supposed to be a DAX 30 company. Three members of a Munich Rotary Club wouldn't sit down to chat about the weather without taking a register and notes of proceedings.

By the time the supervisory board members read the review in April they knew there'd been complaints about a lack of co-operation. KMPG had threatened to resign in early March, which had caused the extension of its term by more than a month. Now they were confronted with a catalogue of obstructions and delays, listed with the furious clarity of the spurned bureaucrat.

Anastassia Lauterbach called a friend. 'It's incredible, you can't believe it. You read the first fifty pages and it's such a bomb. We have to get rid of Markus Braun and the whole management board, we can't trust them.'

It was just one of many calls to and from supervisory board members that night, joined by growing numbers of lawyers and consultants, as hectic and angry discussions stretched through the Monday. If they had suspicions before that Markus Braun was not on the level, a pattern was starting to emerge in his angry denunciation of the whole process. 'A very low-quality report', wasn't that what he said about the Rajah & Tann verdict on their Singapore investigation? The response from Jan Marsalek, after the Austrian had spent six months supposedly focused on the special audit, was only at the eleventh hour to offer co-operation and some actual data. It wasn't what KPMG had asked for, which was examples of real people using their credit cards at merchants supported by Wirecard's partners, so it could see the process from end to end. Instead, one of Marsalek's long-standing cronies in the technology team had produced credit card transactions from December 2019, *after* the special audit was launched. KMPG's forensic auditors were only now invited to conduct a deep dive into these 200 million data points.

Markus Braun's position hung in the balance, along with everything he and Marsalek had worked for two decades to create. It was the first time the company and its problems could be viewed in their totality. He was no longer the final authority, able to hide behind the complexity of Wirecard's arrangements. KPMG had been appointed to settle a simple question: did Wirecard's customers actually exist? Six months and many air miles later, it was unable to say for sure.

There was also the board's own experience to consider. In January, Markus Braun had surprised them by requesting a €35m loan from Wirecard Bank. Billionaire CEOs aren't supposed to use their company like a piggy bank, so a loan would have looked awful even if Wirecard wasn't mired in financial scandal. When the supervisory board objected, however, it was too late. The money was already paid and the request was a post-hoc rubber stamp. (Braun had repaid the loan in March. He'd needed it because his credit wasn't as good as it used to be; Deutsche Bank had refused to refinance the €150m margin loan secured against the value of his stock, and he had to put up cash to avoid a forced sale.) Would it have been too much to ask supervisory board members to connect the dots, to the debt raised from 'SoftBank' and the outflow of huge sums to questionable destinations? How many times does a company need to be accused of fraud for those overseeing it to start playing detective?

Thomas Eichelmann, the forthright new chairman, was the man who had stepped into the spotlight with his media interviews. From a distance he had the look of a new broom, the person on whose shoulders the hopes of investors and short sellers alike rested. He was head of the audit committee, and as he had joined the previous summer would be untarnished if Wirecard fell. His reputation would be enhanced by a robust response to the special audit. Yet Eichelmann was a proud man, and were Wirecard's valuation to drop he could lose membership of an elite club: chairmanship of a vaunted DAX 30 company. In public he had been a steadfast supporter of Braun as intrinsic to the future of the company.

Perhaps the mental leap required was too much. A great many authorities suffered from the failure of imagination required to doubt the evidence of their eyes and ears. The emperor did have clothes on, he was sitting there smirking in a black turtleneck jumper surrounded by several buildings full of staff. Wirecard's largest investors, when asked, quietly voiced their support for Braun as well. He was the man who built it, they thought, and was inseparable from its success. What is harder to explain is the attachment to Jan Marsalek. KPMG provided a thick pile of reasons to fire or suspend the entire management board, and Marsalek was the prime culprit. It was his chaos at the heart of every allegation: the 2015 India deal; the fake contracts in Singapore; the magic black box of profits which couldn't be traced.

No one was fired. Instead a board member, Susana Quintana-Plaza, resigned on the Monday citing personal reasons. She had already signalled an intention to leave, and so departed a few months early. The other five independent directors remained strapped to the ship, warned by their lawyers that it was too late for them to dive overboard; they faced personal liability whatever happened. Late on Monday night they reached a decision: KPMG would be given one more week.

Markus Braun was sent a supervisory board memo indicating what he was to tell investors about this delay: that KPMG had run into obstacles in its investigation, including missing documents and a lack of co-operation, and that the firm could not rebut the allegations raised against Wirecard. Braun threw it in the bin and offered his chairman some free legal advice by text message: 'The supervisory board is personally liable if it allows that a wrong regulatory statement or a wrong ad hoc report destroys value.' Then Braun waited until just after 9 p.m. on Tuesday evening to announce the delay. He blamed KPMG, made no mention of Quintana-Plaza's resignation, and claimed vindication: 'No evidence was found for the publicly raised allegations of balance sheet manipulation,' Wirecard's statement said.

When the announcement appeared Eichelmann was busy chairing another remote meeting. For all their shock, the supervisory board remained silent. Investors all over Germany had waited months for news, and they knew what this long-promised vindication meant:

when trading resumed the next day Wirecard's share price jumped 11 per cent, to close at €141.

Sunday evening, 26 April, found Markus Braun waiting at Wirecard's Aschheim headquarters in a conference room named after New York, the biggest the company had, surrounded by almost two dozen staff and supporters. The crowd included CFO Alexander von Knoop and his deputy Stephan von Erffa, who had overseen the work of Edo Kurniawan in Singapore. Marsalek was there, plus Dagmar Schneider and the lawyer who had accompanied them to Manila and Dubai with the audit teams. Advising Braun was his PR consultant, Rüdiger Assion of Edelman, and the billionaire's old comrade and ally, Burkhard Ley. A representative from the supervisory board's law firm was observing proceedings. The atmosphere was tense, quiet, with little chit-chat as the group waited. When he was stressed, Braun abandoned his usual peppermint tea for cup after cup of coffee, and there were telltale stains at the corners of his mouth. He had lost weight, his hair was thinning and his face was red.

The face of Alexander Geschonneck, the KPMG partner in charge of the audit, appeared on the giant plasma TV in the room. He shared his screen, and began to talk about the details of the report. It was now split in two parts: a seventy-five-page section for publication, and an appendix three times as long into which some of more damaging details and confidential names were shunted. KPMG still had dozens of open questions, and Braun pushed the whole Wirecard team to deliver answers. They desperately tried to find information to shift the auditor's position, to sand down the edges of its conclusions. For ten hours they worked at it, breaking at 4 a.m. so that everyone could get some sleep.

They returned the next day at 11 a.m. to continue, but KPMG gave them little more than an hour. The firm had to finish the report and could accept no more contributions.

Braun protested, a stutter of anger, or incomprehension: there were still inaccurate statements. It was no use, the meeting switched to a waiting game, preparing for the official statements which would have to be issued.

In the early hours of Tuesday morning, KPMG uploaded the document to be published and everyone began to read. The implication was transparent: the accountants could not confirm the existence of Wirecard's Third-Party Acquiring. The company stood accused of inventing its customers and had come up blank.

Marsalek proposed simply refusing to publish. The whole room looked at him with tired incomprehension. Refusing to publish would shred what credibility Wirecard had left. He and Braun left together for a short while, and when they returned Braun was clear: the report would be published.

The room was full of believers. KPMG had not found evidence for the Third-Party arrangements, but if anyone thought Wirecard was hollow they kept their counsel. The company remained misunderstood and chaotic, and Burkhard Ley was one of the sage voices reminding them that they had been through difficulties in the past and survived. Focus shifted to the message. Wirecard had spent a year saying it intended to improve its processes and procedures, tighten up its compliance, and it would reiterate that stance. There was no proof of fraud. The team worked into the night to prepare the communications, and Braun asked for calls with the press and investors to be arranged for the following morning. Alexander von Knoop looked shell-shocked all night and either had a sudden show of backbone or a total attack of the tremors. He went home for the rest of the day.

Wirecard was a favoured stock in the circles of rich men who networked in Munich and Frankfurt, and a considerable number had taken the previous week's announcement as confirmation of what they'd heard privately: that the special audit would clear the air. Many of them had piled in. On Tuesday morning messages rapidly flew around WhatsApp, to sell and sell quickly as the price crashed. It took a little longer for the conclusion to seep out internationally, because the report was only published in German.

The omission of an English-language version gave Markus Braun the chance to spin it, for his international audience at least. Speaking carefully, he told analysts in his usual bloodless tones: 'We can clearly reject today allegations of balance sheet manipulation.' What he admitted to were weaknesses in documentation and processes, 'many of which have already been addressed'. He also claimed the support of the one institution which had backed him through thick and thin for a decade. 'EY informed us this morning that they have no problem at all to sign off on the audit.'

The gambit wasn't entirely true. That very day Wirecard received a letter from Ernst & Young detailing the various pieces of evidence it required to complete the audit, and the publication of the results had been delayed till June (due to Covid, which astonishingly hadn't affected Wirecard's operations, according to Braun). Yet EY was bound by client confidentiality and legally unable to resign. Thomas Eichelmann, so media-savvy when it suited him, remained silent. The board eventually acted in May, by taking away Braun's megaphone; it gave the responsibility for company communications to Alexander von Knoop.

Wirecard's share price stabilized at around €90 as investors, analysts and regulators all waited for the verdict of Ernst & Young. Some of those threw their hands up; the analyst at one French broker, Kepler Cheuvreux, had been honest enough in print to say that his initial favourable reaction to the special audit was published without reading the German report. A week later he withdrew his buy rating, saying the situation was entirely dependent on the audit. Others stuck to their guns. Heike Pauls at Commerzbank told her clients it was a major buying opportunity and that Wirecard was really worth €28bn. Addressing myths about the company pushed by short sellers, she wrote that deficiencies identified by KPMG meant 'major change was happening' and that she expected the firm to forensically validate funds in trustee accounts in due course.

Underpinning Braun's fortune, and the €11bn market capitalization of the company, was the reputation of its auditors. With a couple of signatures the share price would fly. Without them, it was the end of the road.

Martin Dahmen and his colleagues at Ernst & Young weren't all the way there, but they seemed to have a confidence in Wirecard's business which KPMG lacked. The results were scheduled for release on

18 June, and on the 2nd of that month EY shared a draft 'all-clear' accounting opinion with the company. There was, however, a detail to clarify. Was this €1.9bn held in trust really Wirecard's money?

Inside the envelopes handed to Ernst & Young in Manila were two pieces of paper central to the company's future. One listed three accounts at BDO Unibank holding €1.1bn controlled by the Mark Tolentino law office on behalf of Wirecard. The other, signed by an assistant branch manager, detailed three accounts at the Bank of the Philippine Islands (BPI) holding €800m. Both banks had misspelled the name of Wirecard subsidiaries, and EY wasn't completely convinced. On 24 April, unable to return due to pandemic travel restrictions, the EY audit team had held a video call with bank employees to discuss the accounts. The staff members held up their bank identity cards to the screen, and EY staff googled them without success. So far as it was possible to tell from the video, it looked like they were in a bank branch. EY wasn't completely satisfied, and KPMG's report had also placed it under new pressure. For previous audits it had accepted trustee documents, rather than original bank confirmations from the Singapore institution said to hold Wirecard's cash. The sticklers at KPMG had been rather emphatic about the need for independent verification, and had questioned the classification of the money on the balance sheet. It could only be described as 'cash' if Wirecard was able to draw on the money whenever it wanted, without restriction. So EY asked Wirecard to prove it had ready access to the cash by making four transfers, totalling €440m, from the accounts in the Philippines to Wirecard Bank in Germany.

Such payments would be no problem at all, Markus Braun and Jan Marsalek assured the audit team, and anyone else who asked. Marsalek didn't break a sweat as he made every show of chasing the money and his erstwhile trustee. Yet he could only claim the cheque was in the post for so long. Finally, a senior Ernst & Young executive placed calls directly to the CEOs of the two banks. The first formal response arrived from BPI late on Tuesday, 16 June. 'Please be informed that the attached documents are spurious.'

Pretty much every German who saw it reacted the same way: by googling the obscure English word 'spurious'. The language helped quell a rising tide of panic, leaving a tiny space for doubt: was the unusual letter real? Ernst & Young immediately alerted BaFin in Frankfurt, followed by prosecutors in Munich.

At this point, Markus Braun was still calm. 'It's all a big misunderstanding which will soon be resolved,' he said, telling the board that Wirecard was in contact with the bank and would have updates soon.

On Thursday a similar letter arrived from the second Manila bank, BDO, which said the signatures of its staff were forged and the accounts were not real, also calling them 'spurious'. Employees of Ernst & Young were really starting to sound quite nervous, and a degree of bedlam developed as the meetings became larger, longer and more energetic. Word began to leak out inside headquarters, and Braun strode the executive floor offering reassurance that the money really was on the way.

The consequences were hard to look in the face. The head of BaFin, Felix Hufeld, was in regular contact with Wirecard's chairman, Thomas Eichelmann, who briefed the board and those around it on the calls. In one, they discussed the strange aspects of the bank letters and whether the company might yet be the victim of another elaborate plot by short sellers. Could anyone really believe such a desperate excuse at that moment in time?

Wirecard was supposed to announce its results on Thursday morning, the 18th. The €440m had still not arrived. The supervisory board gathered at the office of its lawyers, and Thomas Eichelmann turned to an American outsider. James Freis was a lawyer and former regulator who'd worked at the US Treasury on anti-money-laundering efforts. He'd already agreed to join Wirecard's executive board as its new chief compliance officer, sensibly delaying his arrival until after the special and normal audits were due to be finished. He was about to begin flat-hunting in downtown Munich when he got the call from Eichelmann. 'We're in crisis.' He arrived in shorts and sandals, and was swiftly voted into position.

Marsalek was at Wirecard HQ. 'Everything is possible. We're swaying between catastrophe and all fine,' Marsalek texted a friend at 9.03 a.m. He added: 'We're waiting for input from a bank. If we receive that, everything will be fine. If not, EY will go totally crazy.'

It was Alexander von Knoop who finally took responsibility. Wirecard announced that no sufficient audit evidence could be found for €1.9bn of cash balances and there was evidence that 'spurious account balances' were provided to Ernst & Young. 'The Wirecard management board is working intensively together with the auditor towards a clarification of the situation,' the announcement said. The Wirecard share price dropped like a stone. Marsalek was still texting his friend. If the money didn't reappear, he said, 'then we'll be dead and have a wonderful economic scandal'.

Even at this stage, the two remaining women on the supervisory board were outnumbered by the men; there was no majority to fire Marsalek or Braun. Instead Marsalek was suspended for twelve weeks, and wasn't even escorted from the premises. He strolled around the top floor at Wirecard headquarters whistling to himself as if he had not a care in the world. Before he left, he and Braun held a long and seemingly intense conversation in the CEO's office. One staff member walked in, only to spin right round again when he saw their faces. When Marsalek did finally leave, he told friends he intended to go to Manila to sort out the mess himself. 'I know the money is there, I just need to kick ass.'

At the end of the day there were still signs of hope among Wirecard's ever-faithful investor base. The share price closed at €39.90, valuing the group at €5bn. That night the management board recorded a video, arranged behind a long, thin island topped in Wirecard blue. Braun stood rigid, fingertips pressed to the table in front of him, and was the only one who spoke. The new chief compliance officer, James Freis, was awkwardly introduced, in a light summer jacket borrowed for the appearance. Alexander von Knoop stood there, lips pressed together, staring into the middle distance and rapidly blinking in the manner of a man trying very hard to control his inner demons and stomach. Braun presented himself as the victim. 'At present it cannot be ruled out that Wirecard AG has become the aggrieved party in a case of fraud of considerable proportions,' he said.

The American newcomer Freis retreated to his hotel with bundles of paperwork. Everything was there, a 1,000-piece jigsaw with one piece remaining to place. He pulled up figures for the Philippine banking system. It was a dollarized economy and Wirecard's bank account statements were in euros, an improbably large amount. Wirecard's money wasn't missing, it had never existed in the first place.

As soon as it was a semi-acceptable hour to call, Freis rang Eichelmann and gave the chairman the blunt truth: fraud from inside Wirecard was the only explanation. Another emergency board meeting was called, and the decision was taken to finally oust Braun. He came on to the call and, in a rambling address, resigned before Eichelmann could officially fire him. Freis, as the only person the board could trust, was asked to take over. His first job was to deal with the banks, who were concerned about Wirecard's €2bn credit facility and were threatening to pull the plug, so over the weekend Freis called in debt restructuring advisors to assess the company's prospects.

After that, events began to accelerate. On Monday, 22 June Wirecard admitted that the €1.9bn wasn't missing, but in all probability didn't exist, and got round to firing Marsalek, who hadn't been seen in Munich since everything blew up the previous Thursday. The share price dropped to €14, a market capitalization of €1.8bn. Markus Braun had spent the weekend in Vienna, as usual, and on Monday evening returned to Germany to present himself to prosecutors after a warrant was issued for his arrest on suspicion of false accounting and market manipulation.

Three more days was all that the company could stagger. On Thursday the 25th Wirecard, for the second time, filed for insolvency. It was over.

Conclusion

That Thursday, waiting for the verdict of Ernst & Young, I was home in St Albans at the desk where I'd called Edo Kurniawan eighteen months before. I was up at 6 a.m. again, but with coffee this time and a chat open with the *FT*'s Olaf Storbeck in Frankfurt.

For any other big event telegraphed in advance we'd have copy ready, two skeletons of a story pre-written: guilty or not guilty. This time neither of us had tapped a word because we didn't want to tempt fate. We feared Ernst & Young would be conned once again, yet hoped that it wouldn't. I kept bouncing from tab to tab, refreshing Wirecard's website, Twitter and the business wires. Had I missed anything?

At 8 a.m. the stock market opened, and I felt a little groundswell of optimism. Paul Murphy has a favourite adage – 'Bad numbers take longer to add up than good ones' – and by 8.20 he was feeling confident: 'They are fucked. If the audit was clean the news would be out. Amazing the market doesn't see this. Clear as day.'

Olaf and I started to type. At 9.43 a.m. the statement dropped and I held my breath, trying to take it in. Could it really be? €1.9bn was missing. There was no audit! Then I had my hands up, cheering. I was dancing, it felt like I'd scored the winning goal in an FA Cup Final. I burst into the kitchen, running around the room woo-hooing. 'We did it, we finally did it!' Charlotte and the children were sitting at the counter having a snack, and they joined in, giggling and cheering.

'What are you so excited about?' my daughter asked as I picked her up, the two of us spinning around and laughing. How could I possibly explain?

'The bad guys are going to jail.'

Then I ran back to the computer. News was breaking, there was a story to write, and already there were messages flashing up from the companies desk at the *FT* about when we'd be able to file a 'read' on what was happening.

In Surrey, short seller Matt Earl watched events with a tinge of disappointment that it was auditors who pulled back the curtain. Why weren't the police marching Markus Braun out in handcuffs? Then he heard that Sky News wanted a talking head, and he frantically tidied his study to make a backdrop suitable for national television. His kids enjoyed sticking their heads round the door to see, then going to the living room to watch their dad on the screen telling the lunchtime audience how he'd been targeted for years by a malevolent financial institution.

Earl's persecution by Wirecard was finally in the open. The spyware experts at Toronto's Citizen Lab had traced the phishing emails to their source at an Indian gang called BellTroX, thanks to Wirecard's relentless pursuit of Earl. Sometimes the researchers lost the trail as the hackers' location and tactics shifted, but then another email dropped into Earl's inbox and they picked it up again. The scale of what Citizen Lab discovered was frightening, with 28,000 different web pages set up to target thousands of individuals and hundreds of institutions around the world, including advocacy groups, journalists, elected officials, lawyers, hedge funds and companies. A criminal Federal investigation launched in the US, looking in particular at a range of climate advocacy groups targeted by the hackers, who all appeared to be linked by their prominent opposition to Exxon, the oil giant. (BellTroX denied involvement in hacking and Exxon denied any link to hackers.) In the two years which followed, hopes that the FBI would trace those giving the orders were disappointed, as only one private detective was convicted. Investigators and lawyers of unimpeachable character were once again the circuit breakers protecting those at the top.

*

Leo Perry couldn't believe his luck. As Wirecard clung to life after announcing its cash was missing he took every bet he could, sure the share price would soon be zero. Like the other short sellers who spent years picking away at the company, he knew there was no way back, that any real money inside the company was long gone. He had never given up, the letters to clients of his hedge fund over the years reflecting his frustration that black was white, that he'd never been more certain Wirecard was a fraud. His trades on the Thursday and the Friday finally rewarded their patience, turning a loss-making campaign into a moneymaking one.

Was it worth the effort? There were easier ways to make money. In San Francisco, Eduardo Marques totted up the time he'd dedicated to the fight: at least a day a week for as long as he could remember. On an hourly basis, it was the worst wage he'd ever made. Still, there were other satisfactions to victory, the lessons learned along the way, knowing that the riddle was solved and that it wasn't just about the trade, that some of the fraudsters and money launderers might one day face consequences.

The evening of the collapse, once the stories were done and the kids were in bed, Charlotte and I sat in the corner of our garden that caught the last of the sun with a bottle of champagne. A fortieth birthday present from a connoisseur friend, it had a long, thin neck like a swan, and we'd waited almost two years for a good enough reason to drink it. I don't think anything ever tasted better. I could finally start to take in what had happened, and everyone seemed pretty pleased; Murphy had spent twenty minutes on the phone with an ecstatic Lionel Barber: 'We did it! We finally got those bastards!' Stefania Palma in Singapore was seven hours ahead of us and just as delighted as we basked in the reaction on Twitter.

In the days that followed the scramble was on to find out what was happening at Wirecard in Aschheim. I wondered who had tranquillized the Munich authorities, who were in no hurry to arrest anyone. When they finally got round to issuing arrest warrants on the Monday, Jan Marsalek had disappeared, supposedly to the Philippines. Soon there were reports of flights. Immigration records had him landing in

Manila one day, then jetting off to China the next. Except, when the Philippine police checked the airport cameras, Marsalek never stepped off the plane from Germany. The logs were forged, a false trail to help cover his tracks.

He left behind his long-standing girlfriend, and also significant amounts of money. In the months which followed his friend Colin in Munich was approached by Marsalek on LinkedIn, via an alias he used: Richard Dembrovsky. Marsalek wanted to put a governance structure in place to manage his investments, he said. Without Marsalek around, Colin and Rami El Obeidi had fallen out over finances.

Colin was not about to take instructions from Interpol's most wanted, two pictures of whom now adorned red posters at every train station and airport in the country, one with a Chechen beard, the other without. (Marsalek was by now wanted for 'violation of the German Duty on Securities Act and the Securities Trading Act, criminal breach of trust, [and an] especially serious case of fraud'.) 'Come back and we'll talk,' Colin told him.

Eventually *Süddeutsche Zeitung*, the Munich local paper, pieced together Marsalek's escape. After he was suspended on the Thursday of the collapse Marsalek ate his final dinner in Munich at a tourist-trap Italian restaurant with an illuminated sign. He sat outside, conferring with his personal-life assistant Sabine and Martin Weiss, the former Austrian intelligence agent. For all the warning Marsalek had that the end was nigh, what followed was a last improvisation. The following evening he approached Bad Vöslau, a private airfield on the outskirts of Vienna, by taxi. He was late, and made more so when the driver couldn't find the entrance to the airport building. A Cessna Citation Mustang 510, an entry-level private jet, was waiting for him, allegedly arranged by a former politician for the Far Right FPÖ. Marsalek was travelling light, with just a suitcase and duffle bag. He paid €8,000 to the two pilots in cash, and at 8.03 p.m. it took off, destination Minsk in Belarus.

Weiss was arrested in Austria for his alleged part in the flight, and his other work for Marsalek. He has denied any wrongdoing, and the Austrian authorities continue to investigate the circumstances under which Marsalek received classified information. In October 2021, the country's ambassador to Indonesia was recalled and it was widely reported that prosecutors had accused him of leaking the Novichok nerve gas documents that were later touted by Marsalek.

The fugitive former whizz-kid made his way to Moscow, according to multiple reports that sometimes placed him at specific addresses. Which oligarch supported and protected him remained a matter of speculation, and he appeared to become a pawn of the Russian intelligence agency FSB. In 2021 Germany's secret service, the BND, turned down a meeting with Marsalek on the grounds that it was a trap set by their Russian counterparts. The BND has denied any connection to Marsalek when he was a freewheeling executive, and pictures or details of a clandestine get-together might have been an awkward look. In 2022, the Russian outlet *Dossier Center* published fuzzy video and photographs of a man matching Marsalek's description getting behind the wheel of a car, suggesting that he had learned to drive at last. It was said to be fitted with diplomatic plates for a Gulf state that would allow him to evade surveillance systems in the city. Also published were copies of a possibly fake Russian passport said to be produced by the FSB for Marsalek to use day to day in the name 'German Bazhenov'. Were his new masters mocking the Austrian, or those in the West to whom they expected the document to leak? It is hard to think what a restless workaholic of forty-three years, charm and wits intact but shorn of his connections and prestige, intends for the decades stretching ahead in a country isolated and at war. Perhaps one day, in changed geopolitical circumstances, he will reappear to finally tell his secrets.

Other players also disappeared. PayEasy's Christopher Bauer was reported dead within a month of Wirecard's collapse. His family announced on Facebook that he was hospitalized with a septic boil, died, and was swiftly cremated. Further pictures showed them observing the traditional mourning rituals, including cooking a full pig as a feast on day nine. (The family have rejected any suggestions that Bauer's death was faked.) In the previous year he was seen repeatedly with an Asian man who went by the name 'Michael' and matched the description of Edo Kurniawan, Marsalek's willing gopher. Mr Kurniawan's whereabouts were unknown.

Mark Tolentino, the YouTubing lawyer, protested his innocence in a two-page rant: 'Isn't it ridiculous to appoint me as a "trustee" for billions of dollars . . . they are even making a mockery by making me a trustee of nothing but air.' Events didn't seem to dent his reputation. During the pandemic he became CEO of a company with the exclusive right to distribute China's Sinopharm Covid vaccine in the Philippines. He also continued to broadcast, appearing regularly on a news channel belonging to the network of a Filipino televangelist.

In Singapore the authorities charged Shan, the former trustee and paperwork guy, with multiple counts of forging documents. Henry O'Sullivan was also arrested in August 2021 and charged with abetting Shan, to which he pleaded not guilty and was released on bail. His lawyers said they were instructed not to respond to my questions. In 2022 the Singapore authorities also charged three junior Wirecard staff, and a fourth person, with embezzling funds, where investigations continued.

Marsalek's porn baron friend Ray Akhavan was sentenced in June 2021 to two and a half years in a Federal prison for tricking US banks into processing more than $150m worth of payments for marijuana-related purchases. Their associate Andy Khawaja, who ran Allied Wallet, was fighting extradition from Lithuania to the US, where authorities had charged him in relation to his alleged involvement in a scheme to process payments for a variety of fraudulent schemes using sham merchants.

In Germany, the reverberations were extensive. Wirecard was the first company to crash straight from the Dax 30 Index into insolvency, and the country's largest ever financial fraud. When it collapsed in June 2020 it carried known debts of more than €3bn, but this would prove to be a fraction of the damage. As much as €870m ($1bn) was syphoned off in loans to opaque partners, and estimates for losses ran to more than €20bn.

The head of Germany's financial regulator, Felix Hufeld, and his second-in-command both resigned. Reform of BaFin began, after several staff were found to have personally traded in Wirecard stock. One was under investigation for insider trading related to trades made shortly before Wirecard's failure. In July 2021 the structure of German corporate governance was changed to give supervisory board members the ability to demand information direct from divisional business heads, rather than relying on the management board.

Commerzbank wrote off €175m of bad loans to Wirecard. The bank initially stood by analyst Heike Pauls (who had no role in its lending decisions), then fired her in February 2021. Commerzbank was subsequently forced to reinstate Ms Pauls by an employment tribunal. Deutsche Bank's Alexander Schutz, Markus Braun's friend, who had urged him to 'do this newspaper in', apologized to the *FT* and left the bank's supervisory board in March 2021.

After Wirecard, Ernst & Young tore itself in two. In September 2022 it began a process to split its audit work from its consulting division, a move that if approved by its 10,000 partners in 140 countries will fundamentally reshape the global auditing industry. EY also faced an avalanche of litigation relating to its audits of Wirecard, on which lawyers were expected to feast for years to come. The head of EY Germany, Hubert Barth, stepped down, and the partners involved in the audits were under criminal investigation in Munich over potential violations of professional duties. They and the firm denied wrongdoing. EY was also heavily criticized in a report commissioned by members of Germany's parliament, the Bundestag, for failing to spot indicators of fraud, not fully implementing professional guidelines and, on key questions, relying on verbal assurances from executives.

The criminal investigation into myself and Stefania Palma was swiftly dropped. Olaf Scholz, who as finance minister had ultimate responsibility for the regulator BaFin while it was investigating us, gave a generous speech where he said that our reporting 'did a great service to the rule of law, the common good and – this is something I want to say very explicitly – to Germany as a financial centre'. Of course, ahead of the election that would make him chancellor, Scholz wasn't so foolish as to accept any blame. The Bundestag in Berlin launched a six-month full parliamentary inquiry into Wirecard, and when Scholz appeared he opened with a statement that 'the government does not bear responsibility for this large-scale fraud'. The idea that his ministry had tried to protect the company was an 'absurd fairy tale', he said.

My own appearance at the inquiry came early on, with special dispensation to travel to the becalmed city during Covid restrictions. I watched from another room as the humanitarian Kilian Kleinschmidt testified from North Africa by video link, and then I was ushered in. The committee room held a large circle of desks in the beige laminate of German bureaucracy, each equipped with microphones and earpieces for simultaneous translation. There was a sprawling, unstructured nature to the process. For ten minutes there were questions, as each of the main political groupings spoke in turn while I jotted down notes. Then the floor was mine to answer however I chose and for as long as I needed, at which point the next circuit of questions began. I was only dimly aware that this pattern was repeated until there was nothing more to ask, and the seats were allocated by party rather than person. So the faces changed as the session continued and my stomach rumbled as MPs sat down with generous slices of cake in the afternoon, and then plates of hot food as the evening wore on. There were apologies from the MPs, thanks and point-scoring. Did the Federal Chancellery even have a subscription to the *Financial Times*? asked one opposition MP. They certainly did now, answered another. They were keen to pin the blame on the regulator BaFin and the government, which was far more interested in the failings of Ernst & Young.

Possibly too polite, feeling like a guest in an inscrutable foreign process and disarmed by the novelty of it all, when I was asked what could be done I said the government should do more to protect whistleblowers and inject sunlight into corporate affairs. One of the striking aspects of the scandal was that when the Zatarra Report was published its anonymity was considered problematic by almost everyone, yet the routine corporate secrecy which Wirecard used and abused for itself and customers was not. More disclosure, and forcing secrecy jurisdictions like the British Virgin Islands to open up, would surely help. I didn't hold my breath, as I knew there were hundreds more witnesses to hear and long battles over the minutiae of rules lay ahead. After five and a half hours, with one brief break for a cup of tea, I was very late for dinner with my colleagues at the *FT*'s Berlin bureau. I dashed off to see them, to swap tales and to plot new stories that might one day be told.

Inside Wirecard thousands of staff were left in shock, and then most of them were abruptly fired. So far as they were concerned, they worked for a legitimate company doing serious jobs, and they had been: the core payments processing business was 'real', it just lost money hand over fist. Many of them began to kick themselves over the signs they should have noticed, the odd things they might have considered. Martin Osterloh, the salesman, had always realized that there was a difference between his experience of the company's technology and its public image, but he'd put it down to spin. He knew what it was like trying to get clients through at the bank, facing the same troubles and checks of any compliance department. He spoke for many when he said: 'I'm like the idiot guy in a movie, I got to meet all these guys. The question arises, why were we so naive? And I can't really answer that question.'

It's one that would be asked again and again, about the institutions and people who failed to do their jobs: the auditors who signed the accounts every year; the investors who chose to trust Markus Braun to the bitter end even as alarm bells clanged; the bankers who loaned Wirecard billions; the complacent politicians unable to imagine a fraud of such scale could happen in Germany; the regulators who preferred to chase ghost stories of corrupt foreign journalists; the media organizations happy to regurgitate Wirecard's lies; the prosecutors wowed by a sharp suit, a charming manner and an expensive lawyer.

How that disaster came to be is the story in these pages. Wirecard started life in the shadows where others preferred not to operate, and for a while it thrived. It embraced high risk, financial and then legal, cleaning dirty money. Small crimes, unpunished and unprosecuted, became bigger crimes. In a moment of crisis a talented young man was promoted beyond his ability and he began to improvise. Accounting fraud filled the gaps, producing numbers the stock market demanded;

this imagined, empty Wirecard became huge and rich, a house of cards that those inside must surely have known was one day doomed to topple.

Harder to find are satisfying explanations for why so many were fooled for so long. Complex frauds have a dark magic that challenges our image of the fraudster. We tend to picture a charming grifter such as 'Count' Victor Lustig, who in 1925 personally persuaded two scrap metal dealers that he could sell them a decaying Eiffel Tower, if only they first fronted money to bribe the right official. Modern stock market frauds are different. In his history of financial scams, *Lying for Money*, Dan Davies put it this way: 'the way in which most white-collar crime works is by manipulating institutional psychology. That means creating something that looks as much as possible like a normal set of transactions. The drama comes much later, when it all unwinds.'

What Wirecard abused was trust embedded in the fabric of society. We go through life assuming the businesses we encounter are real, confident that there are institutions and processes in place to check that food standards are met or accounts are prepared correctly. Horse meat smugglers, Enron and Wirecard all abused trust in complex systems as a whole. To doubt them was to doubt the entire structure: surely a company could not get into Germany's Dax 30 without someone checking it was above board? Just think how much wasted effort would be involved to investigate that every large company was what it seemed before making stock market investments. High-trust economies are very efficient in part because every interaction doesn't involve redundant checks. Frauds like Wirecard are insidious precisely because they erode that trust.

What was unusual in this case, however, was how often people did try to check the facts. Think of investigator Susannah Kroeber on a dusty road in Cambodia, short seller Matt Earl trawling through Companies House, or ace reporter Stefania Palma stumbling on to a dog-grooming session in the Philippines. Shareholders, perhaps also Wirecard's regulators and auditors, were invested in its success. With each new set of facts they focused on those that reinforced their expectations and disregarded what didn't; confirmation bias works just as well when investing and regulating as it does with views on climate change, vaccines or politics. So when the *FT* revealed Edo Kurniawan's schemes in Singapore, Wirecard focused on the *amounts* at stake, which were initially small, rather than the unpunished *practices* of forgery and money laundering, which were damning.

I saw accounting fraud from the beginning, every inconsistency another cockroach, because that's what I was looking for. That others didn't was a lesson in how hard it is to change people's minds when money is at stake, and the power of social proof. At Theranos, which falsely claimed to have advanced testing machines able to work miracles with a single drop of blood, it was the board that reassured. Elizabeth Holmes, another aficionado of the black turtleneck, surrounded herself with renowned men: retired general James Mattis, former secretary of state Henry Kissinger and former Wells Fargo chief executive Richard Kovacevich. At Wirecard it was the brands of its enablers and supporters that soothed the faithful: Ernst & Young, Commerzbank, Deutsche Bank, SoftBank, BaFin. And if that didn't work, there was intimidation: in its final year Wirecard spent €45m on professional fees to its serried ranks of lawyers, accountants, private detectives, PR firms, friends of Marsalek and other parasites.

What did Markus Braun think he was buying? When it comes to the proud owner and leader, who protested his innocence after two decades in charge, the whistleblower Pav Gill put it succinctly: 'The CEO can't be that much of a dense dupe, right? If you try to present yourself as some sort of Elizabeth Holmes visionary, you need to have some sense of what is going on in your company. You can't now blame it on the guy who ran away. For all we know, that was the plan all along: Marsalek is missing and everyone else is a victim.'

The trial of Markus Braun began in December 2022 in a bomb-proof courtroom buried five metres underground. It was designed to try gangsters and terrorists, and was connected by tunnel to the huge prison that had held the former billionaire since the summer of his disgrace. There was no jury present, the German system instead relied on a panel of five judges – three professional and two lay members – to reach a verdict. Such was the importance of the case that four more reserve magistrates were also observing, able to step in should any of the presiding five fall ill.

Braun, wearing his familiar rimless glasses and black turtleneck, listened as prosecutors spent four hours reading eighty-nine pages of charges into the record. The former CEO faced four counts of accounting manipulation, twenty-six of market manipulation and six apiece of fraud and embezzlement. The charges carried a potential prison sentence of up to fifteen years.

Alongside him in the dock was Stephan von Erffa, Wirecard's deputy CFO, and Oliver Bellenhaus, the government's star witness. After the company collapsed Bellenhaus flew to Zurich and then drove to Munich, where he surrendered to prosecutors and began to co-operate. His testimony was seen as central to the case, because for all the paperwork left behind in the rubble, the Telegram chats between Braun, Marsalek and the other key men were lost. Bellenhaus could explain how he ran an imaginary business from Dubai, that the clients weren't real, and that the Third-Party structure as Wirecard claimed it existed never made any sense.

As with all cases of accounting fraud, the complexity of the trial lay less in the mechanics of the crime, and more in the tricky question of establishing who was lying. Braun denied wrongdoing; his defence was that he was a victim in this saga as well. In his version of events, Wirecard's outsourced payments processing business was real, but stolen by Marsalek and his cronies. Braun's lawyer told the court that Bellenhaus had 'told a pack of lies', fielding the same arguments he gave to me: there was 'clear and unambiguous evidence' that 'hundreds of millions of Euros of revenues generated by the Third-Party Acquiring business' were embezzled by 'shadow companies' based in Antigua, Indonesia and the British Virgin Islands. The lawyer said events 'were not the product of an attempt to manipulate the balance sheet of Wirecard AG to make it appear to be financially stronger and more attractive to investors in the capital markets' and that 'Markus Braun was not in any way involved in any of these embezzlements or their concealment and had no knowledge of them.'

Stephan von Erffa also denied wrongdoing. His lawyer said that as head of the accounting department he 'did not have the task of materially auditing transactions that came to his attention there' and 'had neither active nor passive knowledge of the events that are being publicly discussed today in connection with the collapse of Wirecard'.

Prosecutors said other senior figures at the company remained under investigation. A notable absence from the list of those charged was Burkhard Ley, Wirecard's chief financial officer for more than a decade, who was arrested and released on bail in 2020. He denied any involvement in or knowledge of Wirecard's fraud. His lawyer told me that every asset purchase on Ley's watch was subject to professional due diligence by lawyers and accountants; Ley himself was not an accountant and so relied on Wirecard's finance team and auditors; that he had a purely professional relationship with Jan Marsalek and no knowledge of his illegal schemes in India or elsewhere.

The trial's initial drama came from the testimony of Bellenhaus, who appeared to be rattled when making his opening statement. Talking in a fast murmur, the chief judge reminded him to take as much time as he needed; hundreds of days in court lay ahead, a product of an archaic system of nineteenth-century rules that required every piece of relevant evidence to be considered. Bellenhaus was admonished again later that day when he became emotional, addressing his fellow defendants directly as he said he 'went to bed with rats and woke up with the plague'.

Bellenhaus apologized for speaking out of turn, and continued. His testimony described a criminal gang at the top of Wirecard. 'There was a system of organized fraud,' he said. 'Braun called the shots, and when he said something, it was done his way.' Bellenhaus said the deception was motivated by the CEO, who was 'obsessed' with reporting growth, and at times specifically instructed him to alter the figures he produced. As for his own motivation, Bellenhaus said the company was his identity, and over time 'small lies became bigger and bigger'. He said: 'Nothing binds men together more closely than a mutually committed crime.'

Elsewhere, life moved on. Fraser Perring's firm Viceroy continued to put out research and attract controversy. In September 2021 Viceroy was fined £2.3m by the South African regulator for publishing 'false, misleading or deceptive statements' about a company in 2018. Perring appealed and the following year a tribunal set aside the fine, finding that the regulator had no jurisdiction over foreign nationals. Perring told the newspaper *Frankfurter Allgemeine Zeitung* that he received twenty to thirty death threats a week. He told me that he had also amassed a portfolio of private equity assets in the British Virgin Islands by assisting firms with their due diligence, and that he was still friends with Ian Hollins, whose real identity he wished to protect.

Pav Gill was as glad as anyone to see Wirecard finally exposed, and his decision to blow the whistle still came at a cost. Even though he knew it wasn't rational, the gentle rattle of his apartment door when the building's lift passed his floor was enough to wake him in a cold sweat. He purchased a large new lock to hold it firmly in place, so he could sleep. His mother Evelyn was well, still in Singapore, and determined as ever to look out for her son.

Gary Kilbey sold Fabric nightclub during the pandemic. He said he was one of the people owed money by Nick Gold, who agreed an Individual Voluntary Arrangement (IVA) with his creditors as an alternative to bankruptcy. Nightclubbing and office supplies were both hit hard by the pandemic, and his financial troubles weren't helped by his generous approach to sharing his spread betting account with other traders who failed to pay up when trades went sour, costing Gold millions.

At the time of writing, Paul Murphy was still trying to get his lodge in Mozambique finished.

Author's Note and
Acknowledgements

This book is informed by my experience of reporting on The Company over seven years. It is based on more than a hundred interviews conducted after Wirecard's collapse, in addition to the hundreds of conversations that took place while attempting to uncover the fraud. I have reviewed many thousands of pages of corporate filings, and more than 500 gigabytes of internal Wirecard emails and documents. I also read countless analyst reports, court records, text messages, transcripts, regulatory notices, message records, contracts, Whois records, and website archives relating to Wirecard and its partners, in an effort to understand and report what happened; where those are quoted verbatim in the text the source is acknowledged. Any errors are mine. The public registers of Companies House in the UK, the Accounting and Corporate Regulatory Authority in Singapore and the Federal Gazette in Germany were models of accessibility that should be applauded and replicated. The Internet Archive was an indispensable free tool of investigative journalism.

Above all, however, the story in these pages is one of people. Without Pav Gill's miraculous truckful of internal documents, and more than a dozen other whistleblowers who took the courageous decision to share what they knew, Wirecard would never have been exposed. They are the heroes whose integrity was the match to its lies, and they have my everlasting gratitude. I am also grateful for the insight, trust, co-operation and patience of everyone who spoke to me, some of them many times over. Each contribution, small and large, was valuable. Some sources agreed to be named, while others appear under pseudonyms or remain entirely anonymous out of a concern for retribution, ongoing investigations and litigation, or a desire for privacy. A small number communicated through surrogates or lawyers. Where speech is reported, those quotes are based on the recollection of participants.

I disappeared down many rabbit holes while researching the sprawling history of Wirecard. I have attempted to weave together some of the stories of its colourful cast – the bankers, bandits, spies, executives, pornographers, enablers, journalists, traders, auditors, prosecutors, lawyers, oddballs and editors – within these pages, and I hope I have done it justice. Some protagonists, like the vanished Jan Marsalek, could not be reached for their input. Henry O'Sullivan, the dealmaker, and his associates involved with the 1A Mauritius investment fund – Amit Shah, Katherine Ardiss and Varun Gupta – did not respond to requests for comment. Neither did Ray Akhavan, the porn baron. My one interview, in December 2014, with the man who led Wirecard is presented. His motivations, and the extent of his knowledge about what happened in Wirecard's name, remain a subject of speculation. Markus Braun himself maintained his innocence and rejected the version of events presented in this book. His lawyer said that 'the allegations/insinuations contained or suggested in your questions are wholly or substantially incorrect and untrue'. My aim has been to chart the rise and fall of Wirecard, and at the time of publication criminal trials lay ahead. I leave it to others to describe the consequences of Wirecard's disgrace.

From the first tip in 2014, Paul Murphy told me to follow my nose and finagled the resources and time so that I could. He has mentored a generation of hacks, me among them, and with Murphy I never fought a battle alone. His support didn't stop when the stake was through Wirecard's heart. I thank him for his contributions to this book, his suggestions, stories, contacts and encouragement. I also owe a debt of gratitude to Nigel Hanson, the *FT*'s badass lawyer, for the untold hours keeping me on the straight and narrow, reviewing copy and seeing off Wirecard's lawyers. We couldn't have done it without him, or without the backing of Lionel Barber, whose guidance, demands for readable copy and restraint when Murphy and I wanted to go all out kept us in the fight. Stefania Palma is a legendary hack. Sam Jones is a magician. All were generous with their time in aid of this project, and I'm grateful to Roula Khalaf for her support, and for giving me a year off to write this book. I'm indebted to Olaf Storbeck for dissecting the final turbulent year of Wirecard's life, for his and Tabby Kinder's unrelenting coverage of Ernst & Young's failings, and for all the leads, research, contacts and feedback he shared as this manuscript took shape.

As I reported on Wirecard I was lucky to do so inside a remarkable institution filled with talented, expert journalists. One of the wonders of the *FT* is the willingness of correspondents across the globe to drop what they are doing and chase leads, offer advice and contacts, hit the phones or go undercover in fancy restaurants. Thank you to Arthur Beesley, Vincent Boland, Sarah O'Connor, Bryce Elder, Nic Fildes, Camila Hodgson, Simeon Kerr, Leo Lewis, Nicole Liu, Izabella Kaminska, David Keohane, Arash Massoudi, Cynthia O'Murchu, John Reed, Khadim Shubber, Robert Smith, Chris Tighe and Don Weinland, who all played a part in the long pursuit. Thank you to Tom Braithwaite, Richard Blackden, Geoff Dyer and Matt Garrahan for their sage editing of the Wirecard stories, and to everyone else who had a hand in their production. Thanks to Peter Spiegel for coining 'Ahab', and to Tom Burgis for his advice on the publishing world as I set about trying to write this book.

As well as the named short sellers who did so much to expose Wirecard's money laundering and fake accounting, there were many who offered advice, thoughts, analysis and support along the way. Thank you to all of them. Marc Cohodes' pep talks were a highlight of the dark times. Sir Chris Hohn's public interventions in the final stages helped keep the pressure up. On the sell side, Toby Clothier and Neil Campling at Mirabaud GTS had a zero-price target on Wirecard from the first moment that they heard Markus Braun speak in 2018, and their constant commentary was always a hilarious breath of fresh air. I want to acknowledge the fine work covering Wirecard and its aftermath by Christoph Giesen and his colleagues at *Süddeutsche Zeitung*, and the digging by Roddy Boyd at the Foundation for Financial Journalism. Thanks also to Stefan Heieck.

My indefatigable agent, Matilda Forbes Watson of WME, is arch negotiator, champion and wise critic. Thanks also to Laura Bonner and Jay Mandel. I was lucky to have the guiding hand of Alex Christofi as editor at Transworld. He saw the essence of a gripping story from the very beginning, his enthusiasm helped me to see the project through, and his deft suggestions were always spot on. Thanks also to Sharika Teelwah for her notes, to Jürgen Diessl at Ullstein for his thoughts and patience, and to Benedict Stoddart and Mark Richards for their sharp-eyed reading.

For the last three years Wirecard took over my life, and I'm lucky to have great friends and family who tolerated this obsession and provided diversion and support when it was needed. Many thanks in particular to James Johnson and Mark Murray, to Jason Smithy for the terrible puns, and to Russ Anderson for the tech support. Above all, my greatest debt is to the loved ones who kept me going, who endured the long days of writing, the absence and the stress, and the deadline crunch that stretched on and on. Bea and Freddie, you are my bright stars. Charlotte, you are my rock, and for your patience, understanding and love I am truly, deeply, grateful.

Index

About the Author

Dan McCrum is a member of the *Financial Times* investigations team. His reporting on Wirecard has been recognized with prizes from the London Press Club, the Society of Editors, the New York Financial Writers' Association, the Overseas Press Club, and the Gerald Loeb awards. He was also awarded the Ludwig Erhard Prize for economic journalism, a Reporters Forum Reporterpreis and a special award by the Helmut Schmidt prize jury for investigative journalism. In 2020, he was named Journalist of the Year at the British Journalism Awards.